# Communications
# in Computer and Information Science  2710

Series Editors

Gang Li , *School of Information Technology, Deakin University, Burwood, VIC, Australia*

Joaquim Filipe , *Polytechnic Institute of Setúbal, Setúbal, Portugal*

Zhiwei Xu, *Chinese Academy of Sciences, Beijing, China*

**Rationale**

The CCIS series is devoted to the publication of proceedings of computer science conferences. Its aim is to efficiently disseminate original research results in informatics in printed and electronic form. While the focus is on publication of peer-reviewed full papers presenting mature work, inclusion of reviewed short papers reporting on work in progress is welcome, too. Besides globally relevant meetings with internationally representative program committees guaranteeing a strict peer-reviewing and paper selection process, conferences run by societies or of high regional or national relevance are also considered for publication.

**Topics**

The topical scope of CCIS spans the entire spectrum of informatics ranging from foundational topics in the theory of computing to information and communications science and technology and a broad variety of interdisciplinary application fields.

**Information for Volume Editors and Authors**

Publication in CCIS is free of charge. No royalties are paid, however, we offer registered conference participants temporary free access to the online version of the conference proceedings on SpringerLink (http://link.springer.com) by means of an http referrer from the conference website and/or a number of complimentary printed copies, as specified in the official acceptance email of the event.

CCIS proceedings can be published in time for distribution at conferences or as postproceedings, and delivered in the form of printed books and/or electronically as USBs and/or e-content licenses for accessing proceedings at SpringerLink. Furthermore, CCIS proceedings are included in the CCIS electronic book series hosted in the SpringerLink digital library at http://link.springer.com/bookseries/7899. Conferences publishing in CCIS are allowed to use Online Conference Service (OCS) for managing the whole proceedings lifecycle (from submission and reviewing to preparing for publication) free of charge.

**Publication process**

The language of publication is exclusively English. Authors publishing in CCIS have to sign the Springer CCIS copyright transfer form, however, they are free to use their material published in CCIS for substantially changed, more elaborate subsequent publications elsewhere. For the preparation of the camera-ready papers/files, authors have to strictly adhere to the Springer CCIS Authors' Instructions and are strongly encouraged to use the CCIS LaTeX style files or templates.

**Abstracting/Indexing**

CCIS is abstracted/indexed in DBLP, Google Scholar, EI-Compendex, Mathematical Reviews, SCImago, Scopus. CCIS volumes are also submitted for the inclusion in ISI Proceedings.

**How to start**

To start the evaluation of your proposal for inclusion in the CCIS series, please send an e-mail to ccis@springer.com.

Minming Li · Jialin Zhang · Zhiping Cai
Editors

# Theoretical Computer Science

43rd National Conference
of Theoretical Computer Science, NCTCS 2025
Kunming, China, August 3–5, 2025
Revised Selected Papers

 Springer

*Editors*
Minming Li
City University of Hong Kong
Hong Kong, China

Jialin Zhang
University of Chinese Academy of Science
Beijing, China

Zhiping Cai
National University of Defense Technology
Changsha, China

ISSN 1865-0929   ISSN 1865-0937 (electronic)
Communications in Computer and Information Science
ISBN 978-981-95-3642-9   ISBN 978-981-95-3643-6 (eBook)
https://doi.org/10.1007/978-981-95-3643-6

© The Editor(s) (if applicable) and The Author(s), under exclusive license to Springer Nature Singapore Pte Ltd. 2026

This work is subject to copyright. All rights are solely and exclusively licensed by the Publisher, whether the whole or part of the material is concerned, specifically the rights of translation, reprinting, reuse of illustrations, recitation, broadcasting, reproduction on microfilms or in any other physical way, and transmission or information storage and retrieval, electronic adaptation, computer software, or by similar or dissimilar methodology now known or hereafter developed.
The use of general descriptive names, registered names, trademarks, service marks, etc. in this publication does not imply, even in the absence of a specific statement, that such names are exempt from the relevant protective laws and regulations and therefore free for general use.
The publisher, the authors and the editors are safe to assume that the advice and information in this book are believed to be true and accurate at the date of publication. Neither the publisher nor the authors or the editors give a warranty, expressed or implied, with respect to the material contained herein or for any errors or omissions that may have been made. The publisher remains neutral with regard to jurisdictional claims in published maps and institutional affiliations.

This Springer imprint is published by the registered company Springer Nature Singapore Pte Ltd.
The registered company address is: 152 Beach Road, #21-01/04 Gateway East, Singapore 189721, Singapore

If disposing of this product, please recycle the paper.

# Preface

The National Conference of Theoretical Computer Science (NCTCS) has emerged as a pivotal academic platform for the field in China. Over the years, NCTCS has been successfully convened in over 20 regions across the country, fostering an environment conducive to exchange and collaboration among researchers in theoretical computer science and allied disciplines.

NCTCS 2025, held from August 3rd to 5th, 2025 in Kunming, Yunnan, was hosted by the China Computer Federation (CCF) and organized jointly by the Theoretical Computer Science Committee of the China Computer Federation and Yunnan University. This event showcased the latest advancements in the field by inviting esteemed scholars to present their work and engaging in a broad spectrum of academic endeavors.

A total of 305 participants registered for NCTCS 2025, with 243 authors submitting 83 papers, of which 54 were ultimately accepted by the conference. The peer-review process, conducted in a single-blind format, involved 81 reviewers from esteemed institutions, with each reviewer assigned an average of 3 papers, and each paper receiving an average of 3 reviews. The submission and review process were facilitated by the Online Submission System (CCF Consys), accessible at https://conf.ccf.org.cn/TCS2025 for further details.

This publication comprises 10 selected papers from NCTCS 2025, categorized under four thematic sections: Algorithm Design, Logic, Artificial Intelligence Theory and Algorithms, and Algorithm Application. These contributions reflect the depth and breadth of research in theoretical computer science today.

The proceedings editors extend their heartfelt gratitude to the diligent Program Committee members and external reviewers for their meticulous efforts in evaluating and selecting the papers. We are also indebted to Springer for their unwavering support and trust in publishing the proceedings of NCTCS 2025.

September 2025                                                                 Minming Li
                                                                              Jialin Zhang
                                                                              Zhiping Cai

# Organization

## Program Committee Chairs

| | |
|---|---|
| Minming Li | City University of Hong Kong, China |
| Jialin Zhang | Institute of Computing Technology, Chinese Academy of Sciences, China |
| Zhiping Cai | National University of Defense Technology, China |

## Area Chairs

| | |
|---|---|
| Yijia Chen | Fudan University, China |
| Qilong Feng | Central South University, China |
| Zhiguo Fu | Northeast Normal University, China |
| Jian Li | Tsinghua University, China |
| Lvzhou Li | Sun Yat-sen University, China |
| Xinwang Liu | National University of Defense Technology, China |
| Zhihao Tang | Shanghai University of Finance and Economics, China |

## Program Committee

| | |
|---|---|
| Rufan Bai | Southeast University, China |
| Kerong Ben | Naval University of Engineering, China |
| Yixin Cao | Hong Kong Polytechnic University, China |
| Yongzhi Cao | Peking University, China |
| Shengminjie Chen | Institute of Computing Technology, Chinese Academy of Sciences, China |
| Wenbin Chen | Guangzhou University, China |
| Zhigang Chen | Central South University, China |
| Baolei Cheng | Soochow University, China |
| Hu Ding | University of Science and Technology of China, China |
| Qilong Feng | Central South University, China |
| Qi Fu | Changsha Institute of Technology, China |
| Zhiguo Fu | Northeast Normal University, China |
| Ling Gai | University of Shanghai for Science and Technology, China |

| | |
|---|---|
| Longkun Guo | Fuzhou University, China |
| Xinxin Han | Shenzhen Polytechnic University, China |
| Kun He | Huazhong University of Science and Technology, China |
| Lingxiao Huang | Nanjing University, China |
| Weiran Huang | Shanghai Jiao Tong University, China |
| Zhaoming Huang | Guangxi Medical University, China |
| Hua Jiang | Yunnan University, China |
| Guiyuan Jiang | Ocean University of China, China |
| Haitao Jiang | Shandong University, China |
| Shaofeng Jiang | Peking University, China |
| Yan Jin | Huazhong University of Science and Technology, China |
| Haibin Kan | Fudan University, China |
| Bo Li | Hong Kong Polytechnic University, China |
| Hongbo Li | Northeast Normal University, China |
| Qian Li | Shenzhen Research Institute of Big Data, China |
| Shaohua Li | Central South University, China |
| Weian Li | Shandong University, China |
| Xingfu Li | Guizhou University of Finance and Economics, China |
| Yaqiao Li | Shenzhen University of Advanced Technology, China |
| Yaochong Li | Shanghai Maritime University, China |
| Yongming Li | Shaanxi Normal University, China |
| Shi Li | Nanjing University, China |
| Shizhong Liao | Tianjin University, China |
| Huawen Liu | Shaoxing University, China |
| Jiyuan Liu | National University of Defense Technology, China |
| Jingcheng Liu | Nanjing University, China |
| Peiqiang Liu | Shandong Technology and Business University, China |
| Shengxin Liu | Harbin Institute of Technology (Shenzhen), China |
| Yanli Liu | Wuhan University of Science and Technology, China |
| Zhendong Liu | Shanghai Polytechnic University, China |
| Junjie Luo | Beijing Jiaotong University, China |
| Lei Luo | National University of Defense Technology, China |
| Weilin Luo | Sun Yat-sen University, China |
| Zhanyou Ma | North Minzu University, China |
| Qiufen Ni | Guangdong University of Technology, China |

| | |
|---|---|
| Haiyu Pan | Guilin University of Electronic Technology, China |
| Yingli Ran | Zhejiang Normal University, China |
| Yun Shang | Academy of Mathematics and Systems Science, Chinese Academy of Sciences, China |
| Feng Shi | Central South University, China |
| Haihe Shi | Jiangxi Normal University, China |
| Yangguang Shi | Shandong University, China |
| Feng Qin | Jiangxi Normal University, China |
| Yun Tan | Central South University of Forestry and Technology, China |
| Zhihao Tang | Shanghai University of Finance and Economics, China |
| Guojing Tian | Institute of Computing Technology, Chinese Academy of Sciences, China |
| Banghai Wang | Guangdong University of Technology, China |
| Changjing Wang | Jiangxi Normal University, China |
| Hanpin Wang | Peking University, China |
| Ke Wang | Guizhou University of Finance and Economics, China |
| Liwei Wang | Wuhan University, China |
| Xiaofeng Wang | North Minzu University, China |
| Yiyuan Wang | Northeast Normal University, China |
| Yalan Wu | Guangdong University of Technology, China |
| Meihua Xiao | East China Jiaotong University, China |
| Chao Xu | Changsha University of Science and Technology, China |
| Yu Yang | Pingdingshan University, China |
| Peisen Yao | Zhejiang University, China |
| Zhen You | Jiangxi Normal University, China |
| Chihao Zhang | Shanghai Jiao Tong University, China |
| Jialin Zhang | Institute of Computing Technology, Chinese Academy of Sciences, China |
| Peng Zhang | Shandong University, China |
| Zhen Zhang | Hunan University of Technology and Business, China |
| Zhijie Zhang | Fuzhou University, China |
| Xiangfu Zhao | Yantai University, China |
| Hong Zheng | East China University of Science and Technology, China |
| Shuming Zhou | Fujian Normal University, China |
| Shuren Zhou | Changsha University of Science and Technology, China |

# Contents

## Algorithm Design

Improved Approximation Algorithms for the Multiple Two-Stage Knapsack Problem ............................................................. 3
   *Kang Zhao, Guangwei Wu, Guozhen Rong, Yunyun Sun, and Feng Shi*

Semi-online Scheduling Problem of Two Identical Machines with Delayed Discount ............................................................. 20
   *Qingyu Luo and Yaru Yang*

## Logic

Sequential Equivalence Checking for Specialized IR via Instrumentation-Based Symbolic Execution ........................... 35
   *Zi Cheng and LeFei Zhang*

Self-learning Modeling of Generalized Possibilistic Decision Processes ....... 50
   *Xintong Zhang, Wuniu Liu, Qing He, and Yongming Li*

## Artificial Intelligence Theory and Algorithm

DPhuman: Generalizable Neural Human Rendering via Point Registration-Based Human Deformation ................................. 77
   *Yongang Yu, Zhigang Chen, and Tangquan Qi*

PSVM-MR: A Parallel Support Vector Machine Algorithm Based on MapReduce ....................................................... 94
   *Bin-bin Guo, Yimin Mao, A Yaser, Neelakandan Chandrasekaran, Le Kang, Wenhao Li, and Decheng Miao*

## Algorithm Application

A Novel Homogenization-Based Method for Population Initialization of Improved Chaotic Artificial Bee Colonies and Convergence Analysis ....... 123
   *Haiyan Yang, Liyong Bao, Dongming Zhou, and Yonghui Si*

A Truthful Resource Allocation and Task Offloading Mechanism of Internet of Vehicles Edge Computing Based on Joint Optimization .......... 153
   *Xing He, Hongyu Pi, Xi Liu, and Xutao Yang*

The State Transition Self-learning Framework Based on Generalized
Intuitionistic Fuzzy Kripke Structure .................................... 182
   *Yuxuan He and Chao Yang*

Spiking Neural Network Based on Bidirectional Variational Anomaly
Detection for Knowledge Tracing ......................................... 204
   *Jinru Hu, Mingkun Chen, Yige Zhu, and Jianrui Chen*

**Author Index** ........................................................ 217

# Algorithm Design

# Improved Approximation Algorithms for the Multiple Two-Stage Knapsack Problem

Kang Zhao[1], Guangwei Wu[1(✉)], Guozhen Rong[2], Yunyun Sun[1], and Feng Shi[3]

[1] School of Computer Science and Mathematics, Central South University of Forestry and Technology, Changsha 410004, China
will99031827@hotmail.com
[2] School of Computer Science and Technology, Changsha University of Science and Technology, Changsha 410114, China
[3] School of computer science and engineering, Central South University, Changsha 410083, China

**Abstract.** This paper studies approximation algorithms on the Multiple Two-stage Knapsack problem, which has received attention recently due to its applications in cloud computing. Given a set of two-stage jobs, the aim is to select a subset of jobs that can be completed by multiple parallel two-stage flowshops (knapsacks) within a time limit, in order to maximize the profit of the selected jobs. The problem is strongly NP-hard even when the number $m$ of flowshops is 2. We focus on the problem where $m$ is part of the input. A natural greedy approximation algorithm is proposed, which iteratively selects a subset of jobs with approximate maximum profit for flowshop from the current unselected jobs. The algorithm is shown to achieve an approximation ratio of $1.582 + \epsilon$ for any constant $\epsilon > 0$, which improves the previously best-known algorithm with an approximation ratio of $3 + \epsilon$. In addition, we provide a faster algorithm with a tight approximation ratio of 4.

**Keywords:** Scheduling · Multiple two-stage flowshops · Knapsack · Approximation algorithm · Cloud computing

## 1 Introduction

In cloud computing environments, modern data centers are equipped with a large number of servers, each comprising processors, network interfaces, and local high-speed I/O [13,19]. Software and data are stored on the servers and serve as resources. Clients dynamically request resources based on their demands, and servers respond by transmitting the requested resources over the network. When

---

This work is supported in part by the National Natural Science Foundation of China under Grant 62072476 and 62302060, and the Hunan Provincial Natural Science Foundation of China under Grant 2025JJ50395.

a request arrives at a server, the server must first retrieve the corresponding resource from secondary storage into the main memory, and then transmit it to the client via the network. As such, each request can be regarded as a two-stage job: disk read (that is, the $R$-operation) followed by network transmission (that is, the $T$-operation), and for a job, its $T$-operation cannot start until the $R$-operation is finished [16]. Correspondingly, each server can be considered as a two-stage flowshop with $R$-processor and $T$-processor, which can perform $R$-operations and $T$-operations of different jobs in parallel, respectively.

Current research on scheduling multiple parallel two-stage flowshop primarily focuses on minimizing the makespan (i.e., the completion time of the last job), with particular emphasis on approximation algorithms. The problem is NP-hard when the number of flowshops is a constant greater than 1, and is strongly NP-hard when the number of flowshops is part of the input [15]. For the case where the number of flowshops is fixed, several Fully Polynomial Time Approximation Schemes (FPTASs) have been developed independently [5,12,15]. For the case where the number of flowshops is a variable, a Polynomial Time Approximation Scheme (PTAS) has been proposed [4]. Some computationally efficient approximation algorithms have also been developed [16,18].

Table 1. A summary of known results for the Multiple Two-stage Knapsack problem and related problems. Our contributions are highlighted with bold font.

| Problem | Hardness | Approximability |
|---|---|---|
| the Single Two-stage Knapsack problem | NP-hard | $3 + \epsilon$ [3] |
| | | $2 + \epsilon$ [2] |
| | | $1 + \epsilon$ [14] |
| the Multiple Two-stage Knapsack problem ($m \geq 2$ is fixed) | Strongly NP-hard | $2 + \epsilon$ [2] |
| | | $1 + \epsilon$ [14] |
| the Multiple Two-stage Knapsack problem ($m \geq 2$ is part of the input) | Strongly NP-hard | $4 + \epsilon$ [2] |
| | | $3 + \epsilon$ [2] |
| | | $1.582 + \epsilon$(**Our works**) |

Recently, another variant of the multiple parallel two-stage flowshop scheduling problem has received attention due to its applications in cloud computing. Each given two-stage job has a profit. The optimization objective is to select a subset of jobs with maximal total profit, which can be completed by the flowshops within a time limit. It is not hard to see that the classical Knapsack problem is a special case of the problem, where every job has its $R$-time (or $T$-time) being 0. Therefore, we refer to the problem as the Multiple Two-stage Knapsack problem. The problem is NP-hard even when the number $m$ of flowshops is 1 (the Single Two-stage Knapsack problem), and becomes strongly NP-hard when $m$ is larger than 1 [2,3]. This implies that there is no FPTAS for the multiple two-stage knapsack problem unless $P = NP$. Very recently, a hybrid problem that combines the Parallel Two-stage Flowshop Scheduling problem with the Bin Packing problem has also been studied [17].

Dawande et al. were the first to address the single two-stage knapsack problem ($m = 1$) [3]. By integrating an FPTAS for the classic knapsack problem, they developed a $(3 + \epsilon)$-approximation algorithm for any constant $\epsilon > 0$ [3]. Chen et al. were the first to study the multiple two-stage knapsack problem [2]. For the case where $m \geq 2$ is a fixed constant, they proposed a $(2+\epsilon)$-approximation algorithm by partitioning jobs into large and small ones based on their sizes (i.e., its $R$-time pluses its $T$-time), enumerating all feasible combinations of a limited number of large and small jobs, and greedily scheduling the remaining small jobs to the flowshops. For the case where $m \geq 2$ is a variable, Chen et al. first proposed a fast 4-approximation algorithm with a time complexity of $O(n^2)$, where $n$ is the number of the two-stage flowshops for selection. Then Chen et al. studied the relationship between the multiple two-stage knapsack problem and the classical multiple knapsack problem. Using a PTAS for the classical multiple knapsack problem, they proposed an approximation algorithm, which has an improved approximation ratio of $(3+\epsilon)$. Tong et al. initially focused on the single two-stage knapsack problem, and proposed a PTAS for the problem with a time complexity of $O(n^{(1/\epsilon)+2})$ [14]. The algorithm first enumerates all possible the most profitable job subset of constant size in polynomial time, and then formulates a linear program to select the cheap jobs based on the enumerations. They showed that most cheap jobs are selected integrally according to the optimal solution of the linear program, and thus discarding the jobs selected fractionally does not cause much loss in terms of profit. Tong et al. further extended their approach to address the Multiple Two-stage Knapsack problem, and developed a PTAS for the problem where the number $m$ of flowshops is fixed. They raised an open question, that is, for the problem when the number of flowshops is part of input, it demands a PTAS or an approximation algorithm with approximation ratio lower than $3 + \epsilon$ (Table 1).

As we have discussed, the multiple two-stage knapsack problem can be regarded as a generalization of the classical knapsack problem. The classical knapsack problem has been extensively studied, which leads to some significant results on the design of approximation algorithms. There exists a FPTAS for the classical knapsack problem [7]. However, for the multiple knapsack problem, where the number of knapsacks is at least two, it has been proven that no FPTAS exists unless $P = NP$. Kellerer et al. were the first to develop a PTAS for the multiple knapsack problem where the number of knapsacks constitutes part of the input [11]. In later studies, the Multiple Knapsack Problem was generalized to scenarios where knapsacks have varying capacities, and several algorithms were developed [1,8,9]. Chekuri et al. developed a PTAS for the multiple knapsack problem with varying knapsack capacities [1]. Furthermore, Jansen et al. developed an EPTAS for the multiple knapsack problem with varying knapsack capacities, which runs in time $O(2^{\frac{1}{\epsilon}\log^4(1/\epsilon)} + poly(n))$ [8,9].

The paper focuses on approximation algorithms for the multiple two-stage knapsack problem, where the number of flowshops $m \geq 2$ is part of the input. Inspired by the strategy used in the Maximum Coverage Problem [6], we propose a natural greedy algorithm for any constant $\epsilon > 0$. By employing the PTAS for the single two-stage knapsack problem, our algorithm continues to seek a job subset with the nearly optimal profit from unselected jobs for the current flowshop, until all flowshops are packed. We show that the algorithm achieves an approximation ratio of $1.582 + \epsilon$ for the multiple two-stage knapsack problem, which significantly improves the previously best-known approximation algorithm with an approximation ratio of $3 + \epsilon$. In addition, a fast 4-approximation algorithm is proposed, which improves the previous fast 4-approximation algorithm [2] by reducing its time complexity from $O(n^2)$ to $O(n \log n)$. A counterexample is also constructed to show that the approximation ratio 4 is tight for both two algorithms.

## 2 Preliminaries

For a set $J = \{J_1, J_2, \cdots, J_n\}$ of two-stage jobs scheduled on $m$ parallel two-stage flowshops $M = \{M_1, M_2, \cdots, M_m\}$, we consider the following setting: each two-stage job $J_i = (r_i, t_i; p_i)$ consists of an $R$-operation and a $T$-operation, and each flowshop is equipped with an $R$-processor and a $T$-processor, which can run in parallel. A two-stage job $J_i$ is assigned to a two-stage flowshop $M_h$, then its $R$-operation and $T$-operation are executed by the $R$-processor of cost $r_i$ (i.e., $R$-time) and by the $T$-processor of cost $t_i$ (i.e., $T$-time), of the same flowshop $M_h$, respectively. For a job, the $T$-operation can start only after the $R$-operation is completed. Each job $J_i$ is associated with a profit $p_i$, which is obtained after $J_i$ is completed by flowshop within the given time limit under a schedule. Without loss of generality, the $R$-times and $T$-times of the jobs in $J$ can be scaled so that the time limit of flowshop is 1. We assume that each job $J_i = (r_i, t_i; p_i)$ in the input satisfies condition $r_i + t_i \leq 1$, otherwise, $J_i$ is directly removed from the set $J$ since it cannot be completed by flowshop within the time limit 1.

A schedule of a two-stage job set on flowshops not only determines the assignment of the jobs to these flowshops, but also considers the execution order (sequence) of the jobs on each flowshop. We say that on multiple two-stage flowshops, a two-stage job set has a feasible schedule, or a schedule is feasible for a two-stage job set, if under the schedule all the jobs in the set are completed by the flowshops within the time limit.

**Definition 1 (The Multiple Two-stage Knapsack problem).** *Given a set of two-stage jobs $J = \{J_i = (r_i, t_i; p_i) \mid 1 \leq i \leq n\}$, where $0 < r_i + t_i \leq 1$, and a set of $m$ two-stage flowshops $M = \{M_1, M_2, \cdots, M_m\}$, the objective is to find a job subset $J^{SEL} \subseteq J$, which has a feasible schedule $S = \{S_1, S_2 \cdots, S_m\}$ for $J^{SEL}$ on the $m$ two-stage flowshops under the time limit 1, such that the total profit of the jobs in $J^{SEL}$ is maximized.*

In general, the paper studies the multiple two-stage knapsack problem, where the number $m$ of the two-stage flowshop is a part of the input. In the subsequent discussion, job is generally regarded as a two-stage job, and flowshop is generally regarded as a two-stage flowshop. The paper mainly considers a type of schedule, named the *permutation schedule*. A permutation schedule on flowshop can be regarded as a job sequence, in which both the $R$-operations and the $T$-operation are executed following the job sequence.

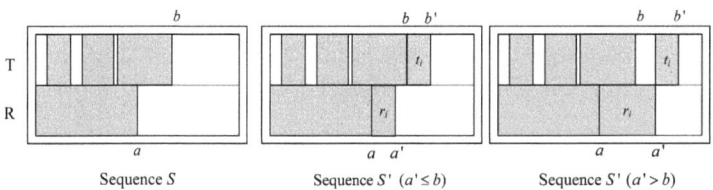

**Fig. 1.** The process of assigning a job to a two-stage flowshop.

**Lemma 1.** *Given a feasible sequence $S = \langle J_1, J_2, \cdots, J_t \rangle$ on flowshop with the completion time of their $R$-operations and $T$-operations, and a job $J_i$ ($J_i \notin S$), then determining whether the new sequence $S' = \langle J_1, J_2, \cdots, J_t, J_i \rangle$ can be completed by flowshop within the time limit 1 takes constant time.*

*Proof.* Let $a$ and $b$ denote the completion times of the $R$-operation and the $T$-operation of the last job $J_t$ on the flowshop under the feasible schedule $S$, respectively. According to Lemma 2.1 in [15], then in the schedule $S'$, the completion time $a'$ of the $R$-operation of the last job $J_i$ is $a + r_i$. The $R$-operation $r_i$ starts immediately after that of the previous job $J_t$ is completed, if our objective is to minimize the completion time of the jobs. The completion time $b'$ of the $T$-operation of $J_i$ is equal to $\max\{a'+t_i, b+t_i\}$. The $T$-operation $r_i$ waits for the completions of the previous $T$-operation and its $R$-operation. Clearly, it takes constant time to determine whether the sequence $S'$ can be completed within the time limit. Figure 1 illustrates the two cases of assigning a job to flowshop. □

For the scheduling problem on a single two-stage flowshop, an optimal solution can be obtained in $O(n \log n)$ time using Johnson's algorithm [10]. We refer to the job scheduling strategy in this algorithm as Johnson's rule, as defined in Definition 2.

**Definition 2 (Johnson's rule [10]).** *Given a set of n two-stage jobs, partition the jobs into two disjoint subsets, where $G_1 = \{(r_i, t_i) \mid r_i \leq t_i\}$ and $G_2 = \{(r_i, t_i) \mid r_i > t_i\}$. The jobs in $G_1$ are executed first in non-decreasing order of their R-times, followed by the jobs in $G_2$ in non-increasing order of their T-times.*

Consider algorithm $A$ for the multiple two-stage knapsack problem. Given a two-stage job set $J$ and an integer $m$, algorithm $A$ produces a job subset $J^{SEL} \subseteq J$ and a feasible schedule $S$ for $J^{SEL}$ on $m$ flowshops. Let $P(S) = \sum_{J_i \in J^{SEL}} p_i$ denote the profit obtained by the algorithm $A$, and let $OPT$ denote the maximum profit of the optimal solution. The algorithm $A$ achieves an approximation ratio $\alpha$, or the algorithm $A$ is an "$\alpha$-approximation algorithm", if

$$\frac{OPT}{P(S)} \leq \alpha.$$

That is, the algorithm $A$ produces $\alpha$-approximate solution for any instance of the multiple two-stage knapsack problem. The approximation ratio is commonly used to evaluate the performance of an approximation algorithm. Based on the approximation ratio and the time complexity, several classes of approximation algorithms have been identified. A Polynomial Time Approximation Scheme (PTAS) is defined as a family of algorithms that, for any given $\epsilon > 0$, can give a $(1+\epsilon)$-approximate solution in time $O(n^{f(\epsilon)})$, where $f(\epsilon)$ is a function independent of the input size $n$. A PTAS is an Efficient Polynomial Time Approximation Scheme (EPTAS), if it produces a $(1+\epsilon)$-approximate solution in time $O(f(\epsilon) \cdot n^{O(1)})$, where again $f(\epsilon)$ is independent of $n$. And a PTAS is a Fully Polynomial Time Approximation Scheme (FPTAS), if it provides a $(1+\epsilon)$-approximate solution in time $O(\epsilon^{O(1)} \cdot n^{O(1)})$, that is, the running time is polynomial in both the input size $n$ and the given constant $\epsilon$.

Tong et al. proposed an algorithm for the single two-stage knapsack problem [14]. The algorithm begins by guessing $\frac{1+\epsilon}{\epsilon}$ most profitable jobs in the optimal solution, denoted as $J^{profitable}$, then determines the selection of the remaining cheap jobs through linear programming (LP), and finally discards the jobs that are selected fractionally by LP. Note that cheap jobs must have their profits no larger than $\epsilon \cdot OPT$, otherwise the total profit of $J^{profitable}$ would exceed $\frac{1+\epsilon}{\epsilon} \cdot \epsilon \cdot OPT = (1+\epsilon)OPT$, which contradicts the optimality. The authors also prove that the number of the fractionally selected cheap jobs is bounded by a constant. Therefore, the final discarding step only causes a loss of $O(\epsilon \cdot OPT)$. The algorithm is a PTAS for the single two-stage knapsack problem.

---

**Algorithm 1:** a $(1.582+\epsilon)$-approximation algorithm for the multiple two-stage knapsack problem

**Input** : an instance $\{J,m\}$ of the multiple two-stage knapsack problem, any constant $\epsilon \in (0,1)$, and a PTAS $A_o$ for the single two-stage knapsack problem;

**Output:** $(J^{SEL}, S)$. $J^{SEL} \subseteq J$ is the subset of the selected jobs, and $S = \{S_1, S_2, \cdots, S_m\}$ is a feasible schedule of $J^{SEL}$ on $m$ flowshops, where each $S_h$ is a job sequence on flowshop $M_h$ with the makespan bounded by the time limit 1.

1 **begin**
2 $\quad \phi \leftarrow 1 + \ln\left(\frac{1+(e-1)\epsilon}{e+(e-1)\epsilon}\right)$
3 $\quad J' \leftarrow J$
4 $\quad J^{SEL} \leftarrow \emptyset$
5 $\quad$ **for** $h \leftarrow 1$ **to** $m$ **do**
6 $\quad\quad (J_h^{SEL}, S_h) \leftarrow A_o(J', \phi)$
7 $\quad\quad J' \leftarrow J' \setminus J_h^{SEL}$
8 $\quad\quad J^{SEL} \leftarrow J^{SEL} \cup J_h^{SEL}$
9 $\quad$ **end for**
10 $\quad$ **return** $(J^{SEL}, S = \{S_1, \cdots, S_m\})$
11 **end**

---

## 3 A $(1.582 + \epsilon)$-Approximation Algorithm

In this section, we present an approximation algorithm for the two-stage multiple knapsack problem, where the number $m$ of two-stage flowshops is part of the input. Our problem instance is given in the form $(J,m)$, where $J = \{J_1, J_2, \cdots, J_n\}$ is the set of two-stage jobs and $m$ is the number of two-stage flowshops. The objective is to select a subset $J^{SEL} \subseteq J$ and schedule the jobs in $J^{SEL}$ on the flowshops that maximize the profit of the selected jobs while subject to the time limit of flowshop.

We first introduce some notation. Given a job set $J' \subseteq J$, let $P(J') = \sum_{J_i \in J'} p_i$ be the profit of $J'$, which equals the sum of the profits of the jobs. The notation can also be slightly generalized. For a solution that contains a schedule $S$ for a selected job subset $J^{SEL}$, its profit is the sum of the profits of the selected jobs, i.e., $P(S) = \sum_{J_i \in J^{SEL}} p_i$.

Consider the algorithm given in Algorithm 1. Let $A_o$ be a polynomial time approximation scheme for the single two-stage knapsack problem. For a given two-stage job set $J$ and a constant $\phi > 0$, $A_o$ finds a job subset from $J$ along with a feasible schedule (job sequence), denoted by $A_o(J, \phi)$, and guarantees that the profit of the job set can reach $(1-\phi)$ times that of the optimal solution for $J$ in one knapsack. Algorithm 1 calls $A_o$ $m$ times, where each $h$-th call $(1 \leq h \leq m)$ finds a job subset from the unselected jobs in $J$ for flowshop $M_h$, and gives a feasible schedule of these selected jobs on $M_h$. More specifically, given a constant $\epsilon > 0$ that determines the approximation ratio of the algorithm, we first set $\phi = 1 + \ln(\frac{1+(e-1)\epsilon}{e+(e-1)\epsilon})$ for $A_o$. The algorithm $A_0$ finds a subset of jobs from $J$, denoted as $J_1^{SEL}$, which admits a feasible scheduled $S_1$ with a profit larger than $(1-\phi)$ times the maximum profit of $J$ on a single flowshop. Then, the selected jobs in $J_1^{SEL}$ are removed from the job set $J$. The same procedure is repeated for each of the remaining two-stage flowshops, until all $m$ flowshops have been packed with corresponding jobs.

The following lemma gives an analysis of the time complexity for Algorithm 1.

**Lemma 2.** *Algorithm 1 runs in polynomial time.*

*Proof.* The time complexity of the algorithm mainly depends on that of the algorithm $A_o$. The first three steps of our algorithm take constant time. The main part of Algorithm 1 is a for-loop which essentially calls Algorithm $A_o$ $m$ times, where $m$ as part of the input is the number of flowshops. Tong et al. [14] have proposed a PTAS for the single two-stage knapsack problem. Its time complexity is $O\left(\bar{n}^{(1/\phi)+2}\right)$, where $\bar{n}$ represents the number of jobs available for selection. The number $\bar{n}$ of unselected jobs initially equals $n$, which is the number of jobs in $J$, and then decreases after each loop. This is because each loop removes the selected jobs from current unselected jobs. Thus the time complexity of each loop from Step 6 to Step 8 is bounded by $O\left(n^{(1/\phi)+2}\right)$, and the for-loop takes time $O\left(mn^{(1/\phi)+2}\right)$. Since $\phi = 1+\ln\left(\frac{1+(e-1)\epsilon}{e+(e-1)\epsilon}\right)$ is a fixed constant, Algorithm 1 runs in polynomial time. □

In the following, we give an analysis of the approximation ratio of Algorithm 1.

Let $OPT(J, m)$ be the profit of the optimal solution for selecting a job subset from the two-stage job set $J$ and scheduling the jobs in the subset on $m$ two-stage flowshops, and let $S^* = \{S_1^*, S_2^*, \cdots, S_m^*\}$ be a feasible schedule for the job subset on $m$ flowshops. Then $OPT(J, 1)$ is the profit of the optimal solution for $J$ on a single flowshop. Given a two-stage job set $J$, we refer to the profit of the two-stage jobs scheduled on the $i$-th flowshop by Algorithm 1 on $J$ as $x_i$, i.e., $x_i = P(S_i)$. Let $y_i$ denote the total profit of the first $i$ flowshops, i.e., $y_i = \sum_{h=1}^{i} x_h = \sum_{h=1}^{i} P(S_h)$, and let $z_i$ denote the difference between the current total profit after $i$ loops for the first $i$ flowshops and the optimal profit, i.e., $z_i = OPT(J, m) - y_i$. According to our definition, $y_0 = 0$, $y_m$ is the total profit of the jobs selected by Algorithm 1 from $J$, and $Z_0 = OPT(J, m)$.

**Lemma 3.** *For any two-stage job set $J$, we have $OPT(J, 1) \geq \frac{OPT(J,m)}{m}$.*

*Proof.* $S^* = \{S_1^*, S_2^*, \cdots, S_m^*\}$ is a feasible schedule for the job subset of an optimal solution of $J$ on $m$ two-stage flowshops. Without loss of generality, we assume that the flowshops have already been sorted in non-increasing order by their profits. That is,

$$P(S_1^*) \geq P(S_2^*) \geq \cdots \geq P(S_m^*),$$

where $P(S_h^*)$ $(1 \leq h \leq m)$ denotes the profit of the job sequence $S_h^*$ on the $h$-th flowshop. We claim that $OPT(J, 1)$ is no less than $P(S_1^*)$, otherwise it contradicts the optimality of $OPT(J,1)$ since the jobs in $S_1^*$ belongs to $J$ and can be schedule to a flowshop within the time limit 1. Combining it with the fact $OPT(J,m) = \sum_{h=1}^{m} P(S_h^*)$, we have:

$$OPT(J,1) \geq \frac{OPT(J,m)}{m}.$$

The equality $OPT(J,1) = \frac{OPT(J,m)}{m}$ holds if and only if $OPT(J,1) = P(S_1^*) = P(S_2^*) = \cdots = P(S_m^*)$. □

The following lemma holds for Algorithm 1.

**Lemma 4.** *For any integer $0 \leq i \leq m$, we have $x_{i+1} \geq \frac{(1-\phi)z_i}{m}$ for any constant $\phi > 0$.*

*Proof.* In each $h$-th loop, $1 \leq h \leq m$, Algorithm 1 selects jobs from unselected jobs and schedules them on the two-stage flowshop $M_h$ by the algorithm $A_o$, which is a PTAS for the single two-stage knapsack problem. Let $J_h^{SEL} \subseteq J$ be the job set selected in the $h$-th loop for $M_h$.

First consider the case $i = 0$. According to the definition of $x_1$ and the fact that $A_o$ is a PTAS, we have:

$$x_1 = A_o(J, 1) = (1 - \phi) \cdot OPT(J, 1). \tag{1}$$

We also have $OPT(J,1) \geq \frac{OPT(J,m)}{m}$ by Lemma 3, and $z_0 = OPT(J,m)$ according to the definition of $z_0$. Combining these with Equality (1) gives:

$$x_1 = (1-\phi)OPT(J,1) \geq (1-\phi)\frac{OPT(J,m)}{m} = \frac{(1-\phi)z_0}{m}.$$

Note that Algorithm 1 removes the jobs in $J_1^{SEL}$ from $J$ after the first loop.

Now consider the case $i \geq 1$. Let $J^{SEL} = \bigcup_{h=1}^{i} J_h^{SEL}$ denote the selected jobs after the first $h$ loops of Algorithm 1. Then the set of current unselected jobs for the $(i+1)$-th loop is $J \setminus J^{SEL}$. Consider a schedule $S' = \{S_1^* \setminus J^{SEL}, S_2^* \setminus J^{SEL}, \cdots, S_m^* \setminus J^{SEL}\}$, where $S_h^*$ is the schedule of an optimal solution on the flowshop $M_h$. We claim that $S'$ is a feasible schedule for $J \setminus J^{SEL}$ on $m$ flowshops, since $S'$ removes the jobs in $J^{SEL}$ from $S^*$ on each flowshop. Furthermore, because $J^{SEL}$ may contain jobs which do not belong to $S^*$, then $\sum_{h=1}^{m} P(S_h^* \setminus J^{SEL}) \geq z_i$. Following a similar analysis as that in Lemma 3, then

$$OPT(J \setminus J^{SEL}, 1) \geq \max_{1 \leq h \leq m} \{P(S_h^* \setminus J^{SEL})\} \geq \frac{z_i}{m},$$

due to that $OPT(J \setminus J^{SEL}, 1)$ represents the optimal profit of the job set $J \setminus J^{SEL}$ on one flowshop. Therefore, for the flowshop $M_{i+1}$,

$$x_{i+1} = A(J \setminus J^{SEL}, 1) \geq (1-\phi) \cdot OPT(J \setminus J^{SEL}, 1) \geq \frac{(1-\phi)z_i}{m}.$$

These complete the proof. □

It is important to note that the profit of the solution by Algorithm 1 is $y_m = x_1 + x_2 + \cdots + x_m$. Lemma 1 gives a lower bound of the profit $x_h$ of the jobs assigned on each flowshop $M_h$ ($1 \leq h \leq m$). To evaluate the approximation ratio of Algorithm 1, based on the lemma, we give a discussion about the upper bound of the difference $z_i$ between the profit of our solution after $i$-th loops and $OPT(J,m)$ of the optimal solution.

**Lemma 5.** *For any integer $0 \leq i \leq m$, the difference between the profit of jobs assigned on the first $i$ two-stage flowshops and the profit of the jobs of the optimal solution is bounded, that is, $z_i \leq \left(1 - \frac{1-\phi}{m}\right)^i \cdot OPT(J,m)$ for any constant $\phi > 0$.*

*Proof.* We prove the lemma by induction on $i$. For the base case $i = 0$, this lemma is obviously true. $z_0 = OPT(J,m)$ since algorithm gains no profit before its first loop. Now suppose inductively that after the first $(i-1)$ loops, the difference between the profit for the jobs in the first $(i-1)$ flowshops and that of the optimal solution is bounded by the following inequality.

$$z_{i-1} \leq \left(1 - \frac{1-\phi}{m}\right)^{i-1} \cdot OPT(J,m).$$

Then we have

$$\begin{aligned} z_{i+1} &= z_i - x_{i+1} \\ &\leq z_i - \frac{1-\phi}{m} z_i = \left(1 - \frac{1-\phi}{m}\right) z_i \\ &\leq \left(1 - \frac{1-\phi}{m}\right)^i \cdot OPT(J,m), \end{aligned}$$

where the first equation holds according to the definition of $z_i$ and $x_i$, the first inequality comes from Lemma 1, and the second inequality holds by the inductive hypothesis. □

Here we come to the main result of the paper.

**Theorem 1.** *Algorithm 1 is a $(1.582+\epsilon)$-approximation algorithm for the multiple two-stage knapsack problem, where the number $m$ of flowshops is part of the input.*

*Proof.* According to Lemma 5, we have

$$z_m \leq \left(1 - \frac{1-\phi}{m}\right)^m \cdot OPT(J,m),$$

where $z_m$ represents the difference between the profit of the optimal solution and the total profit obtained by Algorithm 1 after all $m$ loops for $m$ two-stage flowshops.

Our goal is to evaluate the worst-case performance of the algorithm by maximizing $z_m$, which in turn helps us measure the approximation ratio of the algorithm. We consider the function

$$f(m) = \left(1 - \frac{1-\phi}{m}\right)^m,$$

and find that the function increases monotonically as $m \to \infty$. Thus, the upper bound of the function is:

$$\lim_{m \to +\infty} f(m) = \lim_{m \to \infty} (1 - \frac{(1-\phi)}{m})^m = \lim_{m \to +\infty} e^{\frac{\ln(1-\frac{(1-\phi)}{m})}{\frac{1}{m}}}.$$

Let $t = \frac{1}{m}$. Then we can rewrite the upper bound as:

$$\lim_{t \to 0} e^{\frac{\ln[1-(1-\phi)t]}{t}} = e^{\phi-1}.$$

Therefore, we obtain:

$$z_m \leq \left(1 - \frac{1-\phi}{m}\right)^m \cdot OPT(J,m) \leq e^{\phi-1} \cdot OPT(J,m). \quad (2)$$

The relationship between the profit of the solution $(J^{SEL}, S)$ produced by Algorithm 1 and that of the optimal solution, of a job set $J$, can be expressed as:

$$P(S) = y_m = OPT(J,m) - z_m. \quad (3)$$

Combining Inequality (2) and Equality (3) derives:

$$P(S) \geq (1 - e^{\phi-1})OPT(J,m).$$

According to the definition of approximation ratio, we have:

$$\frac{OPT(J,m)}{P(S)} \leq \frac{1}{1 - e^{\phi-1}} = \frac{1}{1 - e^{-1}} + \epsilon \approx 1.582 + \epsilon.$$

Here the equality holds since Algorithm 1 substitutes $1 + \ln\left(\frac{1+(e-1)\epsilon}{e+(e-1)\epsilon}\right)$ for $\phi$, where $\epsilon > 0$ is a given constant.

These conclude the proof. □

## 4 A Fast 4-Approximation Algorithm

This section presents another approximation algorithm for the multiple two-stage knapsack problem, in which the number $m$ of two-stage flowshops is part of the input. Compared to Algorithm 1, the algorithm has a larger approximation ratio but a much more efficient running time, which makes it more practical for real-world applications.

First, we introduce some new notation. Given a job set $J = \{J_1, J_2, \cdots, J_n\}$, where $J_i = \{r_i, t_i; p_i\}$ for $1 \leq i \leq n$, let $l_i = \frac{p_i}{r_i+t_i}$ be the "density" of the job $J_i$. For a job set $J' \subseteq J$, let $R(J') = \sum_{J_i \in J'} r_i$ be the sum of $R$-times of the jobs in $J'$, let $T(J') = \sum_{J_i \in J'} t_i$ be that of $T$-times of these jobs, and let $W(J') = \sum_{J_i \in J'} r_i + \sum_{J_i \in J'} t_i$ be that of $T$-times and $R$-times of these jobs. Similarly, for a solution that contains a schedule $S$ for a selected job subset $J^{SEL}$, let $R(S) = \sum_{J_i \in J^{SEL}} r_i$, $T(S) = \sum_{J_i \in J^{SEL}} t_i$ and $W(S) = \sum_{J_i \in J^{SEL}} r_i + \sum_{J_i \in J^{SEL}} t_i$ represent the sum of $R$-times, that of $T$-times, and that of $R$-times and $T$-times, of the selected jobs in $J^{SEL}$, respectively.

---

**Algorithm 2:** a fast 4-approximation algorithm for the multiple two-stage knapsack problem

---

**Input** : an instance $\{J, m\}$ of the multiple two-stage knapsack problem;
**Output:** $(J^{SEL}, S)$. $J^{SEL} \subseteq J$ is the subset of the selected job sets, and $S = \{S_1, S_2 \cdots, S_m\}$ is a feasible schedule of $J^{SEL}$ on $m$ flowshops, where each $S_h$ is a job sequence on flowshop $M_h$ with the makespan bounded by the time limit 1.

1  **begin**
2     Sort the jobs in $J$ in non-increasing order by their densities.
3     $i \leftarrow 1, j \leftarrow 1$
4     $S_1, \ldots, S_m \leftarrow \emptyset$
5     $H_1, \cdots H_m, H_{m+1} \leftarrow \emptyset$
6     $J^{SEL} \leftarrow \emptyset$
7     **for** $h \leftarrow 1$ **to** $m$ **do**
8        Find the job index $j$ such that the job sequence $\langle H_h \cup \langle J_i, \ldots, J_j \rangle\rangle$ can be completed by flowshop within the time limit, and the job sequence $\langle H_h \cup \langle J_i, \ldots, J_{j+1} \rangle\rangle$ cannot be completed within the time limit.
9        **if** $P(H_h \cup \langle J_i, \cdots, J_j \rangle) > p_{j+1}$ **then**
10          $S_h \leftarrow \langle H_h \cup \langle J_i, \cdots, J_j \rangle\rangle$ //assign $\langle H_h \cup \langle J_i, \cdots, J_j \rangle\rangle$ to flowshop $M_h$
11          $J^{SEL} \leftarrow J^{SEL} \cup S_h$
12          $H_{h+1} \leftarrow J_{j+1}$
13       **end if**
14       **else**
15          $S_h \leftarrow \langle J_{j+1} \rangle$ //assign $J_{j+1}$ to flowshop $M_h$
16          $J^{SEL} \leftarrow J^{SEL} \cup S_h$
17          $H_{h+1} \leftarrow \langle H_h \cup \langle J_i, \cdots, J_j \rangle\rangle$
18       **end if**
19       $j \leftarrow j+1$
20       $i \leftarrow j$
21    **end for**
22    **return** $(J^{SEL}, S = \{S_1, S_2 \cdots, S_m\})$
23 **end**

Our algorithm is given in Algorithm 2. For the given two-stage job set $J$, we assume that the jobs in $J$ have been sorted in non-increasing order by their densities. Let $H = \{H_1, \cdots H_m, H_{m+1}\}$ denote a group of sequences to record the intermediate state of flowshops during scheduling, where $H_h$ is initialized as $\emptyset$ for each $1 \leq h \leq m+1$. The algorithm then tries to place the current unselected jobs along the sequence $J$, with as much profit as possible, to each flowshop $M_h$ iteratively. Let $i$ be the lowest job index of the current unselected job, and $M_h$ be the current flowshop. The algorithm finds a job index $j$, such that $M_h$ can finish the sequence $\langle H_h \cup \langle J_i, \ldots, J_j \rangle \rangle$, while it cannot finish the sequence $\langle H_h \cup \langle J_i, \ldots, J_j, J_{j+1} \rangle \rangle$, when subject to the time limit 1. If the profit $P(H_h \cup \langle J_i, \cdots, J_j \rangle)$ is greater than the profit $p_{j+1}$ of the job $J_{j+1}$, the algorithm determines the sequence $S_h = \langle H_h \cup \langle J_i, \cdots, J_j \rangle \rangle$ as the schedule for the flowshop $M_h$, and let $J_{j+1}$ be in $H_{h+1}$ prepared for the next flowshop $M_{h+1}$; otherwise, the algorithm schedules $S_h = \langle J_{j+1} \rangle$ to $M_h$ and puts the squence $\langle H_h \cup \langle J_i, \cdots, J_j \rangle \rangle$ in $H_{h+1}$ for $M_{h+1}$. The same procedure is applied $m$ times, until all flowshops $M = \{M_1, M_2, \ldots, M_m\}$ are packed. We note that by carefully recording the profit of $H_h$ ($1 \leq h \leq m$), each job will only be explored once in Algorithm 2.

**Theorem 2.** *The time complexity of Algorithm 2 is $O(n \log n)$.*

*Proof.* The Algorithm 2 first sorts the jobs according to their densities, which takes $O(n \log n)$ time. Then, the for-loop of steps 7 to 21 mainly explores each job $J_i$ once, attempting to pack it into the current flowshop. Given a sequence $H_h$ and a current job $J_i$, checking whether sequence $\langle H_h \cup J_i \rangle$ can be completed within the time limit takes constant time by Lemma 1. Therefore, the for-loop takes $O(n)$ time, and the time complexity of the algorithm is $O(n \log n)$. □

**Theorem 3.** *Algorithm 2 achieves a tight approximation ratio of 4.*

*Proof.* We first consider the approximation ratio of Algorithm 2. The main idea of the proof is similar to that for the fast algorithm of Chen et al. [2], but the use of new notations effectively simplifies the original proof. According to Step 8 of Algorithm 2, $\langle S_h \cup H_{h+1} \rangle$ or $\langle H_{h+1} \cup S_h \rangle$ cannot be scheduled on the same two-stage flowshop subject to the time limit 1, for $1 \leq h \leq m$, then

$$W(S_h) + W(H_{h+1}) = R(S_h) + R(H_{h+1}) + T(S_h) + T(H_{h+1}) > 1,$$

which implies

$$W(S) + W(H) = \sum_{1 \leq h \leq m} W(S_h) + \sum_{1 \leq h \leq m} W(H_{h+1}) > m. \quad (4)$$

Let $S^* = \{S_1^*, S_2^*, \cdots, S_m^*\}$ denote the schedule of the optimal solution. Since $S^*$ is a feasible schedule subject to the time limit 1 and flowshop has an $R$-operation and a $T$-operation, then for any $S_h^*$, $1 \leq h \leq m$,

$$W(S_h^*) = R(S_h^*) + T(S_h^*) \leq 2.$$

Therefore,
$$W(S^*) = \sum_{1 \leq h \leq m} W(S_h^*) \leq 2\,m. \tag{5}$$

Combining the Inequality (4) and Inequality (5) gives
$$W(S) + W(H) > \frac{W(S^*)}{2}. \tag{6}$$

Let $J^{SEL+} = J^{SEL} \cup \{H_{m+1}\}$. Note that Algorithm 2 sorts the jobs in $J$ in non-increasing order by density, and does not discard any job during the scheduling. Then the set $J^{SEL+}$ contains the jobs with the highest density from the original job set $J$. For ease of presentation and without loss of generality, we assume $J^{SEL+} = \langle J_1, J_2, \ldots, J_{m+}\rangle$, satisfying $l_1 \geq l_2 \geq \cdots \geq l_{m+}$. Let $J^{pub} = (S \cup H) \cap S^*$, and let $J_k \in (S \cup H) \setminus J^{pub}$ and $J_{k^*} \in S^* \setminus J^{pub}$. Since $(S \cup H) \setminus J^{pub} \subseteq J^{SEL+}$ and $(S^* \setminus J^{pub} \cap J^{SEL+}) = \emptyset$, we have
$$l_k \geq l_{m+} \geq l_{k^*}. \tag{7}$$

Now consider the profit of the schedule $S$ and $H$ without the jobs in $J^{pub}$.

$$\begin{aligned}
P(S \setminus J^{\text{pub}}) + P(H \setminus J^{\text{pub}}) &= \sum_{J_k \in S \setminus J^{\text{pub}}} P(J_k) + \sum_{J_k \in H \setminus J^{\text{pub}}} P(J_k) \\
&= \sum_{J_k \in S \setminus J^{\text{pub}}} W(J_k)\, l_k + \sum_{J_k \in H \setminus J^{\text{pub}}} W(J_k)\, l_k \\
&\geq l_{m+} \left(W(S \setminus J^{\text{pub}}) + W(H \setminus J^{\text{pub}})\right) \\
&> \frac{l_{m+} W(S^* \setminus J^{\text{pub}})}{2} \\
&> \frac{P(S^* \setminus J^{\text{pub}})}{2},
\end{aligned}$$

where the first and the last inequalities hold from Inequality (7), the second inequality holds from Inequality (6).

The fact $P(S \setminus J^{pub}) + P(H \setminus J^{pub}) > P(S^* \setminus J^{pub})/2$ implies that $P(S) + P(H) > P(S^*)/2$. In each $h$-th loop, where $1 \leq h \leq m$, there is $P(S_h) \geq P(H_{h+1})$, thus $P(S) \geq P(H)$. Therefore,
$$P(J^{SEL}) = P(S) \geq (P(S) + P(H))/2 > p(S^*)/4.$$

As a result, the approximation ratio of Algorithm 2 is 4.

Next, we consider the lower bound of the approximation ratio for Algorithm 2. We construct a counterexample $\{J^{LB}, m\}$ of the multiple two-stage knapsack problem. The two-stage job set $J^{LB}$ can be divided into the following three types of jobs.

$$\begin{aligned}
J^{LB} &= J^{LB_1} \cup J^{LB_2} \cup J^{LB_3} \\
J^{LB_1} &= \{J_i^{LB} = (\tfrac{1}{2} + \epsilon, 0; \tfrac{1}{2} + 2\epsilon) | 1 \leq i \leq m+1\} \\
J^{LB_2} &= \{J_i^{LB} = (1, 0; 1) | m + 2 \leq i \leq 2m+1\} \\
J^{LB_3} &= \{J_i^{LB} = (0, 1; 1) | 2m + 2 \leq i \leq 3m+1\}
\end{aligned}$$

, where $\epsilon$ denotes an arbitrarily small positive constant. $J^{LB_1}$ contains $m+1$ jobs, and $J^{LB_2}$ and $J^{LB_3}$ each contains $m$ jobs.

Now we analyze the approximation ratio of the constructed counterexample. It is not hard to see that in the optimal solution, the jobs in the sets $J^{LB_2}$ and $J^{LB_3}$ are selected, where two jobs from $J^{LB_2}$ and $J^{LB_3}$ are paired into one flowshop. That is, one flowshop obtains a profit of 2. Therefore, the profit gained by the optimal solution is $2m$.

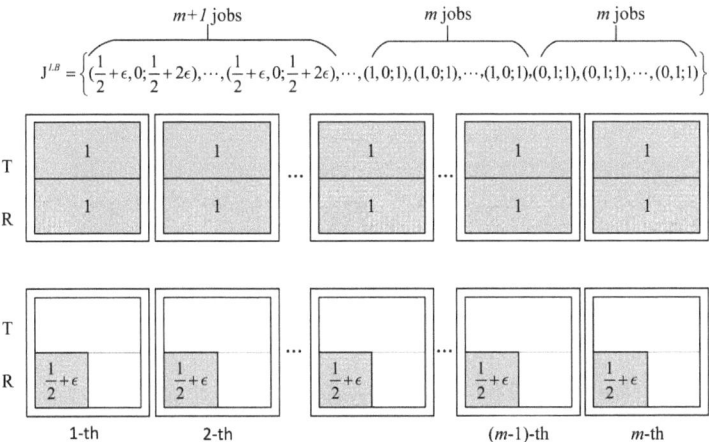

**Fig. 2.** A counterexample and the states of flowshops in the optimal solution and that in the schedule of Algorithm 2 on the counterexample.

Consider Algorithm 2 on the counterexample $\{J^{LB}, m\}$. Algorithm 2 first sorts the jobs in $J^{LB}$ in non-increasing order of their densities. Since the density of $(\frac{1}{2}+2\epsilon)/(\frac{1}{2}+\epsilon)$ of the jobs in $J^{LB_1}$ is slightly greater than that of 1 of the jobs in $J^{LB_2}$ and $J^{LB_3}$, the $m+1$ jobs in $J^{LB_1}$ are first considered by our algorithm. Algorithm 2 repeatedly assigns one job in $J^{LB_1}$ to each flowshop, until all $m$ flowshops have been assigned. The last $(m+1)$-th job in $J^{LB_1}$ prevents the algorithm from further exploring the following jobs in $J^{LB_2}$ and $J^{LB_3}$. As a result, the profit obtained by Algorithm 2 on the counterexample is $m \cdot (\frac{1}{2}+2\epsilon)$. The approximation ratio $\alpha$ of the algorithm on the counterexample is

$$\alpha = 2m / \left(m\left(\frac{1}{2}+2\epsilon\right)\right) \approx 4.$$

Fig. 2 illustrates the states of flowshops in the optimal solution and that in the schedule of Algorithm 2 on the counterexample, respectively.

We conclude that Algorithm 2 for the two stage multiple knapsack problem has an approximation ratio of 4, which is proven to be tight. □

This section proposes a faster approximation algorithm for the Multiple Two-stage Knapsack problem. Compared with the fast algorithm of Chen et al. [2],

Algorithm 2 reduces the time complexity from $O(n^2)$ to $O(n \log n)$ by avoiding reordering jobs within flowshop by Johnson's rule. Meanwhile, the approximation ratio remains 4, which is tight. Furthermore, it is clear that in the lower bound instance, the job sequence (a job of $J^{LB_1}$) scheduled on every flowshop satisfies Johnson's rule, indicating that the instance also applies to Chen et al.'s algorithm. It is worth noting that although Algorithm 2 achieves the same theoretical approximation ratio as that of Chen et al.'s algorithm with better time complexity, in practical applications, Chen et al.'s algorithm may perform better due to its use of Johnson's rule, which is an optimal schedule for jobs assigned on flowshop and thus helps reduce the actual execution time of flowshops.

## 5 Conclusion

This paper focuses on the multiple two-stage knapsack problem, particularly in the case where the number of two-stage flowshops (knapsacks) is part of the input. The problem is a two-stage generalization of the classical multiple knapsack problem. The previously best-known approximation algorithm for the problem has an approximation ratio of $3 + \epsilon$ for any $\epsilon > 0$. In contrast, our proposed algorithm achieves an approximation ratio of $1.582 + \epsilon$, representing significant improvements over the best-known approximation algorithm in terms of the approximation ratio. The result provides a positive answer to an open question proposed by Tong et al. [14] : is it possible to design an algorithm with an approximation ratio better than $3 + \epsilon$.

In addition, we develop a faster 4-approximation algorithm, which optimizes Chen's fast 4-approximation algorithm [2] by reducing the time complexity from $O(n^2)$ to $O(n \log n)$, where $n$ is the number of two-stage jobs. Furthermore, we show that the approximation ratio 4 is tight for our algorithm by establishing a counterexample, which also works to Chen's fast 4-approximation algorithm.

Several directions are worthy of further exploration.

1. Is there a PTAS for the multiple two-stage knapsack problem, where the number of flowshops is a variable?
2. Our fast algorithm essentially adopts a widely used strategy NEXT FIT, and the counterexample shows that the approximation ratio is not affected by the execution order of the assigned two-stage jobs. Are there other strategies that result in approximation algorithms, which take full use of the execution order of jobs, and thus have similar efficiency but better approximation ratio?

## References

1. Chekuri, C., Khanna, S.: A polynomial time approximation scheme for the multiple knapsack problem. SIAM J. Comput. **35**(3), 713–728 (2005). https://doi.org/10.1137/S0097539700382820
2. Chen, J., Huang, M., Guo, Y.: Scheduling multiple two-stage flowshops with a deadline. Theoret. Comput. Sci. **921**, 100–111 (2022). https://doi.org/10.1016/j.tcs.2022.04.004

3. Dawande, M., Gavirneni, S., Rachamadugu, R.: Scheduling a two-stage flowshop under makespan constraint. Math. Comput. Model. **44**(1–2), 73–84 (2006). https://doi.org/10.1016/j.mcm.2004.12.016
4. Dong, J., Jin, R., Luo, T., Tong, W.: A polynomial-time approximation scheme for an arbitrary number of parallel two-stage flow-shops. Eur. J. Oper. Res. **281**(1), 16–24 (2020). https://doi.org/10.1016/j.ejor.2019.08.019
5. Dong, J., et al.: An FPTAS for the parallel two-stage flowshop problem. Theoret. Comput. Sci. **657**, 64–72 (2017). https://doi.org/10.1016/j.tcs.2016.04.046
6. Feige, U.: A threshold of ln $n$ for approximating set cover. J. ACM (JACM) **45**(4), 634–652 (1998). https://doi.org/10.1145/285055.285059
7. Ibarra, O.H., Kim, C.E.: Fast approximation algorithms for the knapsack and sum of subset problems. J. ACM (JACM) **22**(4), 463–468 (1975). https://doi.org/10.1145/321906.321909
8. Jansen, K.: Parameterized approximation scheme for the multiple knapsack problem. SIAM J. Comput. **39**(4), 1392–1412 (2010). https://doi.org/10.1137/080731207
9. Jansen, K.: A fast approximation scheme for the multiple knapsack problem. In: Bieliková, M., Friedrich, G., Gottlob, G., Katzenbeisser, S., Turán, G. (eds.) SOFSEM 2012. LNCS, vol. 7147, pp. 313–324. Springer, Heidelberg (2012). https://doi.org/10.1007/978-3-642-27660-6_26
10. Johnson, S.M.: Optimal two-and three-stage production schedules with setup times included. Naval Res. Logist. Q. **1**(1), 61–68 (1954). https://doi.org/10.1002/nav.3800010110
11. Kellerer, H.: A polynomial time approximation scheme for the multiple knapsack problem. In: Hochbaum, D.S., Jansen, K., Rolim, J.D.P., Sinclair, A. (eds.) APPROX/RANDOM -1999. LNCS, vol. 1671, pp. 51–62. Springer, Heidelberg (1999). https://doi.org/10.1007/978-3-540-48413-4_6
12. Kovalyov, M.: Efficient epsilon-approximation algorithm for minimizing the makespan in a parallel two-stage system. Vesti Academii navuk Belaruskai SSR, Ser. Phiz.-Mat. Navuk **3**, 119 (1985)
13. Rittinghouse, J.W., Ransome, J.F.: Cloud computing: implementation, management, and security. CRC Press (2017). https://doi.org/10.1201/9781439806814
14. Tong, W., Xu, Y., Zhang, H.: A polynomial-time approximation scheme for parallel two-stage flowshops under makespan constraint. Theoret. Comput. Sci. **922**, 438–446 (2022). https://doi.org/10.1016/j.tcs.2022.04.044
15. Wu, G., Chen, J., Wang, J.: Scheduling two-stage jobs on multiple flowshops. Theoret. Comput. Sci. **776**, 117–124 (2019). https://doi.org/10.1016/j.tcs.2019.01.017
16. Wu, G., Chen, J., Wang, J.: On scheduling multiple two-stage flowshops. Theoret. Comput. Sci. **818**, 74–82 (2020). https://doi.org/10.1016/j.tcs.2018.04.017
17. Wu, G., He, H., Rong, G., Shi, F., Yang, Y.: On online approximation algorithms for two-stage bins. In: Fomin, F.V., Xiao, M. (eds.) Computing and Combinatorics. COCOON 2025. LNCS, vol.15983, pp.68–80. Springer Singapore (2026). https://doi.org/10.1007/978-981-95-0215-8_6
18. Wu, G., Zuo, F., Shi, F., Wang, J.: On scheduling multiple parallel two-stage flowshops with Johnson's rule. J. Combinatorial Optim. **47**(12) (2024). https://doi.org/10.1007/s10878-024-01107-z
19. Zhang, Y., Zhou, Y.: TransOS: a transparent computing-based operating system for the cloud. Int. J. Cloud Comput. **1**(4), 287–301 (2012). https://doi.org/10.1504/IJCC.2012.049763

# Semi-online Scheduling Problem of Two Identical Machines with Delayed Discount

Qingyu Luo[✉] and Yaru Yang

School of Mathematics and Statistics, Yunnan University, Kunming, People's Republic of China
1026672013@qq.com

**Abstract.** Firstly, for the processing benefit maximization scheduling problem of $m$ identical machines with a common due date, we prove that the offline optimal value satisfies $F^* = \min\{P_{sum}, md + \delta(P_{sum} - md)\}$. Secondly, we consider the semi-online scheduling problem of two identical machines with delayed discount to maximize the processing benefit, prove that the lower bound of this problem is $\frac{6}{5+\delta}$ and design an optimal semi-online algorithm with a competitive ratio of $\frac{6}{5+\delta}$.

**Keywords:** Processing benefit · Delayed discount · Semi-online · Competitive ratio

## 1 Introduction

Combinatorial optimization encompasses a serious of fundamental problems that arise in various real-world applications, including scheduling [17], resource allocation [13], and facility location. In the context of production and operations management, scheduling problems on identical or parallel machines have been extensively studied. In cloud and edge computing systems, resource allocation problems have attracted significant attention [11,12,19,24]. Facility location continues to be a fundamental problem in combinatorial optimization, and the development of approximation algorithms for its various variants remains an active area of research [29]. This paper mainly studies the processing benefit maximization scheduling problem of identical machines with delayed discount, which further extends the total early work maximization scheduling problem.

Research on early work scheduling is abundant. In 2017, Czerniachowska et al. [27] firstly proposed a new objective of maximizing the total early work, i.e., the total processing time of the jobs processed before their due dates. We can estimate the actual production efficiency or progress based on the target. The processing time of the job processed before its due date is called the early work of the job. Conversely, the processing time of the job processed after its due date is called the late work of the job. The objective to minimize total late work was proposed by Blazewicz et al. [3] in 1984. The total early work maximization scheduling problem is dual to the total late work minimization scheduling problem.

Chen et al. [7] revisited the complexity of late work minimization models, proving that the scheduling problem on $m$ identical machines with a common due date ($m \geq 2$) is binary NP-hard. In this paper, a variant of online scheduling called "online-over-list" is investigated, in which the jobs appear in a certain order and the next job can only appear once the current one has been scheduled. They proposed an online algorithm Extended First Fit for $m$ machines ($EFF_m$) for the total early work maximization scheduling problem with a common due date, i.e., $P\,|d_j = d, online\text{-}over\text{-}list|\max(X)$ and proved that the competitive ratio of the algorithm is $\frac{\sqrt{2m^2-2m+1}-1}{m-1}$. Furthermore, they proved that the online problem on two machines, $P_2\,|d_j = d, online\text{-}over\text{-}list|\max(X)$, has an upper bound equal to $\sqrt{5}-1$, and the $EFF_m$ algorithm is the optimal online algorithm on two machines. Sterna et al. [27] designed a polynomial time approximation scheme (PTAS) for the total early work maximization scheduling problem with a common due date on two machines, i.e., $P_2\,|d_j = d|\max(X)$. In 2020, Chen et al. [10] studied the same problem and proved that the Longest Processing Time first (LPT) algorithm's approximation ratio is at most $\frac{10}{9}$ and gave an example of the problem to show that the lower bound of the LPT algorithm is at least $\frac{12}{11}$. Subsequently, Jiang et al. [16] continued to study the above problem and proved that the tight bound of the LPT algorithm is $\frac{12}{11}$. In 2024, Jiang et al. [17] proved that the classical List Scheduling (LS) algorithm's tight bound for the total early work maximization scheduling problem with a common due date problem on $m$ machines, i.e., $P_m\,|d_j = d|\max(X)$ and proved that the competitive ratio upper bound of the $EFF_m$ algorithm is 1.2956. When the number of machines $m$ is not fixed, Gyorgyi et al. [14] designed a PTAS for the total early work maximization scheduling problem with a common due date, i.e., $P\,|d_j = d|\max(X)$. When the number of machines $m$ is fixed, Chen et al. [7] designed a fully polynomial time approximation scheme (FPTAS) to solve the problem $P_m\,|d_j = d|\max(X)$ based on a dynamic programming approach. In 2022, Li et al. [20] considered the same problem and proposed an efficient polynomial time approximation scheme (EPTAS), which improved the results of Chen et al. [7] and Gyorgyi et al. [14]. In the same year, Chen et al. [8] improved the existing results of the problem $P_m\,|d_j = d|\max(X)$ and they proposed a more efficient dynamic programming algorithm and two FPTAS. In recent years, Xiao et al. [32] have introduced hierarchical constraints into scheduling problems to maximize the total early work. For the online cases on two machines, they gave an optimal online algorithm with a competition ratio of $\sqrt{2}$. In 2025, Li et al. [21] studied the parallel machine scheduling problem with a common due date to maximize the total weighted early work. They presented the first EPTAS for this problem and designed an FPTAS when the number of machines is fixed. In the same year, Li et al. [22] introduced a novel scheduling criterion named as a discounted profit, which could be considered as a generalization of early work. For the online case, they proved the competitive ratio of the LS algorithm is exactly $\frac{4}{3+\delta}$ and proposed a new optimal online algorithm with a competitive ratio of $\frac{\sqrt{2\delta+5}+2\delta-1}{\delta\sqrt{2\delta+5}+1}$ when the number of machines $m = 2$. For the offline case, they proved the approximation ratio of the LPT algorithm is $\frac{\sqrt{2}+1}{2+(\sqrt{2}-1)\delta}$.

In addition, there are many semi-online results. Chen et al. [6] studied several semi-online versions of the problem $P_m |d_j = d| \max(X)$: Under the precondition that the sum of the processing time of all the jobs $P_{sum}$ is known, they designed an optimal semi-online algorithm with a competition ratio of $\frac{6}{5}$; Under the premise that the maximum size of the job is known, they gave a semi-online algorithm with a competition ratio of 1.1357 and proved that the lower bound of the problem is 1.1231; Under the premise that the sum of the processing time of all the jobs and the maximum size of the job are known, they designed an optimal semi-online algorithm with a competition ratio of $\frac{10}{9}$. In 2021, Xiao et al. [31] studied a series of semi-online early work maximization problems on two hierarchical machines. When the total processing time of low or high hierarchy is known, they proposed an optimal algorithm with a competitive ratio of $\sqrt{5} - 1$; When the total processing times of low and high hierarchy are known, they proposed an optimal algorithm with a competitive ratio of $\frac{6}{5}$. Then, Xiao et al. [30] considered the problem of semi-online machine covering on three machines with two hierarchies and designed two optimal algorithms.

The research on the total late work minimization scheduling problem can be traced back to 1984, when Blazewicz [3] first proposed the indicator of "loss of work lost". His research was mainly based on the collection of information in the control system and the information collected after the effective date would be useless. This kind of information can be called "information loss". In 1992, Potts and Van Wassenhove [26] formally introduced the term "late work" and set the goal of these models as the total late work minimization. In 1992, Potts et al. [26] first studied the total late work minimization scheduling problem in a single-machine environment, i.e., $1 || Y$, and proved that the problem is NP-hard in the non-interruptible case. In the same year, they designed a fully polynomial time approximation scheme (FPTAS) to solve this problem [25]. In 1995, they studied the total late work minimization scheduling problem in a single-machine environment with weights, i.e., $1 || Y_w$, and proved that the problem is weakly NP-hard. They also designed a dynamic programming algorithm, a branch-and-bound algorithm [15] and a FPTAS [18] to solve the problem. In 2004, Blazewicz et al. [5] considered the total late work minimization scheduling problem in a free job environment with weights and a common due date, i.e., $O |d_j = d| Y_w$ and they proved that the problem is weakly NP-hard and designed a dynamic programming algorithm. In 2005, they first considered the two-machine non-preemptive flow-shop scheduling problem with a total weighted late work criterion and a common due date, i.e., $F_2 |d_j = d| Y_w$ and proved that the problem is weakly NP-hard; They also designed corresponding heuristic algorithms and precise algorithms for this problem and compared the performance of these algorithms through numerical experiments [4]. In 2006, Lin et al. [23] proved that the two-machine flow-shop scheduling problem of minimizing the total late work with a common due date, i.e., $F_2 |d_j = d| Y$ is NP-hard and designed a meta-heuristic algorithm and a branch-and-bound algorithm respectively for this problem. In 2011, Wu et al. [28] introduced the concept of learning effect into the total late work minimization scheduling problem on a single machine and proposed a series of solving algorithms. In 2014, Abasian et al. [1] studied the total weighted late work minimization scheduling problem with communication delay on parallel machines. In 2015, Xu et al. [33] studied the total weighted late work minimization scheduling problem with a common due date on identical machines i.e., $P|d_j = d|Y_w$ and designed three meta-heuristic algorithms to solve the problem. In 2016, Afzalirad and Rezaeian [2] studied the non-homogeneous machine scheduling problem with hierarchical constraints to minimize the total late work and proposed a hybrid meta-heuristic algorithm to solve it.

Different from the studies mentioned above, we mainly study the semi-online scheduling problem on parallel machines with delayed discount. The scheduling problem on parallel machines with delayed discount is very closely related to the total late work minimization scheduling problem. The late work of the job is the processing time of the job processed after its due date and the delayed discount is the discount of the processing benefit generated by the late work of the job by a certain percentage. When the load of machine exceeds the common due date, this paper hopes that the excess part, i.e., the total late work of all machines, is as small as possible.

We formally introduce the problem as follows: There is a set of $n$ jobs $\mathcal{J} = \{J_1, J_2, \ldots, J_n\}$ and a set of $m$ machines $\mathcal{M} = \{M_1, M_2, \ldots, M_m\}$. It is known that these $n$ jobs must be scheduled on $m$ identical machines in a non-interruptible and non-overlapping manner. The job $J_j$ has a processing time $p_j$ and a due date $d_j$. In this paper we assume that all jobs have a common due date, i.e., $d_j = d$, and the processing time of job $J_j$ is not longer than the common due date, i.e., $p_j \leq d$. Let $C_j$ denotes the completion time of job $J_j$, $X_j$ denotes the early work of job $J_j$, $Y_j$ denotes the late work of job $J_j$. These can be expressed as:

$$X_j = \min\{p_j, \max\{0, p_j - (C_j - d)\}\},$$
$$Y_j = \min\{p_j, \max\{0, C_j - d\}\}.$$

Obviously, the sum of the early work of job $J_j$ and the late work of job $J_j$ is the processing time of job $J_j$, i.e.,

$$X_j + Y_j = p_j,$$

the processing benefit of job $J_j$ can be expressed as:

$$F_j = X_j + \delta Y_j,$$

where $\delta \in [0, 1)$ denotes the processing benefit per unit time of job $J_j$ processed after the common due date. When $\delta = 0$, the problem model is simplified to the total early work maximization scheduling problem.

The goal of this problem is to find a schedule $\sigma : \mathcal{J} \to \mathcal{M}$ that produces the maximum total processing benefits after all the jobs in $\mathcal{J}$ are scheduled on all the machines in $\mathcal{M}$, i.e.,

$$\max F = \max \sum_{j=1}^{n} F_j = \max \sum_{j=1}^{n} (X_j + \delta Y_j).$$

Using the three-filed notation, this problem can be denoted as $P_m |d_j = d|$ $\max(F)$. For convenience, in any feasible scheduling: if $Y_j = 0$, the job $J_j$ is called a early job; If $X_j = 0$, the job $J_j$ is called a full-late job; If $\min\{X_j, Y_j\} > 0$, the job $J_j$ is called a partial-late job.

For an online (or semi-online) scheduling problem with maximizing (or minimizing) objectives, the performance of an algorithm A is measured by its *competitive ratio*, which is defined as follows:

$$R_A = \min\left\{R \mid \frac{C^*(\mathcal{J})}{C^A(\mathcal{J})} \leq R, \forall \mathcal{J}\right\},$$

where $C^A(\mathcal{J})$ denotes the objective value produced by algorithm A and $C^*(\mathcal{J})$ denotes the optimal objective value in the offline version of the problem. The problem has a *lower bound* $\rho$ if no algorithm has a competitive ratio smaller than $\rho$. The algorithm A is called *optimal* if its competition ratio matches the lower bound of the problem.

We organize the rest of the paper as follows: In Sect. 2, we provide some symbolic definitions and prove that the offline optimal value of the problem $P_m |d_j = d| \max(F)$ satisfies $F^* = \min\{P_{sum}, md + \delta(P_{sum} - md)\}$. In Sect. 3, we study the semi-online scheduling problem of two identical machines with delayed discount to maximize the processing benefit, i.e., $P_2 |d_j = d, P_{sum}| \max(F)$. For this problem, we prove that the lower bound of this problem is $\frac{6}{5+\delta}$ and design an optimal semi-online algorithm with a competitive ratio of $\frac{6}{5+\delta}$. Finally, in Sect. 4, we summarize this paper and propose the future research direction.

## 2 Preliminaries

For convenience, the symbols that may be used in this paper are summarized below.

- $L_i^j$: the load of the machine $M_i (1 \leq i \leq m)$ after scheduling the job $J_j (1 \leq j \leq n)$;
- $P_{sum}$: the total processing time of all the jobs, i.e., $P_{sum} = \sum_{j=1}^{n} p_j$;
- $p_{max}$: the largest processing time of all the jobs, i.e., $p_{max} = \max_{1 \leq j \leq n} \{p_j\}$;
- $L_i$: the load of the machine $M_i (1 \leq i \leq m)$ after scheduling all the jobs, i.e., $L_i = \sum_{j:\sigma(j)=i} p_j$;
- $X_{\{i\}}$: the total early work of the machine $M_i (1 \leq i \leq m)$, i.e., $X_{\{i\}} = \sum_{j:\sigma(j)=i} X_j$;
- $Y_{\{i\}}$: the total late work of the machine $M_i (1 \leq i \leq m)$, i.e., $Y_{\{i\}} = \sum_{j:\sigma(j)=i} Y_j$;

- $F_{\{i\}}$: the processing benefit of the machine $M_i$ $(1 \leq i \leq m)$, which can be expressed as follows:

$$F_{\{i\}} = \begin{cases} L_i & \text{if } L_i \leq d; \\ d + \delta(L_i - d) & \text{if } L_i > d, \end{cases}$$

- $F$: the total processing benefit of all the machines, which can be expressed as follows:

$$F = \sum_{j=1}^{n} X_j + \delta \sum_{j=1}^{n} Y_j = \sum_{i=1}^{m} F_{\{i\}}$$
$$= \sum_{i=1}^{m} \min\{L_i, d + \delta(L_i - d)\}.$$

- $F^A(I)$: the total processing benefit of all the machines after scheduling all the jobs by algorithm A, in short $F^A$;
- $F^*(I)$: the total processing benefit of all the machines in the optimal schedule, in short $F^*$.

**Lemma 1.** *The offline optimal value of the problem $P_m |d_j = d| \max(F)$ satisfies*

$$F^* = \min\{P_{sum}, md + \delta(P_{sum} - md)\}.$$

*Proof.* When $P_{sum} \leq md$, there is an optimal offline scheduling scheme, i.e., all jobs are closely arranged on $m$ machines. If the load on all machines does not exceed $d$, then $F^* = P_{sum}$. Otherwise, there exists a machine whose load exceeds $d$ and we can obtain $F^* = md + \delta(P_{sum} - md)$. When $P_{sum} > md$, there is an optimal offline scheduling scheme, i.e., all jobs are closely arranged on $m$ machines, so that the load on all machines are at least $d$, and the part that exceeds the load of machine is minimal, so $F^* = md + \delta(P_{sum} - md)$. In summary, combined with $\delta \in [0, 1)$, we can obtain $F^* = \min\{P_{sum}, md + \delta(P_{sum} - md)\}$. Therefore, the lemma holds.

## 3 Semi-online Scheduling Problem of Two Identical Machines

In this section, we study the processing benefit maximization scheduling problem of two identical machines with delayed discount, mainly in the semi-online case where the total processing time of all the jobs is known in advance, i.e., $P_2 |d_j = d, P_{sum}| \max(F)$. To solve this problem, we designed an optimal semi-online algorithm with a competitive ratio of $\frac{6}{5+\delta}$.

## 3.1 Lower Bound

In order to illustrate the lower bound of this problem, we need to construct the following problem instance to prove it.

**Theorem 1.** *For the problem $P_2 | d_j = d, P_{sum} | \max(F)$, any online algorithm has a competitive ratio of at least $\frac{6}{5+\delta}$.*

*Proof.* Consider the following instance $I$: Suppose that the total processing time of all the jobs $P_{sum} = 6$ and the common due date $d = 3$. At the beginning, the first two jobs $J_1$ and $J_2$ arrive with the same processing time, $p_1 = p_2 = 1$.

**Case 1.** $J_1$ and $J_2$ are scheduled to the same machine by algorithm A.

In this case, the last two jobs $J_3$ and $J_4$ arrive and their processing time $p_3 = p_4 = 2$. So we have $F^*(I) = 6$ and $F^A(I) \leq 5 + \delta(1 + 1 + 2 - 3) = 5 + \delta$. Therefore,

$$\frac{F^*(I)}{F^A(I)} \geq \frac{6}{5+\delta}.$$

**Case 2.** $J_1$ and $J_2$ are scheduled to the different machines by algorithm A.

In this case, the last two jobs $J_3$ and $J_4$ arrive and their processing time $p_3 = 1$ and $p_4 = 3$. So we have $F^*(I) = 6$ and $F^A(I) \leq 5 + \delta(1 + 3 - 3) = 5 + \delta$. Therefore,

$$\frac{F^*(I)}{F^A(I)} \geq \frac{6}{5+\delta}.$$

Above all, the theorem is proved.

## 3.2 The Semi-online Algorithm 1 for the Problem $P_2 | d_j = d, P_{sum} | \max(F)$

We know that the total early work maximization scheduling problem and the total late work minimization scheduling problem are equivalent when considering the offline optimal value, so the problem $P_2 | d_j = d | Y$ and the problem $P_2 | d_j = d | \max(X)$ are equivalent. Furthermore, theorem 1 in reference [9] proves that any optimal value for the makespan minimization problem on two identical parallel machines, i.e., $P_2 || C_{max}$ is also optimal for the problem $P_2 | d_j = d | Y$, so we have the following lemma.

**Lemma 2.** *In the offline case, any optimal value for the problem $P_2 || C_{max}$ is also optimal for the problem $P_2 | d_j = d | \max(X)$.*

Then we prove the competitive ratio of Algorithm 1. If it is equal to the lower bound of the problem, then the Algorithm 1 is an optimal semi-online algorithm.

**Theorem 2.** *For any instance $I$ of the problem $P_2 | d_j = d, P_{sum} | \max(F)$, the competitive ratio of Algorithm 1 is $\frac{6}{5+\delta}$.*

**Algorithm 1.**

1: Initially, let $j = 1$ and $L_1^0 = L_2^0 = 0$.
2: **if** $L_1^{j-1} + p_j \leq \frac{1}{3} P_{sum}$ **then**
3:   Schedule job $J_j$ to the machine $M_1$, set $j := j + 1$ and repeat line 2.
4: **else**
5:   **if** $\frac{1}{3} P_{sum} < L_1^{j-1} + p_j \leq \frac{2}{3} P_{sum}$ **then**
6:     Schedule job $J_j$ to the machine $M_1$ and schedule the rest jobs to the machine $M_2$. Stop.
7:   **else**
8:     **if** $L_1^{j-1} + p_j > \frac{2}{3} P_{sum}$ **then**
9:       Schedule the job $J_j$ to the machine $M_2$ and schedule the rest jobs to the machine $M_1$. Stop.
10:    **end if**
11:   **end if**
12: **end if**

*Proof.* Suppose that $d = 1$, by lemma 1, we have $F^*(I) \leq \min\{P_{sum}, 2 + \delta(P_{sum} - 2)\}$. According to Algorithm 1: If $\max\{L_1, L_2\} \leq 1$, then $F^A(I) = P_{sum} = F^*(I)$; If $L_{min} \geq 1$, then $F^A(I) = 2 + \delta(P_{sum} - 2) = F^*(I)$. In the above two cases, the Algorithm 1 is optimal, so we only consider $L_{min} < 1 < L_{max}$. In this case, there is $F^A(I) = L_{min} + 1 + \delta(L_{max} - 1)$. Then we distinguish two cases to discuss.

**Case 1.** The Algorithm 1 terminates on line 6.
In this case, we have

$$\frac{1}{3} P_{sum} < L_1^n = L_1^{n-1} + p_n \leq \frac{2}{3} P_{sum}.$$

By $L_1^n + L_2^n = P_{sum}$, we have $\frac{1}{3} P_{sum} \leq L_2^n < \frac{2}{3} P_{sum}$, i.e.,

$$\frac{1}{3} P_{sum} \leq L_{min} < 1 < L_{max} \leq \frac{2}{3} P_{sum}.$$

**Case 1.1.** $P_{sum} \leq 2$.
In this case, by $L_{max} \leq \frac{2}{3} P_{sum}$, we have

$$L_{max} - 1 \leq \frac{2}{3} P_{sum} - 1 \leq \frac{2}{3} P_{sum} - \frac{1}{2} P_{sum} = \frac{1}{6} P_{sum}.$$

Therefore, by $F^A(I) = L_{min} + 1 + \delta(L_{max} - 1)$ and $F^*(I) \leq P_{sum}$, we have

$$\frac{F^*(I)}{F^A(I)} \leq \frac{P_{sum}}{L_{min} + 1 + \delta(L_{max} - 1)}$$

$$= \frac{P_{sum}}{P_{sum} - (1-\delta)(L_{max} - 1)}$$

$$\leq \frac{P_{sum}}{P_{sum} - (1-\delta)\frac{1}{6} P_{sum}}$$

$$= \frac{1}{1 - (1-\delta)\frac{1}{6}}$$

$$= \frac{6}{5+\delta}.$$

**Case 1.2.** $P_{sum} > 2$.
In this case, by $L_{min} \geq \frac{1}{3} P_{sum}$ and $F^*(I) \leq 2 + \delta(P_{sum} - 2)$, we have

$$\frac{F^*(I)}{F^A(I)} \leq \frac{2 + \delta(P_{sum} - 2)}{L_{min} + 1 + \delta(L_{max} - 1)}$$

$$= 1 + \frac{1 - L_{min}}{1 + L_{min} + \frac{\delta}{1-\delta} P_{sum}}$$

$$\leq 1 + \frac{1 - \frac{1}{3} P_{sum}}{1 + \frac{1}{3} P_{sum} + \frac{\delta}{1-\delta} P_{sum}}$$

$$\leq 1 + \frac{1 - \frac{2}{3}}{1 + \frac{2}{3} + \frac{2\delta}{1-\delta}}$$

$$= 1 + \frac{1}{5 + \frac{6\delta}{1-\delta}}$$

$$= \frac{6}{5 + \delta}.$$

**Case 2.** The Algorithm 1 terminates on line 9.

In this case, suppose that the last job scheduled to the machine $M_2$ is $J_b$. According to the Algorithm 1, only the job $J_b$ is scheduled to the machine $M_2$, i.e., there is only one job $J_b$ on the machine $M_2$, and the rest jobs are scheduled to the machine $M_1$. Since the Algorithm 1 terminates on line 9, we have

$$L_1^{b-1} + p_b > \frac{2}{3} P_{sum},$$

since $L_1^{b-1} \leq \frac{1}{3} P_{sum}$, we have

$$p_b > \frac{2}{3} P_{sum} - L_1^{b-1} \geq \frac{2}{3} P_{sum} - \frac{1}{3} P_{sum} = \frac{1}{3} P_{sum}.$$

**Case 2.1.** $\frac{1}{3} P_{sum} < p_b \leq \frac{2}{3} P_{sum}$.

In this case, since there is only one job $J_b$ on the machine $M_2$, we have

$$\frac{1}{3} P_{sum} < L_2 = p_b \leq \frac{2}{3} P_{sum},$$

it follows that

$$\frac{1}{3} P_{sum} < L_2 = L_{min} < 1 < L_{max} = L_1 \leq \frac{2}{3} P_{sum}.$$

Therefore from the proof of case 1, we have

$$\frac{F^*(I)}{F^A(I)} \leq \frac{6}{5 + \delta}.$$

**Case 2.2.** $p_b > \frac{2}{3} P_{sum}$.

In this case, according to lemma 2, the offline optimal value of the problem $P_2 || C_{max}$ is also the offline optimal value of the problem $P_2 | d_j = d | \max(X)$. So for the problem $P_2|d_j = d, P_{sum}|\max(F)$, the output solution of the Algorithm 1 in this case is the offline optimal solution of the problem.

Therefore, the theorem is proved and the Algorithm 1 is an optimal semi-online algorithm.

It is worth noting that when $\delta = 0$, the competitive ratio of Algorithm 1 is $\frac{6}{5}$. This matches the optimal competitive ratio for the early work maximization scheduling problem under the assumption that the total processing time $P_{sum}$ is known in advance. This result is consistent with the work of Chen et al. [6], thereby confirming the optimality of Algorithm 1 in this special case.

## 4 Conclusions

In this paper, we study the processing benefit maximization scheduling problem of identical machines with delayed discount, which further extends the total early work maximization scheduling problem of identical machines and the late work minimization scheduling problem of identical machines. And we also analyze and discuss this problem on the basis of existing research results. Firstly, we prove that the offline optimal value of the problem $P_m|d_j = d|\max(F)$ satisfies $F^* = \min\{P_{sum}, md + \delta(P_{sum} - md)\}$. Secondly, we study the semi-online case of two identical machines. Under the precondition that the total processing time of all the jobs $P_{sum}$ is known, we propose an optimal semi-online algorithm with a competitive ratio of $\frac{6}{5+\delta}$.

We can also study more semi-online cases on $m$ machines, such as maximum processing time $P_{max}$ is known in advance, the offline optimal value $OPT$ is known in advance, or the combination of any two of $P_{sum}, P_{max}, OPT$ is known in advance. We can design a better semi-online algorithm and continuously improve the algorithm's competitive ratio to get the best result as far as possible.

## References

1. Abasian, F., Ranjbar, M., Salari, M., Davari, M., Khatami, S.M.: Minimizing the total weighted late work in scheduling of identical parallel processors with communication delays. Appl. Math. Model. **38**(15–16), 3975–3986 (2014)
2. Afzalirad, M., Rezaeian, J.: Design of high-performing hybrid meta-heuristics for unrelated parallel machine scheduling with machine eligibility and precedence constraints. Eng. Optim. **48**(4), 706–726 (2016)
3. Blazewicz, J.: Scheduling preemptible tasks on parallel processors with information. Tech. et Sci. Informatiques **3**, 415–420 (1984)
4. Blazewicz, J., Pesch, E., Sterna, M., Werner, F.: Flow shop scheduling with late work criterion – choosing the best solution strategy. In: Manandhar, S., Austin, J., Desai, U., Oyanagi, Y., Talukder, A.K. (eds.) AACC 2004. LNCS, vol. 3285, pp. 68–75. Springer, Heidelberg (2004). https://doi.org/10.1007/978-3-540-30176-9_9
5. Błażewicz, J., Pesch, E., Sterna, M., Werner, F.: Open shop scheduling problems with late work criteria. Discret. Appl. Math. **134**(1–3), 1–24 (2004)

6. Chen, X., Kovalev, S., Liu, Y., Sterna, M., Chalamon, I., Błażewicz, J.: Semi-online scheduling on two identical machines with a common due date to maximize total early work. Discret. Appl. Math. **290**, 71–78 (2021)
7. Chen, X., Liang, Y., Sterna, M., Wang, W., Błażewicz, J.: Fully polynomial time approximation scheme to maximize early work on parallel machines with common due date. Eur. J. Oper. Res. **284**(1), 67–74 (2020)
8. Chen, X., Shen, X., Kovalyov, M.Y., Sterna, M., Blazewicz, J.: Alternative algorithms for identical machines scheduling to maximize total early work with a common due date. Comput. Ind. Eng. **171**, 108386 (2022)
9. Chen, X., Sterna, M., Han, X., Blazewicz, J.: Scheduling on parallel identical machines with late work criterion: offline and online cases. J. Sched. **19**(6), 729–736 (2016)
10. Chen, X., Wang, W., Xie, P., Zhang, X., Sterna, M., Błażewicz, J.: Exact and heuristic algorithms for scheduling on two identical machines with early work maximization. Comput. Ind. Eng. **144**, 106449 (2020)
11. Deng, B., Guo, H., Li, W.: An alternative mechanism for multiresource fair allocation in heterogeneous cloud computing systems. Concurr. Comput. Pract. Exp. **37**(9–11), e70091 (2025)
12. Guo, H., Deng, B., Li, W.: Multi-resource maximin share fair allocation in the cloud-edge collaborative computing system with bandwidth demand compression. Clust. Comput. **28**(2), 98 (2025)
13. Guo, H., Li, W., Deng, B.: A survey on fair allocation of chores. Mathematics **11**(16), 3616 (2023)
14. Györgyi, P., Kis, T.: A common approximation framework for early work, late work, and resource leveling problems. Eur. J. Oper. Res. **286**(1), 129–137 (2020)
15. Hariri, A.M., Potts, C.N., Van Wassenhove, L.N.: Single machine scheduling to minimize total weighted late work. ORSA J. Comput. **7**(2), 232–242 (1995)
16. Jiang, Y., Guan, L., Zhang, K., Liu, C., Cheng, T., Ji, M.: A note on scheduling on two identical machines with early work maximization. Comput. Ind. Eng. **153**, 107091 (2021)
17. Jiang, Y., et al.: Online early work scheduling on parallel machines. Eur. J. Oper. Res. **315**(3), 855–862 (2024)
18. Kovalyov, M.Y., Potts, C.N., Van Wassenhove, L.N.: A fully polynomial approximation scheme for scheduling a single machine to minimize total weighted late work. Math. Oper. Res. **19**(1), 86–93 (1994)
19. Li, S., et al.: Multi-user joint task offloading and resource allocation based on mobile edge computing in mining scenarios. Sci. Rep. **15**(1), 16170 (2025)
20. Li, W.D.: Improved approximation schemes for early work scheduling on identical parallel machines with a common due date. J. Oper. Res. Soc. China **12**(2), 341–350 (2024)
21. Li, W., Ou, J.: Approximation schemes for parallel machine scheduling to maximize total weighted early work with a common due date. Naval Res. Logist. (NRL) **72**(3), 454–464 (2025)
22. Li, W., Yang, Y., Xiao, M., Chen, X., Sterna, M., Błażewicz, J.: Scheduling with a discounted profit criterion on identical machines. Discret. Appl. Math. **367**, 195–209 (2025)
23. Lin, B.M., Lin, F.C., Lee, R.C.: Two-machine flow-shop scheduling to minimize total late work. Eng. Optim. **38**(04), 501–509 (2006)
24. Liu, X., Liu, J., Li, W.: Truthful mechanism for resource allocation and pricing in vehicle-assisted mobile edge computing. IEEE Trans. Veh. Technol. **74**, 8171–8186 (2025)

25. Potts, C.N., Van Wassenhove, L.N.: Approximation algorithms for scheduling a single machine to minimize total late work. Oper. Res. Lett. **11**(5), 261–266 (1992)
26. Potts, C.N., Van Wassenhove, L.N.: Single machine scheduling to minimize total late work. Oper. Res. **40**(3), 586–595 (1992)
27. Sterna, M., Czerniachowska, K.: Polynomial time approximation scheme for two parallel machines scheduling with a common due date to maximize early work. J. Optim. Theory Appl. **174**(3), 927–944 (2017)
28. Wu, C.C., Chen, H.M., Cheng, S.R., Hsu, C.J., Wu, W.H.: Simulated annealing approach for the single-machine total late work scheduling problem with a position-based learning. In: 2011 IEEE 18th International Conference on Industrial Engineering and Engineering Management, pp. 839–843. IEEE (2011)
29. Xiao, H., Zhang, J., Zhang, Z., Li, W.: A survey of approximation algorithms for the universal facility location problem. Mathematics **13**(7), 1023 (2025)
30. Xiao, M., Du, Y.F., Li, W.D., Yang, J.H.: Semi-online machine covering problem on three hierarchical machines with bounded processing times. J. Oper. Res. Soc. China, 1–13 (2023). https://doi.org/10.1007/s40305-023-00477-1
31. Xiao, M., Liu, X., Li, W.: Semi-online early work maximization problem on two hierarchical machines with partial information of processing time. In: International Conference on Algorithmic Applications in Management, pp. 146–156. Springer (2021). https://doi.org/10.1007/s10878-023-01086-7
32. Xiao, M., Liu, X., Li, W., Chen, X., Sterna, M., Blazewicz, J.: Online and semi-online scheduling on two hierarchical machines with a common due date to maximize the total early work. Int. J. Appl. Math. Comput. Sci. **34**(2), 253–261 (2024)
33. Xu, Z., Zou, Y., Kong, X.: Meta-heuristic algorithms for parallel identical machines scheduling problem with weighted late work criterion and common due date. Springerplus **4**(1), 1–13 (2015). https://doi.org/10.1186/s40064-015-1559-5

# Logic

# Sequential Equivalence Checking for Specialized IR via Instrumentation-Based Symbolic Execution

Zi Cheng and LeFei Zhang[✉]

School of Computer Science, Wuhan University, Wuhan, China
{2019302110244,zhanglefei}@whu.edu.cn

**Abstract.** High-Level Synthesis (HLS) tools automatically convert high-level algorithmic descriptions into hardware implementations, enabling rapid prototyping and design space exploration. As these tools perform complex transformations, Formal Equivalence Checking (FEC) becomes essential to verify that the generated hardware maintains the same behavior as the original high-level specification. Google's open-source XLS tool represents a new generation of HLS frameworks that achieves a balance between flexibility and simplicity through its specialized intermediate representation (IR). However, unlike traditional LLVM IR, XLS's functional SSA-style IR lacks structural continuity across transformations and optimization passes, and its semantics are based on Kahn Process Networks that differ from the CDFG-based LLVM IR, posing new challenges for equivalence checking. In this paper, we address the Sequential Equivalence Checking (SEC) between the scheduled XLS IR and the generated RTL. We propose an instrumentation-based pipeline-stage-wise symbolic execution approach with two main contributions: First, we prove that stage-by-stage verification of output transition functions and the concerned state transitions is sufficient to establish sequential equivalence. To overcome the symbolic execution difficulties, we record mapping relationships and construct symbolic constraint formulas through instrumentation during the code generation process. Experimental results show that our method effectively verifies the sequential equivalence, offering a practical approach to equivalence checking for modern HLS tools.

**Keywords:** High-Level Synthesis (HLS) · symbolic execution · equivalence checking · register-transfer level (RTL)

# 1 Introduction

High-Level Synthesis (HLS) is a widely used design methodology that converts algorithmic descriptions written in high-level languages like C/C++ into hardware implementations like Verilog or VHDL [7]. By raising the abstraction level of hardware development, HLS enables faster design exploration and improves overall productivity. Formal equivalence checking (FEC) [9] has become a key verification technique to ensure functional correctness is maintained across synthesis stages.

**Problem Statement.** As one of the major notions of equivalence, sequential equivalence, also called cycle-accurate equivalence, concerns whether two models generate identical outputs at the same times for equivalent inputs, without requiring full correspondence of internal states. A common use case in sequential equivalence checking (SEC) is comparing an unpipelined behavioral RTL with its pipelined counterpart by applying identical input sequences and comparing outputs after the pipeline fills. Symbolic simulation is widely used in SEC to represent large input spaces compactly via symbolic variables, enabling the efficient detection of functional equivalence without exhaustive enumeration [19]. In this work, we perform SEC between a customized IR and its generated RTL within a relatively new HLS framework by symbolic execution.

**Challenges.** Traditional HLS tools like Vivado HLS [2], Catapult [1], and LegUp [5] convert C/C++ or SystemC code into RTL via LLVM-based control data flow graphs (CDFGs). These tools hide low-level synthesis details, which limit opportunities for RTL optimization. In contrast, Google's XLS [3] adopts a mid-level synthesis approach. It compiles DSLX or restricted C++ into a custom intermediate representation that preserves high-level modeling while exposing key hardware structures such as pipeline stages and dataflow. This structural visibility enables designers to guide scheduling and resource usage more directly than in traditional HLS. XLS IR differs from traditional HLS IRs in both semantics and structure. Semantically, it follows a dataflow model with functions, channels, and procs, aligning more with Kahn Process Networks (KPNs) [11] than with imperative LLVM CDFGs. It models continuous sequential behavior over data streams, rather than isolated combinational executions. Structurally, XLS uses a purely functional, SSA-based IR where each transformation generates a fresh set of nodes without structural continuity. Unlike traditional HLS tools that incrementally update a mutable CDFG while preserving node identity and topology, XLS breaks structural continuity after transformations, such as optimization passes. This leads to two key challenges: (1) The customized IR requiring semantic-level analysis; (2) Tracking node correspondence is difficult, as transformations replace node sets entirely.

**Prior Work.** Traditional high-level synthesis (HLS) verification adopts a phase-wise methodology, independently validating each transformation step compilation [21], scheduling [6,14], resource binding [12], and datapath/controller synthesis [13] to ensure functional equivalence. This work focuses on the post-scheduling phase. A representative approach [13] models both the input (CDFG after binding) and output (datapath and controller) as finite-state machines with datapaths (FSMDs), establishing equivalence through structural matching of control and data signals. However, as highlighted in the recent survey [16], such FSMD-based methods are fundamentally limited when the structure alignment is not possible, an issue inherent in the transformation strategies employed by XLS IR. Consequently, their approach does not generalize to our setting.

**Our Work.** We propose an instrumentation-based symbolic execution method [15,21] to check the equivalence between scheduled XLS IR and its generated RTL. To enable semantic comparison, we model both the XLS IR and the RTL as Mealy machines [17], which are widely used to describe synchronous digital systems. We show that if the transition functions at each pipeline stage are equivalent, then the two systems exhibit bisimulation [20]. This ensures that both systems produce identical output sequences for the same input sequences and maintain consistent internal state behavior throughout execution. Assuming a correct handshake protocol, we apply symbolic execution to systematically explore the behavior of each pipeline stage under symbolic input. This technique generates expressions representing all feasible input values and their associated path conditions. This instrumentation-based symbolic execution approach enables the identification of corresponding elements across structurally divergent implementations, which is essential for reasoning about the non-structural transformations introduced by the XLS IR design flow.

## 2 Equivalence Checking Framework

Sect. 2.1 analyzes the behavior of XLS IR and RTL using Mealy machines, and formally defines how to partition the verification task based on bisimulation. Section 2.2 discusses the challenges of symbolic execution and presents our solutions.

### 2.1 Modeling

**Circuit Architecture Overview.** The pipelined circuit generated by XLS in this work accepts two types of inputs: (1) **data inputs**, corresponding to the receive channels in XLS IR, and (2) **control signal inputs**, originating from external modules to manage communication. The outputs are similarly divided into **data outputs**, mapped to XLS IR send channels, and **control outputs**, sent to external components. Internally, the circuit maintains three classes of registers: (1) **pipeline registers**, which separate adjacent computation stages; (2) **control registers**, used to store state and synchronization signals; and (3) **state registers**, which implement the persistent state elements of XLS IR procs. Control signals follow a handshake protocol that governs the temporal behavior of the data flow. They can insert bubbles when data is invalid or stall the pipeline when downstream modules are not ready, ensuring safe and synchronized operation. The state registers realize the semantics of the XLS IR protocols. Each state element is initialized on the first activation and updated thereafter, so that the activation $N+1$ observes the values written during the activation $N$.

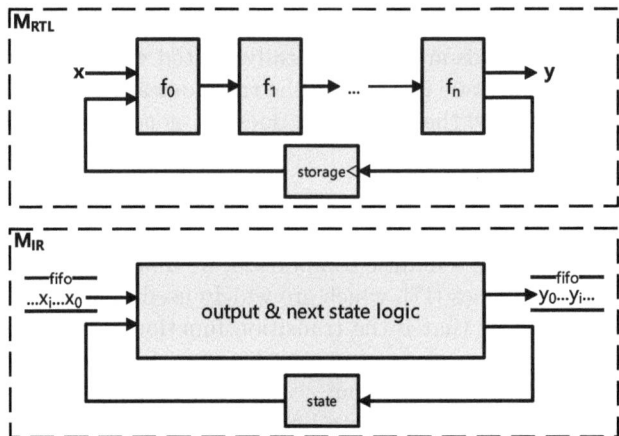

**Fig. 1.** We adopt a Mealy machine perspective to describe both the RTL and IR behavior. The RTL implementation of $F$ is decomposed into a sequence of stage-wise transfer functions $f_j$. These are further refined in Eq. 4 into output-specific functions $f_{i,j}$ for each output $y_i$. The bold symbol **x** denotes the concatenation of all input signals (with possibly different widths) as defined in Eq. 1. The modified input vector **x**$'$ excludes pipeline control signals and consists only of the data-carrying RTL inputs.

**Formal Model for RTL and IR.** In the following, the formal Mealy machine models for both are constructed.

**Definition 1 (Mealy Machine).** *A (deterministic) Mealy machine is defined as a tuple $M = (X, Y, S, s_0, \delta, \lambda)$, where:*

- *$X$ is a finite non-empty set of inputs;*
- *$Y$ is a finite non-empty set of outputs;*
- *$S$ is a finite set of states;*
- *$s_0 \in S$ denotes the initial state;*
- *$\delta : S \times X \to S$ is a state transition function;*
- *$\lambda : S \times X \to Y$ is an output function.*

For convenience, here we coalesce the above transition function and the output function into a single transition function $F : S \times X \to S \times Y$. The components of the RTL above are modeled in detail as $M_{RTL} = (X, Y, S, s_0, F)$. The inputs, outputs, and states received by the system at a time can be defined as follows: the set of possible values $X^{(j)}$ of each $x^{(j)}$ constitutes the total set of $X$, where $\|$ means concatenation:

$$\mathbf{x} = x^{(1)} \| x^{(2)} \| \cdots \| x^{(m)}, \quad x^{(j)} \in X^{(j)}, \; X = \prod_{j=1}^{m} X^{(j)} \qquad (1)$$

$$\mathbf{y} = y^{(1)} \| y^{(2)} \| \cdots \| y^{(n)}, \quad y^{(i)} \in Y^{(i)}, \; Y = \prod_{i=1}^{n} Y^{(i)} \qquad (2)$$

$$\mathbf{s} = s^{(1)} \| \cdots \| s^{(p)}, \quad s^{(k)} \in S^{(k)}, \; S = \prod_{k=1}^{p} S^{(k)}. \qquad (3)$$

For each output $y^{(i)}$, let $x_i \in X_i \subseteq X$ be the concatenation of all its dependent inputs, and define the transition function $F_i : S \times X_i \to S \times Y^{(i)}$. Each $F_i$ can be realized as the composition below, where $f_{i,n}$ denotes the combinational circuit function of the pipeline stage $n$:

$$F_i(s_0, y^{(i)}) = f_{i,n} \circ f_{i,n-1} \circ \cdots \circ f_{i,0}(s_0, y^{(i)}) \qquad (4)$$

where "$\circ$" denotes function composition, like $(g \circ h)(u) = g(h(u))$. Concretely, each $f_{i,n}$ is defined in detail as follows, where $(s_{i,0}, u_{i,0})$ can be initialized as $(s_0, x_i)$:

$$f_{i,j}(s_{i,j-1}, u_{i,j-1}) = (s_{i,j}, u_{i,j}) \quad (0 \leq j \leq n) \qquad (5)$$

The global transitionoutput function $F$ then aggregates all outputs:

$$F(s_0, \mathbf{x}) = \left(s', y^{(1)} \| \cdots \| y^{(n)}\right) \qquad (6)$$

Similarly, a KPN-based IR can be formally modeled as a Mealy machine $M_{IR} = (X_{IR}, Y_{IR}, S_{IR}, s_{0_{IR}}, F_{IR})$. Like Eq. 1, $X_{IR}$ and $Y_{IR}$ are formed by concatenating values from receive and send channels, respectively. The state space $S_{IR}$ combines all internal states, with execution starting from $s_{0_{IR}}$ and evolving under $F_{IR}$. The Fig. 1 illustrates the IR and RTL from the Mealy machine perspective.

**Definition 2 (Trace of Mealy Machine).** *Mealy machines progress by receiving inputs at discrete ticks $t_0, t_1, t_2, \ldots$ and transitioning states accordingly, which induces a causal trace function* $\mathrm{Trace}(F) : X^\omega \to Y^\omega$. *Ignoring specific state transfer details, given an input stream* $\mathbf{x} = (x_0, x_1, \ldots) \in X^\omega$, *the output stream* $\mathbf{y} = (y_0, y_1, \ldots) \in Y^\omega$ *is generated by*

$$(s', \mathbf{y}) = \mathrm{Trace}(F)(s, \mathbf{x}) \qquad (7)$$

**Definition 3 (Observable Equivalence).** *Two Mealy machines $M_1$ and $M_2$ are trace-equivalent (or observable-equivalent [4]), denoted $M_1 \approx M_2$, if and only if:*

$$\forall \mathbf{x} \in X^\omega : \mathrm{Trace}(F_1)(\mathbf{x}) = \mathrm{Trace}(F_2)(\mathbf{x}). \qquad (8)$$

A bisimulation relation between two deterministic Mealy machines suffices to prove that their trace functions coincide, and hence their observable behaviors are equivalent [18,20]. The following is a formal definition of the Mealy Machines bisimulation relation.

**Definition 4 (Bisimulation of Mealy Machine).** *Let $M_1 = (S_1, s_{01}, F_1)$ and $M_2 = (S_2, s_{02}, F_2)$ be two Mealy machines over the same input set $X$. We say that a relation $R \subseteq S_1 \times S_2$ is a bisimulation between $M_1$ and $M_2$ if all the following are satisfied:*

1. **Initial state:** $(s_{01}, s_{02}) \in R$.
2. **Output and State Consistency:** *For every $(s_1, s_2) \in R$ and input $x \in X$, if $F_1(s_1, x) = (s_1', y_1) \wedge F_2(s_2, x) = (s_2', y_2)$, and fulfill $y_1 = y_2 \wedge (s_1', s_2') \in R$.*

According to Definition 4, the key problem we need to deal with is how to verify $F_{IR}$ and $F_{RTL}$, which is sufficient to prove the observable equivalence of $M_{IR}$ and $M_{IR}$. After aligning $S'_{RTL} \subseteq S_{RTL}$ with $S_{IR}$ that is explicitly defined by XLS IR, and verifying the transition functions of them, sequential equivalence can be proved.

## 2.2 Equivalence Checking by Symbolic Execution

**Analysis and Simplification.** To facilitate the verification of functional equivalence between $F_{IR}$ and $F_{RTL}$, we introduce a key simplification that significantly simplifies the analysis: control inputs do not affect the values of data outputs. This assumption, commonly adopted in HLS verification, has been formally validated in Sect. 3.1. Control signals are solely responsible for managing pipeline execution. Their variations induce exactly three operational behaviors: (1) normal execution; (2) bubble insertion; and (3) pipeline stalling. In the Mealy machine model, bubble insertion corresponds to skipping state transitions due to invalid inputs, while stalling results in repeated self-loops that preserve the current state and output. We can safely ignore the auxiliary inputs, outputs, and registers introduced for pipeline control logic, as they only affect the timing of data propagation, not the data values themselves.

By abstracting away pipeline control signals, the equivalence checking task reduces to comparing the per-output transition functions $F_i$ of the IR and RTL under a common initial state. The verification process proceeds in three steps:

1. For each data output $y_i$, identify the corresponding transition functions $F_i^{IR}$ and $F_i^{RTL}$. Then, decompose $F_i^{IR}$ into a sequence of stage-wise functions $f_{i,0}^{IR}, f_{i,1}^{IR}, \ldots, f_{i,n}^{IR}$, as defined in Eq. 4.
2. For each stage $j$, verify the equivalence of $f_{i,j}^{IR}$ and $f_{i,j}^{RTL}$ using symbolic execution, under the assumption that corresponding inputs and states are identical. Output equivalence at each stage implies functional consistency.
3. Since the KPN-based IR performs state updates only after a full activation, it is sufficient to verify that the overall state transition behavior matches between the IR and RTL under all possible inputs.

**Definition 5 (Symbolic Execution).** *Symbolic execution [15] is a program analysis technique that uses symbolic inputs to explore multiple execution paths simultaneously. Given programs $P, S$ with input space $I$ and output space $O$, let $\mathcal{S}_P, \mathcal{S}_S$ be their sets of symbolic paths. For each $\pi_P \in \mathcal{S}_P, \pi_S \in \mathcal{S}_S$, let $pc_P, pc_S$ denote path conditions over inputs $i \in I$, and $o_P, o_S \in O$ the outputs under inputs satisfying $pc_P, pc_S$.*

**Algorithm 1.** CODEGEN-INSTRUMENTED-SYMBOLIC-EXECUTION($IR$)

**Input:** $IR$: all nodes of the XLS Intermediate Representation (IR)
**Output:** $RTL$: Register Transfer Level code
1: $ec \leftarrow$ NEWEQUIVALENCECHECKER()
2: $BlockIR \leftarrow$ TOBLOCKIRANDTRACE($IR, ec$)     ▷ Generate Block IR
3: $ec$.CHECKIRTOBLOCKIRBYSTAGE()
4: $RTL \leftarrow$ TORTLANDTRACE($BlockIR, ec$)     ▷ Generate RTL
5: $ec$.CHECKBLOCKIRTORTLBYSTAGE()

---

**Methods of Instrumented Symbolic Execution.** Based on the above analysis, equivalence checking between $F_{IR}$ and $F_{RTL}$ reduces to comparing matched functional units $f_{i,j}^{IR}$ and $f_{i,j}^{RTL}$, which form the basic units of symbolic execution. According to Definition 5, we aim to prove that each matched pair produces identical outputs under the same symbolic inputs, whenever their path conditions are simultaneously satisfiable. To this end, our method performs path partitioning, symbolic execution, inputoutput mapping at each stage, and constructs equivalence checking formulas for the corresponding outputs.

*Path Partition.* Path partitioning follows naturally from the scheduled XLS IR and its generated RTL. The IR is already divided into stages, and the pipeline registers in the RTL mark the corresponding combinational paths, ensuring consistent partition boundaries across both representations.

*Symbolic Execution.* In XLS, the Codegen transformation involves multiple stages: scheduled XLS IR, Block IR, optimized Block IR, and RTL. Each stage generates a fresh set of nodes, replacing rather than modifying previous ones. This approach simplifies internal management but breaks the structural continuity and consistency of names in two representations, which traditional verification methods rely on to establish mappings [21]. To address this, we employ an instrumentation-based symbolic equivalence checking method that runs alongside the Codegen process. Algorithm 1 summarizes this approach: NewEquivalenceChecker initializes the symbolic execution environment; ToBlockIRandTrace and ToRTLandTrace perform transformation and tracing simultaneously. Since Block IR adopts a static single assignment (SSA) form closely aligned with RTL semantics, the entire process can be unified into a single Trace procedure (Algorithm 2). The verification of equivalence across stages is handled by the CheckByStage algorithm, which applies a consistent logic for all transformation phases.

*Stage-wise Mapping.* This section explains how the Trace algorithm maps IR nodes to RTL nodes during the Codegen process. Although new RTL nodes may be introduced without a one-to-one correspondence to IR nodes, the essential data dependency relationships are preserved. Specifically, while the length of data dependency chains may change, the core dependencies remain intact. Furthermore, control dependencies are implicitly encoded as data dependencies using operations such as select, effectively reducing control logic to data dependency at the IR level. Codegen transforms the SSA-based data dependencies into a tree-like structure in RTL. The Trace function propagates symbolic constraints along these dependencies as IR nodes are transformed into RTL nodes. The behavior of Trace depends on the RTL node type:

- For operational nodes, Trace constructs SMT-based symbolic constraints based on the semantics of node and the symbolic values of its operands, which are available from previous Trace calls.
- For InputPort or RegisterRead nodes, which represent matched inputs between IR and RTL, a unified symbolic variable *symbol* is created and bounded to both IR and RTL nodes, then propagates through dataflow.
- For OutputPort or RegisterWrite nodes, RecordMapping records output mappings and associates outputs with pipeline stages and other information for final equivalence checking.

*Equivalence Checking.* After symbolic execution, CheckByStage (Algorithm 3) verifies the equivalence of each mapped functional unit $f_{i,j}$ by comparing IR and RTL outputs at each pipeline stage. Let the symbolic output formulas be $\alpha_{i,j}^{\text{IR}}$ and $\alpha_{i,j}^{\text{RTL}}$. The equivalence miter formula is defined as: $\neg \left( \alpha_{i,j}^{\text{IR}} = \alpha_{i,j}^{\text{RTL}} \right)$ If the SMT solver returns SAT, a counterexample input is found, indicating functional inequivalence. If UNSAT, equivalence is confirmed for all possible inputs.

---

**Algorithm 2.** TRACE($n_{IR}, n_{RTL}, message$)
---
**Input:** $n_{IR}$: an IR node,   $n_{RTL}$: generated RTL node,   *message*: auxiliary information
1: **if** type($n_{RTL}$) ∈ {InputPort, RegisterRead} **then**
2:   *symbol* ← CREATESYMBOL(type($n_{IR}$))   ▷ Create symbol with the same type as $n_{IR}$
3:   BINDINGSYMBOL(*symbol*, $n_{IR}$)
4:   BINDINGSYMBOL(*symbol*, $n_{RTL}$)
5: **else**
6:   **if** type($n_{RTL}$) ∈ {OutputPort, RegisterWrite} **then**
7:     RECORDMAPPING($n_{IR}, n_{RTL}, message$)        ▷ Record IRRTL mapping
8:   **else**
9:     $ops_{IR}$ ← GETSYMBOLICCONSTRAINTS($n_{IR}.operands$)
10:    CREATESYMBOLICCONSTRAINTS($n_{IR}, ops_{IR}$)
11:    $ops_{RTL}$ ← GETSYMBOLICCONSTRAINTS($n_{RTL}.operands$)
12:    CREATESYMBOLICCONSTRAINTS($n_{RTL}, ops_{RTL}$)
13:   **end if**
14: **end if**

**Algorithm 3.** CHECK-BY-STAGE()

**Input:** mappings organized by stage already recorded in the equivalence checker
**Output:** $FLAG$: Boolean indicating the equivalence
1: stages ← GETSTAGES
2: **for** each stage $s$ in stages **do**
3:     units ← GETMAPPINGSBYSTAGE($s$)
4:     **for** each $(n_{IR}, n_{RTL}, msg)$ in units **do**
5:         formula$_{IR}$ ← GETSYMBOLICOUTPUTFORMULA($n_{IR}$)
6:         formula$_{RTL}$ ← GETSYMBOLICOUTPUTFORMULA($n_{RTL}$)
7:         miter ← ¬(formula$_{IR}$ == formula$_{RTL}$)
8:         **if** SMTSOLVER(miter) == SAT **then**
9:             **return** FALSE           ▷ Found an inequivalent unit
10:        **end if**
11:     **end for**
12: **end for**
13: **return** TRUE            ▷ All units are equivalent

## 3 Experiments

We implemented the proposed equivalence checking algorithm in XLS using Z3 [8] as SMT solver and applied it to large-scale industrial designs and the standard CHStone [10] benchmark suite. The designs in CHStone (DFADD and DFMUL) were rewritten into a restricted subset of C++ acceptable to XLS. We do not have a baseline to compare against, as other symbolic execution tools cannot be applied directly to XLS IR. All experiments were conducted on a Ubuntu 22.04 LTS, equipped with a 3.70 GHz Intel Core i9-10900X CPU (10 cores, 20 threads) and 251 GB of RAM.

We conduct experiments to answer the following research questions.

- **RQ1.** Is the simplification assumption of pipeline control signals valid?
- **RQ2.** Can our method provide equivalence verification results for large-scale inputs in a reasonable time?
- **RQ3.** Can our method detect non-equivalence cases?

### 3.1 RQ1: Validity of the Simplification Assumption via Formal Pipeline Verification

Our equivalence checking framework assumes that pipeline control affects only the timing of output data tokens (i.e. $\mathbf{y^t}$, where $t$ denotes the time it was generated) in output streams, not their values or relative order. To justify this assumption, we prove via bounded model checking that under the XLS valid/ready protocol in appendix A.1. Any input sequence produces an output sequence with:

- **Preserved relative order.** There does not exist two tokens that swap order.
- **No loss or duplication.** The number of non-bubble outputs equals the number of non-bubble inputs.

– **Temporal-only deviations.** The only deviations from ideal behavior are inserted "bubble" tokens or temporary pauses in output generation.

**Results.** All assertions in appendix A.2 were encoded in SMT-LIB2 and checked with Z3 [8]. Each query was reformulated to search for a counterexample and Z3 returned `unsat`, confirming that there are no violations. Thus, the valid/ready protocol may delay data via bubbles or stalls but never corrupt or reorder them, justifying the core simplification of our methods.

### 3.2 RQ2:Efficient Execution of Equivalence Checking

**Table 1.** We performed 10 runs and calculated the average execution times for two scenarios: running Codegen alone, and running Codegen with equivalence checking. The EC time is defined as the difference between these two average execution times, representing the additional overhead introduced by equivalence checking. This approach allows us to approximate the total time overhead introduced by the equivalence checking process, which includes both symbolic execution and miter formula solving

| Design | AVG | DLY_UI | FFCR | DFADD | DFMUL |
|---|---|---|---|---|---|
| Lines of IR | 4368 | 2637 | 13873 | 479 | 238 |
| Lines of RTL | 18307 | 5923 | 18730 | 1602 | 792 |
| Codegen Time (s) | 3.081 | 0.435 | 20.623 | 0.071 | 0.113 |
| Codegen&EC Time (s) | 3.917 | 0.582 | 21.172 | 0.257 | 0.462 |
| EC Time(s) | 0.836 | 0.147 | 0.549 | 0.186 | 0.349 |

Table 1 reports the average runtime over ten runs for five representative algorithms of varying code sizes. Since our equivalence checker is tightly integrated with the Codegen pipeline, the checking time is derived by subtracting the standalone Codegen time from the total execution time. The results show that the overall checking overhead remains low, even for input designs with tens of thousands of lines of code. In general, larger programs take more time to check due to heavier symbolic execution and SMT solving. However, this is not always the case. For example, DFMUL and DLY_ UI exhibit longer runtime than expected relative to their code sizes. This is because their IR contains more complex bit-level operations, which lead to harder constraint solving. To reduce such overhead, we introduce higher-level abstractions for these operations. For instance, we replace long chains of `and/or` gates with Z3's `ite` (if-then-else) expression. This simplifies the symbolic formulas and helps the solver run faster without affecting correctness.

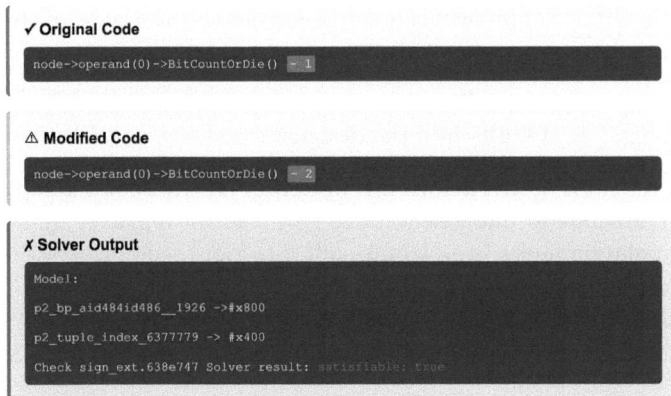

**Fig. 2.** When the equivalence checking is performed individually for each output of each stage one by one, and the solver successfully finds the location of the bug.

### 3.3 RQ3:Ability to Detect the Bug

In addition to verifying sequential equivalence, we evaluated the method's ability to detect functional mismatches through experiments involving both real and artificial bug cases. Among 315 public commits related to Codegen reports in the XLS code repository, only two directly stemmed from RTL generation errors. The rest involve feature extensions, IR-level issues, or are unrelated to our goals. Due to the limited availability of relevant real-world bugs, we systematically injected design faults to perform controlled evaluations of our effectiveness in detecting non-equivalence. We analyze the real bugs of XLS as follows:

- **Detectable Bug: Arithmetic Overflow Not Handled.**
  In XLS IR, arithmetic operations follow idealized semantic behavior. For example, fixed-width operands are typically zero-extended to ensure precise arithmetic. In contrast, the generated RTL reflects only the raw logic from Codegen, without such semantic safeguards. As a result, when adding fixed-width bit-vectors like $start + i$, overflow may occur in RTL if not explicitly handled, while the IR's behavior remains mathematically correct. Our symbolic execution detects this mismatch by leveraging the Z3 solver, which exposes the divergence between IR and RTL semantics when overflow is possible.
- **Undetectable Bug: Scalar vs. Vector Mismatch.**
  In the IR, the statement $foo[start+ : 1] = update\_value$ implies a bit-vector update. However, XLS IR does not distinguish scalar from vector types. During RTL generation, this ambiguity causes Codegen to emit indexed updates unconditionally. If $foo$ is a scalar (e.g., a single-bit register), this results in an invalid part-select operation in Verilog, leading to a compilation error. Our method cannot detect this issue because both scalars and vectors are uniformly represented as bit-vectors of Z3, lacking the expressiveness to capture syntactic constraints that distinguish scalars from vectors. This reflects

a limitation of our approach: it assumes syntactic correctness of the RTL and focuses purely on semantic equivalence.

We also evaluated the ability of methods to detect non-equivalence by injecting three categories of faults into the designs:

- **Errors in RTL generation for specific IR nodes.** Examples include incorrect arithmetic implementations (e.g., adder replaced by subtractor), bit manipulation faults (e.g., wrong shift direction), and incorrect conditional select logic.
- **Bit-width mismatches in truncation or extension.** These involve faulty data truncation or sign/zero-extension, such as erroneously truncating a 32-bit output to 16 bits.
- **State transition logic errors.** This includes incorrect transition conditions, wrong initial state value and update logic for state in XLS IR.

In all cases, the solver successfully returns a satisfiable (SAT) result, confirming behavioral divergence between the IR and RTL. By adjusting the granularity of miter formulas, such as checking equivalence at the level of individual outputs or pipeline stages. We can localize the source of the discrepancy for targeted diagnosis. Figure 2 illustrates a representative case involving an injected fault in the RTL translation of a `SignExt` node. By performing stage-wise and output-level checking, the solver accurately pinpoints the incorrect result. These results demonstrate the approach's effectiveness in identifying functional mismatches and its robustness in handling both structural and semantic discrepancies across representations.

## 4  Conclusion

We present a symbolic execution-based approach for verifying sequential equivalence between scheduled XLS IR and its automatically generated RTL. By modeling both representations as Mealy machines, we reduce the problem to stage-wise checking of output and state transition functions. Our method performs instrumentation-based symbolic tracing during code generation to capture mappings and generate SMT formulas for equivalence checking. The key contributions are: (1) Modeling XLS IR and RTL as Mealy machines to formalize pipeline-stage equivalence; (2) Designing a symbolic execution framework that handles structural discontinuity across transformations; (3) Supporting fine-grained discrepancy localization by adjusting miter construction granularity. Experiments demonstrate that our method efficiently verifies large-scale designs and detects functional mismatches introduced by various faults. Future work includes optimizing symbolic execution and SMT solving, and extending the approach to other high-level synthesis frameworks.

## A  Formal Modeling and Verification of Pipeline Properties

We use an n-stage pipeline as a representative example. Let $t \in \{0, \ldots, K\}$ index clock cycles and $s \in \{0, 1, \ldots, n\}$ index pipeline stages, where stage $n$ is a virtual final stage with no contribution to the output computation. The handshake signals received from downstream modules are defined as Boolean function $a\_vld(t)$, $b\_vld(t)$, and $d\_rdy(t)$, where $a\_vld(t)$ and $b\_vld(t)$ serve as valid signals indicating the presence of valid input data at cycle $t$, and $d\_rdy(t)$ serves as a ready signal indicating readiness of downstream modules to accept data at cycle $t$.

### A.1  Modeling

In the following, we define the Boolean functions corresponding to the pipeline control signals. These functions are expressed using first-order logic. All definitions are based on the signal generation rules employed in XLS.

**valid(t,s)** indicates whether stage s holds valid input data. All of these are initialized as 0 at $t = 0$.

$$valid(t+1, s) \equiv \begin{cases} a\_vld(t) \wedge b\_vld(t) \wedge enable(t, 0), & s = 0, \\ enable(t, s)?valid(t, s-1) : valid(t, s), & s \in [1, n-1] \end{cases}$$

**not_valid(t, s)** indicates that stage $s{-}1$ does not hold valid data at time $t$, allowing stage $s$ to accept new data due to upstream emptiness.

$$\forall t, s \in [1, n], \quad not\_valid(t, s) \equiv \neg valid(t, s{-}1)$$

**data_enable(t, s)** indicates whether the data produced in stage $s$ at time $t$ should be written to its pipeline registers.

$$data\_enable(t, s) \equiv \begin{cases} enable(t, 0) \wedge a\_vld(t) \wedge b\_vld(t) & s = 0, \\ enable(t, s) \wedge valid(t, s{-}1) & s \in [1, n-1] \end{cases}$$

**enable(t, s)** indicates whether stage $s$ is active at time $t$, i.e., ready to process and forward data.

$$enable(t, s) \equiv \begin{cases} data\_enable(t, s{+}1) \vee not\_valid(t, s{+}1) & s \in [0, n-2], \\ stage\_done(t) \vee not\_valid(t, n) & s = n-1 \end{cases}$$

**stage_done(t)** indicates whether the last pipeline stage contains valid data and the downstream modules are ready to consume.

$$\forall t, \quad stage\_done(t) \equiv valid(t, n-1) \wedge d\_rdy(t)$$

## A.2 Key Assertions

To ensure pipeline correctness and maintain output order in the presence of bubbles and stalls, we construct assertion formulas covering three critical properties: pipeline completion, stall handling, and bubble propagation.

**(A1) Pipeline Completion.** This property asserts that if inputs remain valid and the output remains ready over time, then all input data is eventually processed. It guarantees no data is lost and establishes the basis for preserving output order.

$$\forall t > n-1, \quad a\_vld(t) \wedge b\_vld(t) \wedge \_rdy(t) \Rightarrow stage\_done(t)$$

**(A2) No Writes Into Stalled Full Stages.** This property states that if the pipeline output is stalled ($d\_rdy = 0$) at time $t_0$, and stage $s$ along with all downstream stages (up to stage $n-1$) are full, then no new data should be enabled into stage $s$ or any of its downstream stages. This ensures data integrity by preventing overwriting valid data and preserves data order during backpressure.

$$\forall t \geq t_0,\ s \in [0, n-1], \quad \neg d\_rdy(t) \wedge \bigwedge_{s'=s}^{n-1} valid(t, s') \Rightarrow \neg data\_enable(t, s')$$

**(A3) Full Bubble Propagation.** We define a bubble injection predicate at time $t_0$ and no additional bubbles are injected afterward as the equation:

$$\forall t > t_0, \quad BubbleInject(t_0) \triangleq \neg(a\_vld(t_0) \wedge b\_vld(t_0)) \wedge a\_vld(t) \wedge b\_vld(t)$$

This property requires that when a bubble is injected, it must propagate correctly through all pipeline stages. Specifically, the valid signal for stage $s$ should be false at time $t_0 + s + 1$, ensuring empty slots are preserved and input data maintains order without skipping stages.

$$\forall s \in [0, n-1] \quad BubbleInject(t_0) \Rightarrow \bigwedge_{t'=t_0+1}^{t_0+1+s} \neg valid(t', s)$$

## References

1. Catapult high-level synthesis and verification. https://eda.sw.siemens.com/en-US/ic/catapult-high-level-synthesis/
2. Xilinx. n.d. vivado design suite user guide: High-level synthesis UG902 (v2020.1). https://docs.amd.com/v/u/en-US/ug902-vivado-high-level-synthesis. Accessed 15 May 2025
3. XLS: Accelerated hw synthesis. https://google.github.io/xls/
4. Aarts, F., Vaandrager, F.: Learning I/O automata. In: Proceedings of the 21st International Conference on Concurrency Theory, pp. 71–85 (2010)

5. Canis, A., Choi, J., Aldham, M., Zhang, V., Kammoona, A., Czajkowski, T., et al.: LEGUP: an open-source high-level synthesis tool for FPGA-based processor/accelerator systems. ACM Trans. Embed. Comput. Syst. **13**(2) (2013). https://doi.org/10.1145/2514740
6. Chouksey, R., Karfa, C.: Verification of scheduling of conditional behaviors in high-level synthesis. IEEE Trans. Very Large Scale Integr. (VLSI) Syst. **28**(7), 1638–1651 (2020). https://doi.org/10.1109/TVLSI.2020.2978242
7. Cong, J., Lau, J., Liu, G., Neuendorffer, S., Pan, P., et al.: FPGA HLS today: successes, challenges, and opportunities. ACM Trans. Reconfigurable Technol. Syst. **15**(4) (2022). https://doi.org/10.1145/3530775
8. De Moura, L., Bjørner, N.: Z3: an efficient SMT solver. In: Proceedings of the Theory and Practice of Software, 14th International Conference on Tools and Algorithms for the Construction and Analysis of Systems, pp. 337–340 (2008)
9. Drane, T., Kiran Kumar, M.V.A.: High-level formal equivalence. In: Chattopadhyay, A. (ed.) Handbook of Computer Architecture, pp. 1–26. Springer Nature Singapore (2022). https://doi.org/10.1007/978-981-97-9314-3.pdf
10. Hara, Y., Tomiyama, H., Honda, S., Takada, H., Ishii, K.: CHSTONE: a benchmark program suite for practical c-based high-level synthesis. In: 2008 IEEE International Symposium on Circuits and Systems (ISCAS), pp. 1192–1195 (2008)
11. Kahn, G.: The semantics of a simple language for parallel programming. In: Information Processing, Proceedings of the IFIP Congress 74, pp. 5–10 (1974)
12. Karfa, C., Mandal, C., Sarkar, D., Reade, C.: Register sharing verification during data-path synthesis. In: 2007 International Conference on Computing: Theory and Applications (ICCTA 2007), pp. 135–140 (2007)
13. Karfa, C., Sarkar, D., Mandal, C.: Verification of datapath and controller generation phase in high-level synthesis of digital circuits. IEEE Trans. Comput. Aided Des. Integr. Circuits Syst. **29**(3), 479–492 (2010). https://doi.org/10.1109/adcom.2007.55
14. Karfa, C., Sarkar, D., Mandal, C., Kumar, P.: An equivalence-checking method for scheduling verification in high-level synthesis. IEEE Trans. Comput. Aided Des. Integr. Circuits Syst. **27**(3), 556–569 (2008). https://doi.org/10.1109/TCAD.2007.913390
15. King, J.C.: Symbolic execution and program testing. Commun. ACM **19**(7), 385–394 (1976). https://doi.org/10.1145/360248.360252
16. Mahmoud, A.T., Mohammed, A.A., Ayman, M., Medhat, W., Selim, S., Zayed, H., et al.: Formal verification of code conversion: a comprehensive survey. Technologies **12**(12), 244 (2024). https://doi.org/10.3390/technologies12120244
17. Mealy, G.H.: A method for synthesizing sequential circuits. Bell Syst. Tech. J. **34**(5), 1045–1079 (1955). https://doi.org/10.1002/j.1538-7305.1955.tb03788.x
18. Park, D.: Concurrency and automata on infinite sequences. In: Deussen, P. (ed.) GI-TCS 1981. LNCS, vol. 104, pp. 167–183. Springer, Heidelberg (1981). https://doi.org/10.1007/BFb0017309
19. Pixley, C.: A theory and implementation of sequential hardware equivalence. IEEE Trans. Comput. Aided Des. Integr. Circuits Syst. **11**(12), 1469–1478 (2002). https://doi.org/10.1109/43.180261
20. Sangiorgi, D.: On the origins of bisimulation and coinduction. ACM Trans. Programm. Lang. Syst. **31**(4) (2009). https://doi.org/10.1145/1516507.1516510
21. Yang, Z., Hao, K., Cong, K., Ray, S., Xie, F.: Equivalence checking for compiler transformations in behavioral synthesis. In: 2013 IEEE 31st International Conference on Computer Design (ICCD), pp. 491–494 (2013)

# Self-learning Modeling of Generalized Possibilistic Decision Processes

Xintong Zhang[1], Wuniu Liu[2], Qing He[1], and Yongming Li[2](✉)

[1] School of Artificial Intelligence and Computer Science, Shaanxi Normal University,
Xi'an, Shaanxi, China
{zhangxint,heqing}@snnu.edu.cn
[2] School of Mathematics and Statistics, Shaanxi Normal University,
Xi'an, Shaanxi, China
{liuwuniu,liyongm}@snnu.edu.cn

**Abstract.** Self-learning modeling is a technique used to automatically learn and optimize model parameters from data, which is significant for modeling in process of possibilistic model checking. Self-learning modeling based on generalized possibility Kripke structure (GPKS) has been studied to some extent. Recently, model checking based on generalized possibilistic decision process (GPDP) has become a research focus. However, the lack of effective self-learning methods for constructing GPDP models limits the practical applications of GPDP-based model checking. For complex GPDP models, manually generating fuzzy states and possibility transitions is extremely time-consuming and resource-consuming. To address this issue, we developed an online supervised learning algorithm capable of learning the fuzzy states and possibilistic transition matrices of a GPDP. By using Gaussian fuzzy functions to associate external variables with fuzzy states, our new GPDP model with fuzzifier sets (GPDP-FS) maps the values of external variables to the atomic proposition values of fuzzy states in the GPDP model. For the action set of the GPDP model, we set the transition mechanism of each action in the action set as different atomic proposition evolution matrix. The algorithm uses stochastic gradient descent to emulate the state transition process and build the possibility transition matrix which is an essential component of model checking. Results indicate that our method can derive fuzzy states, state transition mechanisms, and possibility transition matrices solely from external variables. This approach enables GPDP modeling through a self-learning process, overcoming the modeling problem of possibilistic decision processes in practical applications.

**Keywords:** generalized possibilistic decision process (GPDP) · self-learning modeling · supervised learning · possibility theory · model checking

# 1 Introduction

In recent years, as system complexity increases, the need for the verification of system correctness is growing, model checking techniques have gained widespread attention and application. As a formal automated verification technique, the fundamental principle of classical model checking is to use a model checker to verify whether certain properties specified by temporal logic formulas hold for a given finite-state model of a system. However, the classical model checking method is typically based on Boolean transition systems or Boolean-state Kripke structures. Hence, classical model checking method is highly effective, it falls short in dealing with systems containing non-deterministic information, such as medical diagnosis systems. To better handle non-determinism, various quantitative model checking techniques have been proposed in recent years, including timed, probabilistic, stochastic, multi-valued, quantum model checking [1,2] and possibilistic model checking for quantitative verification of fuzzy systems [1,3–6], etc. These methods provide more flexibility for addressing complex situations involving non-determinism.

The generalized possibilistic measure provides an effective tool for dealing with fuzziness and non-determinism of possibilistic model checking. Possibilistic model checking is based on the combination of model checking principles and possibility theory, which was introduced by Zadeh in the 1970s [7] as an extension of fuzzy sets and logic. This approach, proposed by Li et al., has been the subject of extensive research and development in recent years. In 2015, Li et al. proposed the generalized possibilistic computation tree logic (GPoCTL) on Generalized Possibilistic Kripke Structures (GPKS), and they studied its model checking problem. This measure quantifies non-additive fuzzy events and is suitable for describing problems with fuzzy and non-determinism. However, existing GPKS models are mainly for closed systems, i.e., the model does not interact with the environment, which here refers to non-determinism, such as non-deterministic choices in a possibilistic distribution. These models lack the ability to deal with non-deterministic choices in open systems, i.e., systems involving non-deterministic choices in the possibilistic distribution. Therefore, new approaches are needed to model open systems that interact with their environment. To address this problem, an extended model of GPKS called the generalized possibilistic decision process (GPDP) [5,8] has been proposed. The GPDP model is a variant of GPKS that is able to handle non-deterministic choices in possibilistic distributions. Its main feature is that state transitions can be achieved through different kinds of actions, and there is nondeterminism in different actions and to resolve this nondeterminism, the concept of strategy is given and we also give the GPDP the ability to make a decision that when all possible strategies are considered, we can obtain the optimal strategy.

Traditional modeling processes usually require expert knowledge and experience to manually model a system. However, expert knowledge is usually subjective and may lead to modeling deviations or inconsistencies. Self-learning modeling method automatically learn the model states and the parameters in model through algorithms, which greatly reduces modeling deviations, greatly eliminates subjectivity in the modeling process, and improves the objectivity and reliability of the model. For complex models, manually generating a large number of fuzzy states and transitions is very time-consuming and resource-consuming. Self-learning modeling method can automatically abstract information from data and construct models, greatly reducing manual intervention, improving modeling efficiency and allowing for automatic optimization and improvement. In addition, these methods are highly adaptive and can learn and update the model based on changes in the environment or system dynamically, thus maintaining the accuracy of the model.

This article introduces a model checking self-learning modeling approach based on the generalized possibilistic decision process (GPDP), which further promotes the practical application of the GPDP. For example, in healthcare systems, this approach can help doctors to determine the best treatment strategy for their patients, thus improving the science and accuracy of decision making.

## 1.1 Motivations

Although generalized possibilistic Kripke structures (GPKS) can deal with fuzzy events, they are mainly designed for closed systems and lack the ability to model possibilistic decisions in open systems. To address this problem, it is necessary to introduce extended modeling approaches, such as generalized possibilistic decision processes (GPDP), to enhance the handling of environmental interactions and non-deterministic choices. Traditional modeling processes rely on expert knowledge, which can easily lead to biases and inconsistencies [9,10]. Self-learning modeling approaches that use automatic algorithms to learn states and parameters can improve modeling efficiency and objectivity, when dealing with fuzzy states and transitions in GPDP models. In conclusion, the motivation of this article is to improve the modeling efficiency and reduce the modeling computation cost by introducing a self-learning modeling approach based on GPDP, aiming for practical application in real-world.

## 1.2 Main Idea

This study tackles the challenges of modeling fuzzy states, possibility transition matrices $P$, and state transition mechanisms in practical applications. To address these issues, we present an online learning algorithm designed to enable a GPDP to autonomously learn its fuzzy states and possibility transition matrix, thereby eliminating the need for subjective expert input. The algorithm assumes that while the fuzzy states of the system are unknown, they are correlated with sensor variables whose values are accessible, a scenario frequently encountered in real-world settings. To put this approach into practice, we propose the generalized possibilistic decision making process with fuzzy sets (GPDP-FS), a model that integrates the traditional GPDP framework with a set of Gaussian fuzzy functions. These functions serve as the critical interface linking the atomic propositions of system states to sensor variables, thereby connecting sensor observations to atomic propositions. Using the stochastic gradient descent principle, we derive an online learning algorithm that is able to estimate the elements in the atomic propositions evolution matrix. This study demonstrates the applicability of the learning algorithm in situations where the system state is not directly observable but external sensor data is available.

### 1.3 Related Work

This work is inspired by self-learning modeling in possibilistic model checking of GPKS [11] and supervised learning of multi-event transition matrices in fuzzy discrete-event systems (FDES) [12–15]. First, Liu et al. developed a self-learning modeling approach for model checking based on generalized possibility Kripke structures (GPKS). They consist of a graph where nodes represent reachable system states, edges represent transitions between system states, and a labeling function associates each state with a set of atomic propositions for property verification in model checking. Second, FDES [16–18] is well suited for the control of fuzzy systems including supervised control [15,19,20], distributed control [13,21] and online control [22]. In FDES, multi-event transition matrices are used to represent state transition relations under the influence of multiple fuzzy events. Traditional discrete-event systems usually describe the dynamic behavior through event-triggered state transitions. However, in fuzzy discrete event systems, a more flexible representation is needed since both events and states may have fuzzy characteristics. Multi-event transition matrices extend single-event state transitions by allowing multiple events to affect the system simultaneously. The elements of the matrix represent the possibility or degree of membership of a transition from one fuzzy state to another. This representation captures the complex behavior of dynamics affected by multiple fuzzy events and better reflects the ambiguity and non-determinism of the system.

### 1.4 Main Contributions

This article presents two key contributions to the field of possibilistic model checking and GPDP modeling. First, we introduce the GPDP with fuzzifier sets (GPDP-FS), a model that integrates Gaussian fuzzy functions into the traditional GPDP model. This integration establishes a direct connection between sensor variables and atomic propositions in GPDP model, enabling the system to learn fuzzy states and possibility transition matrices. Second, we introduce self-learning modeling into the field of generalized possibilistic decision processes significantly advancing its practical applicability. By using an online learning algorithm, it enables GPDP models to autonomously learn fuzzy states and possibility transition matrices from sensor data without requiring subjective expert input. This work reduces modeling deviations, eliminates manual dependencies, and improves the overall objectivity and reliability of GPDP models.

## 2 Preliminaries

This section introduces the foundational concepts of possibility theory and the generalized possibilistic decision process (GPDP).

## 2.1 Generalized Possibility Theory

Possibility theory, a framework designed to address non-determinism in cases of incomplete information, offers an alternative to traditional probability theory. Unlike probability theory, which relies on a single measure, possibility theory uses two dual set-functions: the possibility and necessity measures. Zadeh first presented this theory in the late 1970s as an extension of fuzzy sets and logic [7,23]. Subsequent studies, such as those by Dubois and Prade [24,25], further developed this concept.

For simplicity, we assume that the universe of discourse $U$ is a nonempty set, and that all its subsets are measurable. A possibility measure is a function $\Pi$ from the powerset $2^U$ to the interval $[0,1]$, with the following properties:

$$1)\ \Pi(\emptyset) = 0, \quad 2)\ \Pi(U) = 1, \quad 3)\ \Pi\left(\bigcup_{i \in I} E_i\right) = \bigvee_{i \in I} \Pi(E_i),$$

for any subset family $\{E_i\}$ of $U$, where $\bigvee$ denotes the supremum (least upper bound) of the family of real numbers $\{a_i\}_{i \in I}$; similarly, $\bigwedge$ represents the infimum (greatest lower bound).

If only the first and third conditions are satisfied, the measure $\Pi$ is referred to as a generalized possibility measure. The generalized possibility measure on a nonempty set can be determined by its behavior on singletons, as given by:

$$\Pi(E) = \bigvee_{x \in E} \Pi(\{x\}).$$

The function $\pi : U \to [0,1]$ defined by $\pi(x) = \Pi(\{x\})$ is known as the possibility distribution of $\Pi$, which uniquely defines the measure, i.e., $\Pi$ is fully determined by the possibility distribution $\pi$.

Possibility theory involves two key concepts: the possibility and the necessity of an event. For any set $E$, the necessity measure $N$ dual to the possibility measure $\Pi$ is defined as:

$$N(E) = 1 - \Pi(U - E).$$

A necessity measure $N$ is a function from the powerset $2^U$ to $[0,1]$ that satisfies:

$$1)\ N(\emptyset) = 0, \quad 2)\ N(U) = 1, \quad 3)\ N\left(\bigcap E_i\right) = \bigwedge N(E_i),$$

for any family of subsets $\{E_i\}$ of $U$.

## 2.2 Generalized Possibilistic Decision Process

**Definition 1.** *A generalized possibilistic decision process (GPDP) is represented as a tuple*

$$M = (S, Act, P, I, AP, L),$$

where $S$, $I$, $AP$, and $L$ have the same definitions as in generalized possibilistic Kripke structures (GPKS). The primary distinction between GPKS and GPDP lies in the addition of an action set $Act$ and the inclusion of actions in the transition function $P$.

1) $S$ is a countable, nonempty set of states.
2) $Act$ is a set of actions.
3) $\boldsymbol{P}: S \times Act \times S \to [0,1]$ is the possibilistic action transition function, such that for all $s \in S$, there exist $\alpha \in Act$ and $t \in S$ satisfying

$$\boldsymbol{P}(s, \alpha, t) > 0.$$

4) $I: S \to [0,1]$ is the possibilistic initial distribution function, with $I(s) > 0$ for some state $s \in S$.
5) $AP$ is a set of atomic propositions.
6) $L: S \times AP \to [0,1]$ is the possibilistic labeling function, mapping a state $s$ to a fuzzy set of atomic propositions. That is, $L(s, a)$ denotes the possibility or truth value of the atomic proposition $a$ holding in state $s$.

Additionally, let

$$Act(s) = \{\alpha \in Act \mid \bigvee_{t \in S} P(s, \alpha, t) > 0\},$$

ensuring that $Act(s)$ is nonempty. Each state $t$ for which $P(s, \alpha, t) > 0$ is considered an $\alpha$-successor of state $s$.

Verification algorithms are limited to finite GPDPs, where a GPDP is considered finite if the state space $S$, action set $Act$, and atomic proposition set $AP$ are all finite.

## 3 Generalized Possibilistic Decision Process with Fuzzifier Sets

This model which has been proposed by Liu et al. [11] extends the standard GPDP model by introducing a set of fuzzifiers to connect external (sensor) variables to the state space of the model. The GPDP-FS model is represented as a tuple $G = (\lambda, M_\lambda, Fuzzifier)$, where $\lambda$ denotes the modeling accuracy, $M_\lambda$ is a GPDP with a state space $S_\lambda$, and the $Fuzzifier$ is a set of fuzzy membership functions that map the values of variables $V$ to states in the state space $S_\lambda$.

### 3.1 Setting of the States

We analyze a state pair from the sample set, where the value of the atomic proposition of state $s$ is mapped from an external variable $x$. State $s$ can transition gradually to states $t_L$ through different types of actions $Act_1, Act_2, \cdots, Act_L$. This can be expressed as

$$x \Rightarrow s \xrightarrow{p_{s \to t_1} \to \cdots \to t_L} t_L \Leftarrow z.$$

In this study, we focus on the situation where $s$ transitions to $t_L$ through all actions in the action set, and the true value of the atomic proposition of $t_L$ is mapped from an external variable $z$. In this work, the values of external variables are known, which corresponds to real-world conditions. By learning the value of external variable $z$, we compare the learned values with the true values to observe the learning performance.

We refer to the state $s$ as the *current state* and $t_L$ *successor state*, and $t_k$ refers to the state obtained through the atomic proposition evolution matrix $\mathbf{T}_k$, where $k = 1, 2, \cdots, L$ and $|L|$ is the number of act. Let $s = [l_1, l_2, \ldots, l_n]$ where $n = |AP|$. Suppose the value of $l_j$ is unknown, but it can be obtained by mapping the value of the external variables $x = [x_1, x_2, \ldots, x_n]$ to the interval $[0, 1]$ through the function $\theta_j$. Similar to the method used by Liu et al. [11], the $\theta_j$ function is set to the Gaussian type:

$$l_j = \theta_j(x_j \mid g_j, h_j) = exp(-\frac{(x_j - g_j)^2}{2h_j^2}), \tag{1}$$

where $j \in [1, n]$, $g_j$ and $h_j$ represents the means and standard deviations of the sample set, respectively. For the convenience of learning, we use the sample means and standard deviation to replace the true values, as the true means and standard deviations are unknown. The state $s$ which represents the current state in system becomes

$$s = [\theta_1(x_1), \theta_2(x_2), \ldots, \theta_n(x_n)].$$

In an actual system, the atomic proposition value of state $t_L = [c_1^L, c_2^L, \ldots, c_n^L]$ is also unknown, but correlated with external variables $\mathbf{z} = [z_1, z_2, \ldots, z_n]$ that is available. Specifically, define estimated variables as $\hat{\mathbf{z}} = [\hat{z}_1, \hat{z}_2, \ldots, \hat{z}_n]$, and use the inverse Gaussian function to link the estimated successor states $\hat{c}_j^L$ to the external variables:

$$\hat{c}_j^L = \theta_j(\hat{z}_j \mid g_j, h_j) = exp(-\frac{(\hat{z}_j - g_j)^2}{2h_j^2}).$$

And

$$\hat{z}_j = \theta_j^{-1}(\hat{c}_j^L \mid g_j, h_j) = g_j \pm h_j\sqrt{-2ln\hat{c}_j^L}, \tag{2}$$

when $\hat{z}_j \geq g_j$ use + and − will be used in other situations. The rest of the ± signs in the article follow the same principle.

### 3.2 Atomic Positions Evolution Matrix(APEM)

In practice, the transition method between states is unknown and is difficult to obtain. Typically, in GPDP, state transitions operate as a black-box model; for instance, a patient may shift from a poor to a better physical condition through specific medications, but the mechanism behind the drugs' effects is still unknown. We can represent the state transition process through the evolution of atomic propositions, as states are defined by atomic propositions. Fortunately, this complex transition mechanism can be learned, and we represent the effect of these $L$ drugs by atomic propositions transition matrix $T_1, \ldots, T_L$.

$$\mathbf{T}_k = \begin{bmatrix} \tau_{11}^k & \cdots & \tau_{1n}^k \\ \vdots & \ddots & \vdots \\ \tau_{n1}^k & \cdots & \tau_{nn}^k \end{bmatrix},$$

where $k = 1, 2, \ldots, L$ and $n = |AP|$. The transition between state $s = [l_1, l_2, \ldots, l_n]$ and $\hat{t}_k = [\hat{c}_1^k, \hat{c}_2^k, \ldots, \hat{c}_n^k,]$ is

$$s \circ \mathbf{T}_1 \circ \cdots \circ \mathbf{T}_k = \hat{t}_k.$$

The operation $\circ$ denotes max-product operation. Here we are discussing the case where state $s$ reaches state $t_k$ after passing through $Act_1, Act_2, \cdots, Act_k$ sequentially.

Hence,

$$\begin{aligned}
\hat{c}_j^1 &= \bigvee_{m=1}^n l_m \cdot \tau_{mj}^1, \\
\hat{c}_j^2 &= \bigvee_{m=1}^n \hat{c}_m^1 \cdot \tau_{mj}^2, \\
&\vdots \\
\hat{c}_j^L &= \bigvee_{m=1}^n \hat{c}_m^{L-1} \cdot \tau_{mj}^L.
\end{aligned} \quad (3)$$

To achieve accurate learning, we approximated the function in (3) using the exponential penalty function [26], i.e.,

$$\begin{aligned}
\hat{c}_j^1 &= \bigvee_{m=1}^n l_m \cdot \tau_{mj}^1 \approx \frac{1}{k} \ln(\sum_{m=1}^n e^{k l_m \cdot \tau_{mj}^1}), \\
\hat{c}_j^2 &= \bigvee_{m=1}^n \hat{c}_m^1 \cdot \tau_{mj}^2 \approx \frac{1}{k} \ln(\sum_{m=1}^n e^{k \hat{c}_m^1 \cdot \tau_{mj}^2}), \\
&\vdots \\
\hat{c}_j^L &= \bigvee_{m=1}^n \hat{c}_m^{L-1} \cdot \tau_{mj}^L \approx \frac{1}{k} \ln(\sum_{m=1}^n e^{k \hat{c}_m^{L-1} \cdot \tau_{mj}^L}),
\end{aligned} \quad (4)$$

where $k > 0$ is a hyper-parameter that controls the precision of the approximation.

## 4 Possibilistic Transition Defined by Similarity

In practical applications, the successor state of a system is unknown. To address this issue, Liu et al. proposed the concept of state similarity [11]. This concept computes the reachability degree of all possible successor states $t$ for a given state $s \in S$ to be evaluated. The main idea is that the higher the similarity between states, the higher the similarity of their successor states. Based on this theory, we define the most possible next state $s \circ T_k$ that state $s$ transitions to under the action $Act_k$. Specifically, the possibility of transition from state $s$ to $s \circ T_k$ is $P(s, s \circ T_k) = 1$. For other successor states $t$ (where $t \neq s \circ T_k$) transition from the action $Act_k$, the possibility $P(s,t)$ is calculated based on the similarity between states. The specific concept of distance and similarity of fuzzy states are introduced by Liu et al. [11].

Figure 1 summarizes the basic components of the GPDP-FS model and their corresponding mathematical notations.

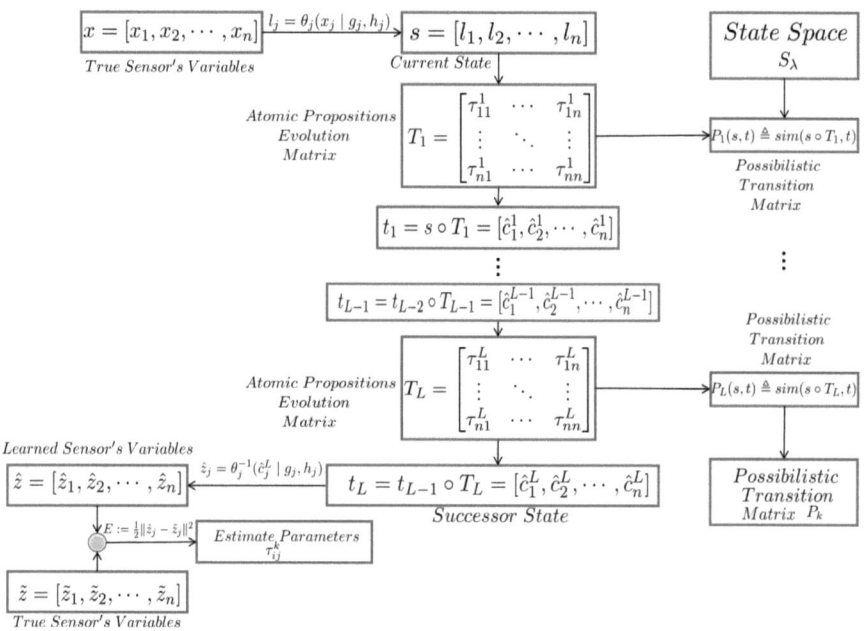

**Fig. 1.** Summary of the GPDP-FS learning model configuration.

## 5 Learning Algorithms of Parameters for the GPDP-FS Model

Suppose $R$ states sample pairs $\{(x_i, z_i)\}_{i=1}^{R}$ are available. We learn the elements in the atomic propositions evolution matrix $\tilde{\mathbf{T}}_k = (\tilde{\tau}_{ij}^k)_{n \times n}$ in the GPKS-FS model using the stochastic gradient descent algorithm. Stochastic gradient descent is a commonly used optimization algorithm in machine learning and deep learning, especially for large-scale datasets. The goal of the gradient descent method is to minimize the loss function, and the objective function in this study is:

$$E := \frac{1}{2}\|\hat{z} - \tilde{z}\|^2 = \frac{1}{2}\sum_{j=1}^{n}(\hat{z}_j - \tilde{z}_j)^2, \quad (5)$$

where $\hat{z}_j$ represents the simulated value of the external variable, and $\tilde{z}_j$ represents the true value of the external variable.

Based on (1), (2) and (4), the function of computed $\hat{z}_j$ is

$$\hat{z}_j = g_j \pm h_j\sqrt{-2ln\hat{c}_j^L} = g_j \pm h_j\sqrt{-2ln[\frac{1}{k}ln(\sum_{m=1}^{n}e^{k\hat{c}_m^{L-1}\tau_{mj}^L})]}, \quad (6)$$

where

$$\hat{c}_j^L = \bigvee_{m=1}^{n}\hat{c}_m^{L-1}\tau_{mj}^L = \frac{1}{k}ln(\sum_{m=1}^{n}e^{k\hat{c}_m^{L-1}\tau_{mj}^L}). \quad (7)$$

### 5.1 Learning Algorithms for $\tau_{ij}^k$

On the basis of gradient descent learning principle,

$$\tau_{ij}^{new} = \tau_{ij} - \lambda_\tau \frac{\partial E}{\partial \tau_{ij}}. \quad (8)$$

The hyperparameter *new* represents the updated parameter value that replaces the original parameter value after one iteration of the learning process. The hyperparameter $\lambda_\tau$ represents the learning rate for $\tau_{ij}$.

Based on (6) and (7), we have

$$\frac{\partial E}{\partial \tau_{ij}^k} = \frac{\partial E}{\partial \hat{z}_j}\frac{\partial \hat{z}_j}{\partial \tau_{ij}^k} = (\hat{z}_j - \tilde{z}_j)\frac{\partial \hat{z}_j}{\partial \tau_{ij}^k}, \quad (9)$$

where $k = 1, 2, \cdots, L$, and

$$\frac{\partial \hat{z}_j}{\partial \tau_{ij}^k} = \frac{\partial \hat{z}_j}{\partial \hat{c}_j^L}\frac{\partial \hat{c}_j^L}{\partial \tau_{ij}^k} = \mp\frac{h_j}{\hat{c}_j^L\sqrt{-2ln\hat{c}_j^L}}\frac{\partial \hat{c}_j^L}{\partial \tau_{ij}^k}. \quad (10)$$

When $k$ takes different values, we first calculate $\frac{\partial \hat{c}_j^L}{\partial \tau_{ij}^k}$,

$$\frac{\partial \hat{c}_j^L}{\partial \hat{c}_j^{L-1}} = \frac{\tau_{jj}^L e^{k\hat{c}_j^{L-1}\tau_{jj}^L}}{\sum_{m=1}^{n}e^{k\hat{c}_m^{L-1}\tau_{mj}^L}},$$

$$\frac{\partial \hat{c}_j^{L-1}}{\partial \hat{c}_j^{L-2}} = \frac{\tau_{jj}^{L-1} e^{k\hat{c}_j^{L-2}\tau_{jj}^{L-1}}}{\sum_{m=1}^{n}e^{k\hat{c}_m^{L-2}\tau_{mj}^{L-1}}},$$

$$\vdots$$

$$\frac{\partial \hat{c}_j^2}{\partial \hat{c}_j^1} = \frac{\tau_{jj}^2 e^{k\hat{c}_j^1\tau_{jj}^2}}{\sum_{m=1}^{n}e^{k\hat{c}_m^1\tau_{mj}^2}}.$$

Let
$$o_{jj}^p = \frac{e^{k\hat{c}_j^{p-1}\tau_{jj}^p}}{\sum_{m=1}^n e^{k\hat{c}_m^{p-1}\tau_{mj}^p}}, \quad p = 2, 3, \ldots, L. \tag{11}$$

If $k = L$,
$$\frac{\partial \hat{c}_j^L}{\partial \tau_{ij}^L} = \frac{\hat{c}_i^{L-1} e^{k\hat{c}_i^{L-1}\tau_{ij}^L}}{\sum_{m=1}^n e^{k\hat{c}_m^{L-1}\tau_{mj}^L}} = \hat{c}_i^{L-1} o_{ij}^L, \tag{12}$$

where
$$o_{ij}^p = \frac{e^{k\hat{c}_i^{p-1}\tau_{ij}^p}}{\sum_{m=1}^n e^{k\hat{c}_m^{p-1}\tau_{mj}^p}}, p = 2, 3, \cdots, L. \tag{13}$$

If $k = L-1$, by (4), we have
$$\frac{\partial \hat{c}_j^L}{\partial \tau_{ij}^{L-1}} = \frac{\partial \hat{c}_j^L}{\partial \hat{c}_j^{L-1}} \frac{\partial \hat{c}_j^{L-1}}{\partial \tau_{ij}^{L-1}} = \tau_{jj}^L o_{jj}^L \hat{c}_i^{L-2} o_{ij}^{L-1},$$

if $k = L-2$, we have
$$\frac{\partial \hat{c}_j^L}{\partial \tau_{ij}^{L-2}} = \frac{\partial \hat{c}_j^L}{\partial \hat{c}_j^{L-1}} \frac{\partial \hat{c}_j^{L-1}}{\partial \hat{c}_j^{L-2}} \frac{\partial \hat{c}_j^{L-2}}{\partial \tau_{ij}^{L-2}} = \tau_{jj}^L o_{jj}^L \tau_{jj}^{L-1} o_{jj}^{L-1} \hat{c}_i^{L-3} o_{ij}^{L-2},$$

$\vdots$

if $k = 1$, we have
$$\frac{\partial \hat{c}_j^L}{\partial \tau_{ij}^1} = \frac{\partial \hat{c}_j^L}{\partial \hat{c}_j^{L-1}} \frac{\partial \hat{c}_j^{L-1}}{\partial \hat{c}_j^{L-2}} \cdots \frac{\partial \hat{c}_j^2}{\partial \hat{c}_j^1} \frac{\partial \hat{c}_j^1}{\partial \tau_{ij}^1}$$
$$= \tau_{jj}^L o_{jj}^L \tau_{jj}^{L-1} o_{jj}^{L-1} \cdots \tau_{jj}^2 o_{jj}^2 \frac{\partial \hat{c}_j^1}{\partial \tau_{ij}^1},$$

$$\hat{c}_j^1 = \bigvee_{m=1}^n l_m \tau_{mj}^1 \approx \frac{1}{k} ln(\sum_{m=1}^n e^{kl_m\tau_{mj}^1})$$

$$\frac{\partial \hat{c}_j^1}{\partial \hat{\tau}_{ij}^1} = \frac{l_i e^{kl_i\tau_{ij}^1}}{\sum_{m=1}^n e^{kl_m\tau_{mj}^1}}.$$

Let
$$o_{ij}^1 = \frac{e^{kl_i\tau_{ij}^1}}{\sum_{m=1}^n e^{kl_m\tau_{mj}^1}}, \tag{14}$$

so we have
$$\frac{\partial \hat{c}_j^L}{\partial \tau_{ij}^1} = \tau_{jj}^L o_{jj}^L \tau_{jj}^{L-1} o_{jj}^{L-1} \cdots \tau_{jj}^2 o_{jj}^2 l_i o_{ij}^1.$$

Eventually, we have
$$\frac{\partial E}{\partial \tau_{ij}^k} = \mp \frac{(\hat{z}_j - \tilde{z}_j) h_j}{\hat{c}_j^L \sqrt{-2ln\hat{c}_j^L}} \frac{\partial \hat{c}_j^L}{\partial \tau_{ij}^k}, \tag{15}$$

where $k = 1, 2, \cdots, L$.

We found that the learning performance under this parameter setting is poor because the minimum values of $o_{ij}^1$ and $o_{ij}^p$ are close to zero, which causes the gradients to update very little, resulting in poor learning performance. To address the issue of parameter dependence, we introduce the solution below, which is to enhance $o_{ij}^k$ using the following equation:

$$o_{ij}^1 := \frac{e^{kl_i\tau_{ij}^1}}{\bigwedge_{i=1}^{n} e^{kl_i\tau_{ij}^1}}, \tag{16}$$

$$o_{ij}^p := \frac{e^{k\hat{c}_i^{p-1}\tau_{ij}^p}}{\bigwedge_{i=1}^{n} e^{k\hat{c}_i^{p-1}\tau_{ij}^p}}, \; p = 2, 3, \cdots, L. \tag{17}$$

### 5.2 Improved Learning Algorithms for $\tau_{ij}^k$

The poor learning performance of these parameters $\tau_{ij}^k$ is not limited to GPDP model modeling. This issue was first noted by Ying et al. during their work on learning algorithms for the FDES model and was further extended by Liu et al. in the context of GPKS model learning algorithms. The reason for the poor learning performance of $\tau_{ij}^k$ here is the same as that in the GPKS model. Although we have smoothed the max function in Eq. (4), the algorithm sometimes performs poorly during the learning task because the gradient calculation includes the computation of $o_{ij}^k$ defined in Eqs. (13) and (14), whose values in turn depend on the learning of $\tau_{ij}^k$. In Eqs. (13) and (14), the minimum values of $o_{ij}^1$ and $o_{ij}^p$ are close to zero, which would lead to gradients being nearly unupdated, thereby resulting in poor learning of $\tau_{ij}^k$. To address the issue of parameter dependence, we introduce the solution below, which is to enhance $o_{ij}^k$ using the following equation:

$$o_{ij}^1 := \frac{e^{kl_i\tau_{ij}^1}}{\bigwedge_{i=1}^{n} e^{kl_i\tau_{ij}^1}},$$

$$o_{ij}^p := \frac{e^{k\hat{c}_i^{p-1}\tau_{ij}^p}}{\bigwedge_{i=1}^{n} e^{k\hat{c}_i^{p-1}\tau_{ij}^p}}, \; p = 2, 3, \cdots, L.$$

By substituting the updated $o_{ij}^k$ into Eq. (15) instead of the previous ones, we ensure that $o_{ij}^k$ remains within the range $[1, e^k]$, preventing it from becoming zero. This adjustment effectively resolves the parameter dependency issue encountered in subsequent simulations. Additionally, the $o_{ij}^k$ in Eqs. (13) and (14) has been replaced with the updated $o_{ij}^k$, resulting in improved learning performance compared to previous implementations.

## 6 Learning Performance

The learning algorithm derived from the proposed theory appears to be feasible; however, its performance must be evaluated through computer simulations. The learning performance of the GPDP-FS model is influenced by many parameters, including the initial values, learning rate, sample size, and elapsed time. Therefore, determining the optimal parameter values requires extensive testing and refinement.

### 6.1 Learning Accuracy Criteria

Learning accuracy criteria are the means by which we measure the learning effect of the algorithms and can analyze the reasons for poor results through learning effectiveness in order to adjust the parameters. We need to compare the final learned parameter values with the true parameter values and evaluate their error to assess the learning performance, then adjust the system structure and parameters based on the learning results. Furthermore, the overall effect for the learned model should also be assessed to ensure its accuracy and reliability. We suggest using the following criteria:

$$Normalized\ Overall\ Error = \frac{1}{nR}\sum_{i=1}^{R}\sum_{j=1}^{n}|\hat{z}_j^i - \tilde{z}_j^i|, \tag{18}$$

$$Normalized\ \mathbf{T}_k\ Error = \frac{1}{n^2}\sum_{i=1}^{n}\sum_{j=1}^{n}|\hat{\tau}_{ij}^k - \tilde{\tau}_{ij}^k|; \tag{19}$$

$$Normalized\ \mathbf{P}_k\ Error = \frac{1}{L^2}\sum_{i=1}^{L}\sum_{j=1}^{L}|\hat{\mathbf{P}}_k(s_i, s_j) - \tilde{\mathbf{P}}_k(s_i, s_j)|. \tag{20}$$

In practical applications, the true values of parameters are often unavailable, so the normalized output error becomes the primary evaluation metric. Unlike black-box model evaluation, which typically requires training, validation, and testing datasets along with separate fitting steps, GPDP-based modeling does not require these steps. The testing error of the GPDP model is indirectly reflected through the goodness of fit of the learned parameter values-the smaller the deviation between the final parameter values and the true values, the smaller the implied testing error. We also obtain the normalized overall error, $\mathbf{T}_k$ error, and $\mathbf{P}$ error, which can help reflect and adjust parameter values in time.

### 6.2 Simulation Settings

We implemented the learning algorithm and used MATLAB (version 2020b) to generate the necessary sample pairs $\{(x_i, \tilde{z}_i)\}_{i=1}^{R}$ for evaluating performance.

- A Gaussian random number generator is used to produce the external variable $\tilde{x}_i$, where $i = 1, 2, \ldots, R$, ensuring it follows a Gaussian distribution.
- Uniformly distributed random numbers are created to construct the atomic propositions evolution matrix $\tilde{T}_k$ for $k = 1, 2, \ldots, L$. The sample means $g_j$ and standard deviations $h_j$ are used for this process.

- The Gaussian fuzzy sets, along with their means $g_j$ and standard deviations $h_j$, are mapped to the external variable $x_i$ to derive the true current state $s_i$ for $i = 1, 2, \ldots, R$. These states, combined with $\hat{T}_k$, help generate the next states $\tilde{t}_k$ for $k = 1, 2, \ldots, L$.
- Using the inverse of the Gaussian fuzzy sets, the true next variables $\tilde{z}_i$ are computed for $i = 1, 2, \ldots, R$. The function in Eq. (2) is a one-to-two mapping, so alternating between addition and subtraction operations ensures proper distribution.

This process generates $R$ sample pairs $\{(x_i, \tilde{z}_i)\}_{i=1}^{R}$, and the designed program sequentially processes the system parameters in each epoch. The process of handling all samples constitutes one learning epoch, some epochs are grouped to form a single trial, where each epoch reads the sample pairs in the same order. The initial parameter values of all trials are same: $\tau_{ij}$ is initialized to 0.5, $g_j$ is set to the mean of the samples, and $h_j$ is set to the standard deviation of the samples, with these statistical values assumed to be known from the data. It was observed that when $L > 1$, simultaneous learning of $g_j$, $h_j$, and $\tau_{ij}$ is less effective if the true values of $g_j$ and $h_j$ are unknown. To address this, $g_j$ and $h_j$ are fixed as known values, and only $\tau_{ij}$ is updated during learning. This approach is practical, as in real-world, the mean and standard deviation of the sample data can be directly computed, and with a sufficient number of samples, these values approximate the true $g_j$ and $h_j$. Additionally, to ensure stability during iterations, any new value of $\tau_{ij}$ that becomes less than or equal to zero is reset to $10^{-6}$, while values bigger than one are set as one. The learning process then continues with these adjustments.

Importantly, the hyper-parameters in the learning process need to be set empirically. These hyper-parameters include the learning rate $\lambda_\tau$, the weighting factor $k$ and the number of epochs. Some effort was made to manually explore the effects of different values of these hyper-parameters on learning performance.

### 6.3 Simulation Results

Below, we present the learning results of the GPDP-FS model with action numbers $L = 1$, $L = 2$, and $L = 3$, where the precision of state atomic proposition values is set to $\lambda = 1$. Each state is associated with 3 atomic propositions, and each atomic proposition corresponds to an external sensor variable. In this case, the system consists of 1331 states and approximately 1.77 million transitions. The goal of the learning algorithm in this article is to derive the values of the atomic proposition evolution matrix and the possibility transition matrix solely based on the values of external variables. Under these three action numbers, we found that the best performance was achieved when $k = 3.5$. Therefore, we set $k = 3.5$. The value of $\lambda_\tau$ and the number of learning epochs need to be set differently depending on the number of actions, and we will provide a detailed explanation for each case.

We have the following results during the simulations.

*Result* 1: When the number of actions is 1, i.e., $L = 1$, the GPDP model simplifies to the GPKS model. In this case, it aligns with the situation studied by Liu et al. [11], and we will not describe more where $L = 1$. The results obtained through learning are as follows (Figs. 2, 3 and 4).

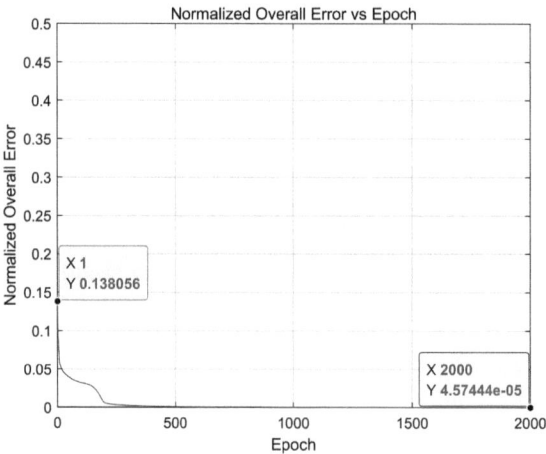

**Fig. 2.** The Normalized Overall Error when L = 1.

The red line is the true value and the blue solid line is learned values at end of each epoch are used to form the plots (this also applied to the rest of the figures of this subsection). To better demonstrate the learning effect, we show in the figure both the initial error values and the values after learning (Fig. 5).

*Result* 2: For two actions, that is, $L = 2$, after several simulations, we found that the best performance was achieved when $\lambda_\tau = 0.0005$ and $epoch = 4000$ and we found that when $L > 1$, the learning effect of $\tau$ is not ideal, mainly due to gradient propagation and decay. In gradient descent algorithms, gradients are passed layer by layer through the chain rule. In the formulas, we can see that the gradient at each layer, $\frac{\partial E}{\partial \tau_{ij}^k}$, depends on the gradient from the previous layer. Specifically,

$$\frac{\partial E}{\partial \tau_{ij}^k} = (\hat{z}_j - \tilde{z}_j)\frac{\partial \hat{z}_j}{\partial \tau_{ij}^k},$$

the gradient propagation depends on the error $\hat{z}_j - \tilde{z}_j$ and the derivative of that layer $\frac{\partial \hat{z}_j}{\partial \tau_{ij}^k}$. In a multi-layer network, the gradient propagates layer by layer, and the gradient at each layer is calculated as the product of the previous layer's gradient and that layer's derivative. This means that if the derivatives at each layer are small, the gradients decay as they propagate through the layers, which leads to the final gradient becoming very small.

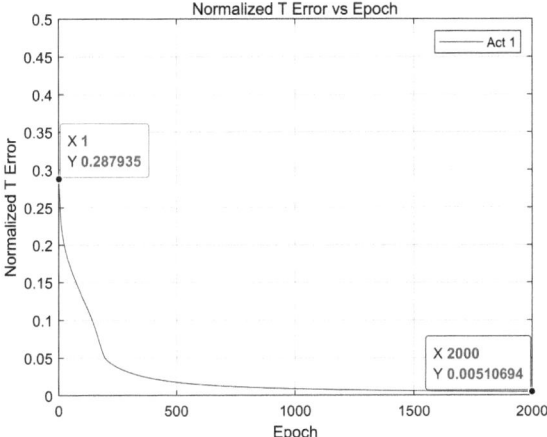

**Fig. 3.** The Normalized **T** Error when L = 1.

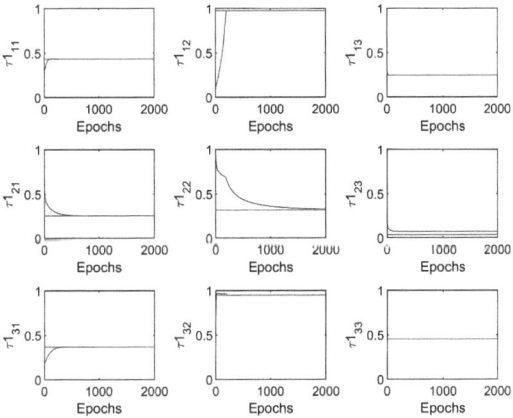

**Fig. 4.** The learning process of the atomic propositions evolution matrix elements when L=1.

However, the reason that the final result obtained after computation has a small error compared to the true values is that the APEM is, in a certain sense, not unique. That is, for the same current state, two different atomic propositions evolution matrices can generate the same next state because the max-product operator is not one-to-one but many-to-one. Therefore, the normalized overall error can decrease to an ideal value after one learning epoch. Let's illustrate with an example.

*Example 1.* Suppose the state is given as $s = [0.7, 0.5, 0.3]$, atomic propositions evolution matrices are given as $A_1 = \begin{bmatrix} 0.5 & 0.2 & 0.1 \\ 0.3 & 0.7 & 0.5 \\ 0.2 & 0.1 & 0.9 \end{bmatrix}$ and $A_2 = \begin{bmatrix} 0.5 & 0.3 & 0.2 \\ 0.2 & 0.7 & 0.4 \\ 0.1 & 0.2 & 0.9 \end{bmatrix}$,

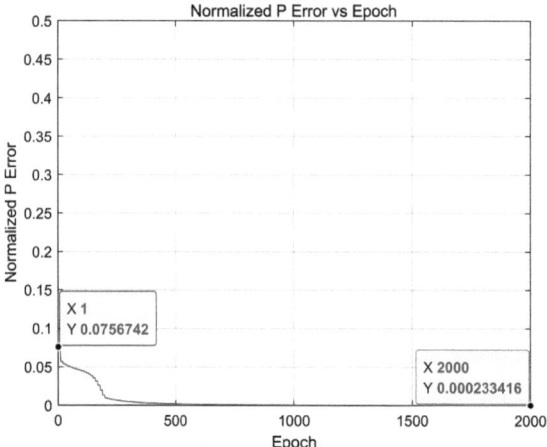

**Fig. 5.** The Normalized **P** Error when L = 1.

$B_1 = \begin{bmatrix} 0.5 & 0.4 & 0.3 \\ 0.2 & 0.6 & 0.1 \\ 0.4 & 0.3 & 0.7 \end{bmatrix}$ and $B_2 = \begin{bmatrix} 0.5 & 0.3 & 0.3 \\ 0.1 & 0.6 & 0.5 \\ 0.2 & 0.4 & 0.7 \end{bmatrix}$. We calculate $s$ with $A_1$, $B_1$ and $A_2$, $B_2$, and obtain the results as

$$s \circ A_1 \circ B_1 = [0.7, 0.5, 0.3] \circ \begin{bmatrix} 0.5 & 0.2 & 0.1 \\ 0.3 & 0.7 & 0.5 \\ 0.2 & 0.1 & 0.9 \end{bmatrix} \circ \begin{bmatrix} 0.5 & 0.4 & 0.3 \\ 0.2 & 0.6 & 0.1 \\ 0.4 & 0.3 & 0.7 \end{bmatrix} = [0.175, 0.21, 0.189],$$

$$s \circ A_2 \circ B_2 = [0.7, 0.5, 0.3] \circ \begin{bmatrix} 0.5 & 0.3 & 0.2 \\ 0.2 & 0.7 & 0.4 \\ 0.1 & 0.2 & 0.9 \end{bmatrix} \circ \begin{bmatrix} 0.5 & 0.3 & 0.3 \\ 0.1 & 0.6 & 0.5 \\ 0.2 & 0.4 & 0.7 \end{bmatrix} = [0.175, 0.21, 0.189].$$

Through the example above, we can observe that when the same state $s$ is computed using max-product with $A_1 B_1$ and $A_2 B_2$, even though the matrices are different, the results are still the same. This demonstrates that the max-product operation is a many-to-one mapping. This is why $\tau$ can't effectively learn the true values, yet the normalized overall error can still decrease to an ideal value.

Figure 6 shows the decrease in the normalized overall error during the learning process for two actions. The error decreases from an initial value of 0.221318 to $3.10414 \times 10^{-5}$ after 4000 learning epochs.

Figure 7 shows the error when $L = 2$ calculated by (19). From the formula (19), it is clear that the error is obtained through the calculation of $\tau$. Due to gradient vanishing, the learning effect of $\tau$ is poor, which leads to the worse decrease in the normalized **T** error when $L = 2$ compared to when $L = 1$.

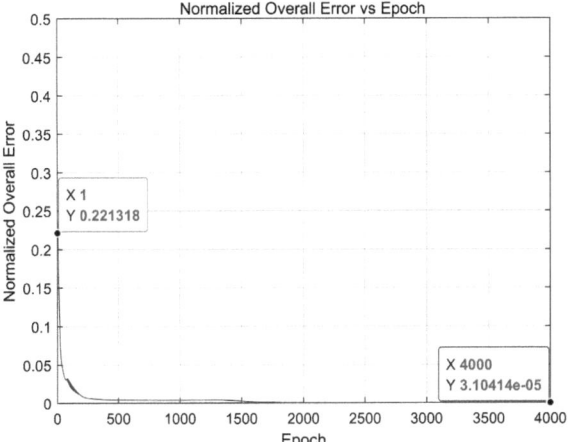

**Fig. 6.** The Normalized Overall Error when L=2.

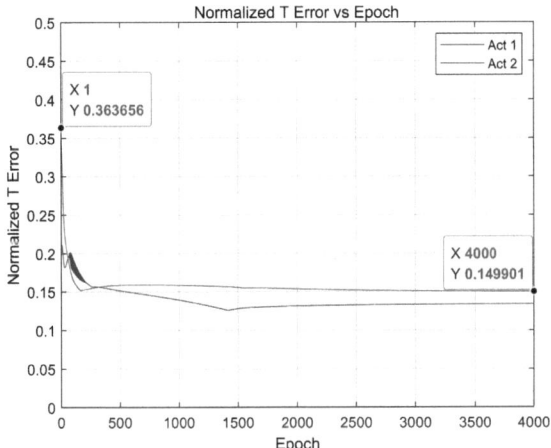

**Fig. 7.** The Normalized **T** Error when $L = 2$.

Figure 8 show the learning process of the elements in two atomic propositions evolution matrices when $L = 2$. It can be observed that only a part of the elements have learned the true values.

Figure 9 illustrates the progressive reduction of the normalized **P** error across successive learning epochs. From the formula of distance and similarity of state, it can be seen that **P** is also computed using $\tau$, so the normalized **P** error is also affected by the learning effect of $\tau$. To reduce runtime, we still record the error every 10 epochs.

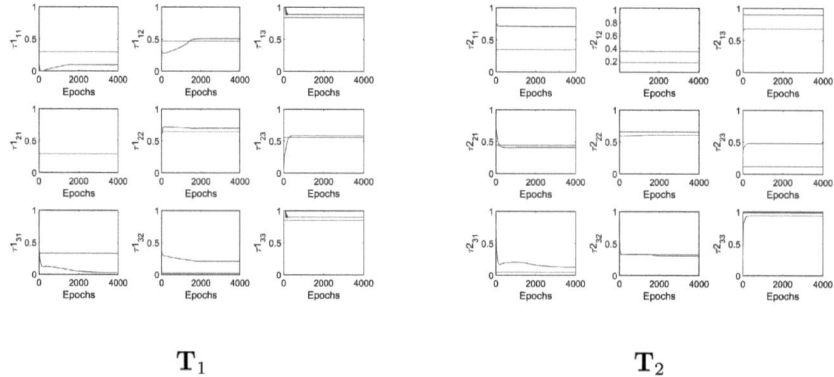

**Fig. 8.** The learning process of the atomic proposition evolution matrix elements when L = 2.

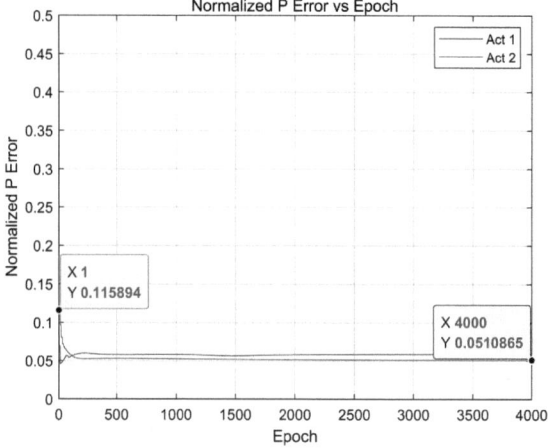

**Fig. 9.** The Normalized **P** Error when L = 2.

*Result* 3: For three actions, that is, $L = 3$, after several simulations, we found that the best performance was achieved when $\lambda_\tau = 0.0002$ and $epoch = 4000$. Figure 11 show how the normalized overall error when L = 3. When L = 3, the learning of the model parameters is not very effective, this is due to the reason that when the number of actions increases, more different atomic proposition evolution matrices can be computed to the same result, which causes the learning to be ineffective. To solve this problem the one-to-one computation can be chosen, and this problem can be continued to be studied subsequently (Fig. 10).

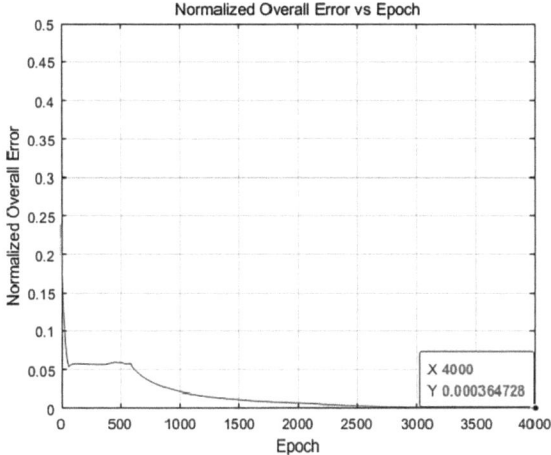

**Fig. 10.** The Normalized Overall Error when L = 3.

## 7 Example of Possibilistic Model Checking Based on GPDP-FS

In this section, we will use an example of traffic management to illustrate the application of the learning algorithm in model checking [4,11]. In this example, we are managing the traffic flow at a major city intersection. The physical state of the traffic can be determined by three fuzzy atomic propositions representing key traffic indicators, such as $AP = \{congested, uncrowded, recovery\}$, where:

- *congested* represents traffic flow is congested,
- *uncrowded* represents traffic flow has returned to being uncrowded,
- *recovery* represents the process of traffic flow recovering from being congested to uncrowded.

And the set of act $Act = \{\alpha, \beta\}$ have two actions $\alpha$ and $\beta$. Action $\alpha$ represents a traffic optimization solution (e.g., adjusting traffic signals, allocating lanes, etc.), action $\beta$ represents another optimization solution (e.g., increasing road guidance, setting speed limits, etc.). The property is that the traffic flow will be uncrowded next minute as

$$\varphi = \bigcirc uncrowded.$$

We generated a system with three samples using the above learning algorithm, i.e., the system contains three states, the state space is $S = \{congested, uncrowded, recovery\}$ where each state contains three atomic propositions and $I(congested) = 1$. The atomic proposition evolution matrix $T_1$ and $T_2$ and the possibility transition matrix $P$ learned from randomly generated external variables are as follows:

$$T_1 = \begin{bmatrix} 0.0446 & 0.4570 & 0.2142 \\ 1 & 0.0482 & 0.2650 \\ 0.9999 & 0.7415 & 0.7110 \end{bmatrix},$$

$$T_2 = \begin{bmatrix} 0.5288 & 0.3929 & 0.5364 \\ 0.1325 & 0.4576 & 0.4484 \\ 0.8616 & 0.6690 & 0.1936 \end{bmatrix}.$$

We round the data of the obtained possibilistic transition matrix to one decimal place.

$$P_\alpha = \begin{bmatrix} 0.8 & 0.8 & 0.8 \\ 0.9 & 0.6 & 0.7 \\ 0.9 & 0.7 & 0.8 \end{bmatrix},$$

$$P_\beta = \begin{bmatrix} 0.8 & 0.7 & 0.9 \\ 0.8 & 0.8 & 0.9 \\ 0.9 & 0.7 & 0.8 \end{bmatrix}.$$

Since the possibility transition matrix $P_\alpha$, $P_\beta$ obtained through the learning algorithm is dense, for observation purposes we divide this GPDP-FS model into two GPKS based on the kind of action $\alpha$, $\beta$.

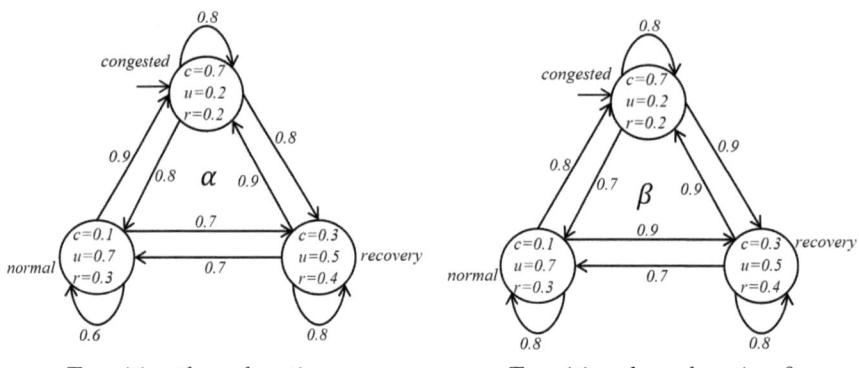

**Fig. 11.** GPDP-FS model.

What are the optimal strategy and maximal possibility that congested will get normal in the next minute? We have the following formula:

$$Po_{max}(congested \models \bigcirc n) = \bigvee_{\alpha \in Act(s)} P_\alpha \circ D_n \circ r_{sup}(congeated), \quad (21)$$

$$r_{sup} = \left( \bigvee_{\alpha \in Act} P_\alpha \right)^+ \circ \left( \bigvee_{\alpha \in Act} P_\alpha^+(s,s) \right)_{s \in S}, \quad (22)$$

where + denotes the transitive closure of a fuzzy matrix.

$$r_{sup} = \left(\bigvee_{\alpha \in Act} P_\alpha\right)^+ \circ \left(\bigvee_{\alpha \in Act} P_\alpha^+(s,s)\right)_{s \in S}$$

$$= \left(\begin{bmatrix} 0.8 & 0.8 & 0.8 \\ 0.9 & 0.6 & 0.7 \\ 0.9 & 0.7 & 0.8 \end{bmatrix} \vee \begin{bmatrix} 0.8 & 0.7 & 0.9 \\ 0.8 & 0.8 & 0.9 \\ 0.9 & 0.7 & 0.8 \end{bmatrix}\right)^+ \circ \begin{bmatrix} 0.8 \\ 0.8 \\ 0.8 \end{bmatrix}$$

$$= \begin{bmatrix} 0.8 \\ 0.8 \\ 0.8 \end{bmatrix},$$

$$Po_{max}(congested \models \bigcirc n) = \bigvee_{\alpha \in Act(s)} P_\alpha \circ D_n \circ r_{sup}(congested)$$

$$= \left(\begin{bmatrix} 0.8 & 0.8 & 0.8 \\ 0.9 & 0.6 & 0.7 \\ 0.9 & 0.7 & 0.8 \end{bmatrix} \vee \begin{bmatrix} 0.8 & 0.7 & 0.9 \\ 0.8 & 0.8 & 0.9 \\ 0.9 & 0.7 & 0.8 \end{bmatrix}\right)$$

$$\circ \begin{bmatrix} 0.2 & 0 & 0 \\ 0 & 0.7 & 0 \\ 0 & 0 & 0.5 \end{bmatrix} \circ \begin{bmatrix} 0.8 \\ 0.8 \\ 0.8 \end{bmatrix} (congested)$$

$$= 0.7,$$

and an optimal strategy corresponding to 0.7 is to choose $\alpha$ action in state congested.

This example illustrates the use of self-learning modeling of GPDP models for model checking in practical applications, where the algorithm learns to obtain the atomic propositions evolution matrix and the possibility transfer matrix.

## 8 Conclusion

This research solves the problem of modeling fuzzy states and possibility transition matrices **P** and state transfer mechanisms in GPDP models in practical applications. The research focuses on developing an online learning algorithm for generalized possibilistic decision process (GPDP) to self-learning APEM and possibilistic transition matrix without relying on subjective expert knowledge. The approach assumes that the fuzzy state of the system model, although unknown, is related to sensor variables that can be acquired through samples, which is reasonable in practical applications. To this end, this article proposes a new GPDP model, the generalized possibilistic decision process with fuzzy set (GPDP-FS), which combines the standard GPDP with a Gaussian fuzzy function in order to connect the value of atomic propositions of the state to the sensor variables. Inspired by self-learning modeling in possibilistic model checking and supervised learning of multi-event transition matrices in fuzzy discrete event systems (FDES), this study aims to improve the ability of GPDP models to deal with non-determinism in open systems and to complement the lack of the traditional generalized possibilistic Kripke structure (GPKS). The GPDP-FS, by allowing for state transition through different types of actions, the extends GPKS to better cope with non-deterministic choices between possibilistic distributions in open systems. The algorithm using stochastic gradient principle learns the elements of multiple atomic propositional evolution matrices (APEM) $\mathbf{T}_k$. The method constructs models by automatically extracting information from data, which greatly improves the efficiency and objectivity of modeling GPDP models. At the same time, it provides a flexible and adaptive approach that allows the model to be dynamically updated according to changes in the environment or system. The method's potential applications, such as optimizing treatment strategies in medical decision-making systems, demonstrate the importance of resolving non-determinism in practical applications.

This article provides an algorithmic foundation for self-learning modeling of generalized possibilistic decision processes, and there are still many issues worth studying here, such as the problem of learning effects decreasing when the number of actions increases.

**Acknowledgments.** This work was supported in part by the National Natural Science Foundation of China under Grant 12471437 and Grant 12071271, Shaanxi Fundamental Science Research Project for Mathematics and Physics under Grant 23JSZ011, and the China Association for Science and Technology Youth Talent Support Project.

# References

1. Li, Y., Lei, L., Li, S.: Computation tree logic model checking based on multi-valued possibility measures. Inf. Sci. **485**, 87–113 (2019)
2. Liu, W., Li, Z., Li, Y.: Quantum reachability games. IEEE Trans. Emerg. Topics Comput. Intell., 1–15 (2024)
3. Liu, W., Wang, J., He, Q., Li, Y.: Model checking computation tree logic over multi-valued decision processes and its reduction techniques. Chin. J. Electron. **33**(6), 1399–1411 (2024)
4. Liu, W., Li, Y.: Optimal strategy model checking in possibilistic decision processes. IEEE Trans. Syst. Man Cybern. Syst. **53**(10), 6620–6632 (2023)
5. Li, Y., Liu, W., Wang, J., Yu, X., Li, C.: Model checking of possibilistic linear-time properties based on generalized possibilistic decision processes. IEEE Trans. Fuzzy Syst. **31**(10), 3495–3506 (2023)
6. Li, Y., Wei, J.: Possibilistic fuzzy linear temporal logic and its model checking. IEEE Trans. Fuzzy Syst. **29**(7), 1899–1913 (2021)
7. Zadeh, L.A.: Fuzzy sets as a basis for a theory of possibility. Fuzzy Sets Syst. **1**(1), 3–28 (1978)
8. Liu, W., He, Q., Li, Y.: Computation tree logic model checking over possibilistic decision processes under finite-memory scheduler. In: Cai, Z., Li, J., Zhang, J. (eds.) NCTCS 2021. CCIS, vol. 1494, pp. 75–88. Springer, Singapore (2021). https://doi.org/10.1007/978-981-16-7443-3_6
9. Dawson, N.V.: Physician judgment in clinical settings: methodological influences and cognitive performance. Clin. Chem. **39**(7), 1468–1478 (1993). https://doi.org/10.1093/clinchem/39.7.1468

10. Cooke, R.M.: Experts In Uncertainty: Opinion and Subjective Probability in Science. Oxford Academic, New York, NY (1991)
11. Liu, W., He, Q., Li, Z., Li, Y.: Self-learning modeling in possibilistic model checking. IEEE Trans. Emerg. Topics Comput. Intell. **8**(1), 264–278 (2024)
12. Lin, F., Ying, H.: Modeling and control of fuzzy discrete event systems. IEEE Trans. Syst. Man Cybern. B **32**(4), 408–415 (2002)
13. Cao, Y., Ying, M.: Observability and decentralized control of fuzzy discrete-event systems. IEEE Trans. Fuzzy Syst. **14**(2), 202–216 (2006)
14. Deng, W., Qiu, D.: BiFuzzy discrete event systems and their supervisory control theory. IEEE Trans. Fuzzy Syst. **23**(6), 2107–2121 (2015)
15. Qiu, D.: Supervisory control of fuzzy discrete event systems: a formal approach. IEEE Trans. Syst. Man Cybern. B **35**(1), 72–88 (2005)
16. Ying, H., Lin, F.: Self-learning fuzzy automaton with input and output fuzzy sets for system modelling. IEEE Trans. Emerg. Topics Comput. Intell. **7**(2), 500–512 (2023)
17. Ying, H., Lin, F.: Online self-learning fuzzy discrete event systems. IEEE Trans. Fuzzy Syst. **28**(9), 2185–2194 (2020)
18. Ying, H., Lin, F.: Learning fuzzy automaton's event transition matrix when post-event state is unknown. IEEE Trans. Cybern. **52**(6), 4993–5000 (2022)
19. Cao, Y., Ying, M.: Supervisory control of fuzzy discrete event systems. IEEE Trans. Syst. Man Cybern. B **35**(2), 366–371 (2005)
20. Deng, W., Qiu, D.: Supervisory control of fuzzy discrete-event systems for simulation equivalence. IEEE Trans. Fuzzy Syst. **23**(1), 178–192 (2015)
21. Deng, W., Qiu, D.: State-based decentralized diagnosis of bi-fuzzy discrete event systems. IEEE Trans. Fuzzy Syst. **25**(4), 854–867 (2017)
22. Yin, X.: A belief-evolution-based approach for online control of fuzzy discrete-event systems under partial observation. IEEE Trans. Fuzzy Syst. **25**(6), 1830–1836 (2017)
23. Zadeh, L.A.: Fuzzy sets. Inf. Control **8**(3), 338–353 (1965)
24. Dubois, D.: Possibility theory and statistical reasoning. Comput. Statist. Data Anal. **51**(1), 47–69 (2006)
25. Dubois, D., Prade, H.: Possibility theory and its applications: where do we stand? In: Kacprzyk, J., Pedrycz, W. (eds.) Springer Handbook of Computational Intelligence, pp. 31–60. Springer, Heidelberg (2015). https://doi.org/10.1007/978-3-662-43505-2_3
26. Bertsekas, D.P.: Minimax methods based on approximation. In: Proceedings John Hopkins Conference Information Science System, pp. 463–465 (1976)

# Artificial Intelligence Theory and Algorithm

# DPhuman: Generalizable Neural Human Rendering via Point Registration-Based Human Deformation

Yongang Yu[1], Zhigang Chen[2,3](✉), and Tangquan Qi[4]

[1] Big Data Institute, Central South University, Changsha 410083, Hunan, China
[2] School of Computer Science and Engineering, Central South University, Changsha 410083, Hunan, China
[3] Hunan Provincial Key Laboratory of Philosophy and Social Sciences of Urban Smart Governance, Central South University, Changsha 410083, Hunan, China
czg@csu.edu.com
[4] Wondershare Technology, Central South University, Changsha 410125, Hunan, China

**Abstract.** Animating virtual avatars with free-view control through implicit Neural Radiance Field rendering (NeRF) has attracted considerable attention. Previous methods for generalizable neural human rendering employed explicit constraints to improve both quality and functional accuracy. However, directly optimizing coordinates on a complex surface leads to a dynamic semantic contradiction between the character's pose and explicit constraints, which in turn reduces the generalizability of neural rendering for human motion. Tackling these issues, we present a novel framework named DPhuman, which optimizes the prefitted SMPL with a concise and consistent Hypergraph representation, integrating point registration and forward deformation into a unified model of shared rigid motion while simultaneously capturing the global topological structure. Specifically, the Hypergraph representation simplifies complex human meshes and establishes associations with human joints. Then, the Mapping-based Deformable Radiance Fields (MDRF) translate human motion into rigid translation through point registration, enabling human deformation based on specific semantic parts while mapping points. Finally, the Fine-grained module is employed to further improve fine-grained consistency, weighted from the aligned SMPL model. Extensive experiments demonstrate the superiority of our proposed DPhuman over state-of-the-art methods, and the ablation study illustrates the effectiveness of our approach.

**Keywords:** Neural Radiance Fields (NeRF) · Human Avatar Reconstruction · Explicit Constraints · SMPL Priors

## 1 Introduction

Producing high-fidelity, free-viewpoint videos of dynamic human performers is essential for various applications. Previous research [14,23,24,37] in human pose control has demonstrated that explicit constraints can be integrated into neural radiance fields. Several works [3,23,39] have extended explicit mesh constraints (*e.g.*, SMPL [15]) to include topological adjustments for geometric alignment, significantly enhancing the quality of human rendering. However, the inherent contradictions between explicit constraints and pose-driven dynamics greatly hinder the application of such methods. Targeting these issues, [20] proposed to learn the painted SMPL model under the canonical space and captures the global relationships between human parts with transformers, addressing pose ambiguity and extend it to sequence models for a more generalizable human rendering.

Previous methods [2,12,37] for generalizable neural human rendering mainly employ an explicit constraint to improves the aesthetic quality and the functional accuracy of the neural human rendering. Human-specific methods typically assume a SMPL to constrain the motion space. Recent works [4,17,26,41] have extended the explicit constraint into a mesh-based driven approach to achieve a pose-independent generalizable neural human rendering. The mesh-based human driven approach mainly suffers from the following two aspects: 1) Directly optimizing 3D coordinates on the complex surface is inherently problematic, which lead to solutions where the sample coordinates no longer correspond to any point on the actual surface, thereby deviating from realistic human anatomical features [23]. 2) Although the SMPL model integrates mesh and pose parameters into a cohesive framework, there exists a dynamic semantic contradiction between the character's pose and explicit constraints imposed by the mesh (*e.g.* [1,17,28]). As shown in Fig. 1, this contradiction arises because the pose parameters, designed to capture a wide range of human motions, often conflict with the mesh's ability to conform to these movements without distorting. As a result, maintaining both accurate pose representation and the integrity of the mesh structure becomes a complex challenge.

To address the aforementioned issues, we present the DPhuman, a novel neural human rendering framework that shows superior generalization ability with high efficiency. DPhuman is composed of Mapping-based Deformable Radiance Fields (MDRF), Hypergraph representation, and the Fine-grained Continuous Module. We first introduce the Hypergraph representation, which simplifies complex human meshes and establishes associations with human 3D joints. This representation integrates point mapping and forward deformation into a unified model, enabling shared rigid transformations. MDRF allows for the deformation of the mesh based on specific semantic parts, mapping points in canonical space to the mesh while considering their global spatial relationships. The core idea of MDRF is to translate human motion into rigid deformation through point registration, thereby avoiding conflicts between the dynamic SMPL mesh and pose without computing Linear Blend Skinning (LBS) weights. By utilizing Hypergraph Representation and the MDRF, human representation incorporates coarse information based on human priors while capturing fine-grained details directly from the mesh representation. Therefore, similar to [20], we propose to further integrate detailed features from mesh alignment based on the guidance of the final human representations.

Extensive experiments on ZJU-MoCap [26] and H36M [10] demonstrate the superior generalization ability across poses and dynamic mesh and high efficiency of DPhuman.

Our contributions are summarized as follows:

- We propose a novel framework DPHuman for addressing the challenging task of generalizable and transferable neural human rendering. This framework achieves significant performance improvements while maintaining high efficiency, reaching the current state-of-the-art level.
- We propose processing the pre-fitted SMPL model in canonical space to eliminate pose alignment issues during training phases. By using MDRF, we deform the model back to the observation space, enabling robust queries based on topological structures.
- To the best of our knowledge, we make the first exploration to the transformer-based deformation around the point registration for capturing the global topological and implicit relation between human parts.

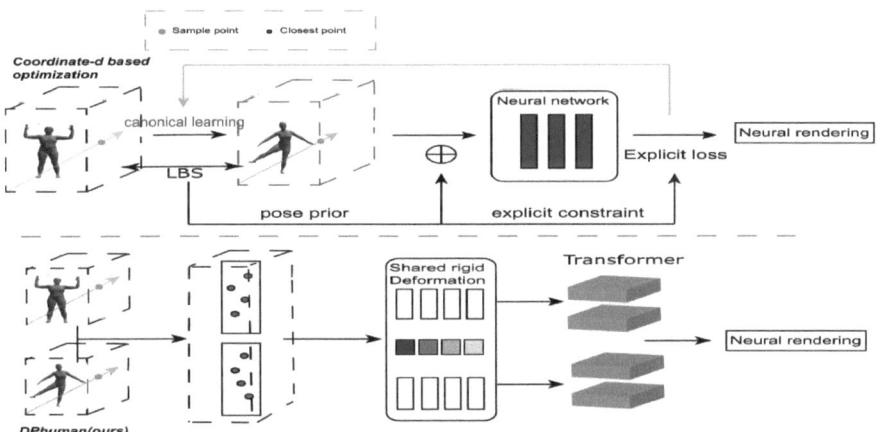

**Fig. 1.** Comparisons between existing SPC-based and our point registration-based human representations: Given the pose aligned SMPL, the coordinate-based method directly optimizes vertex coordinates under the canonical space with human motion, assisted by LBS weights. Instead, our point registration-based deformation integrates point registration and forward deformation into a unified model of shared rigid deformation.

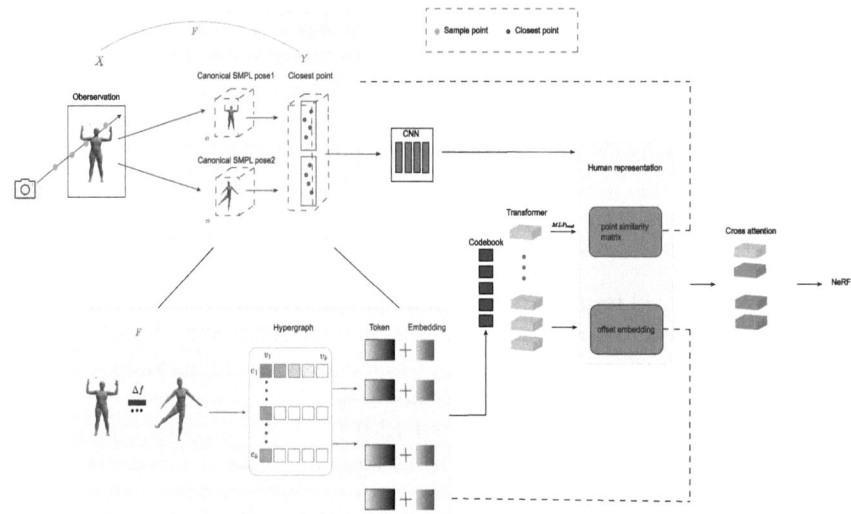

**Fig. 2.** Method Overview: The Hypergraph representation simplifies complex human meshes by reducing multidimensional data into a more manageable form, establishing direct associations between the vertices of human meshes and the corresponding skeletal joints. Then the Mapping-based Deformable Radiance Fields (MDRF) translate human motion into rigid translation through point registration, enabling human deformation based on specific semantic parts while mapping points. Finally, the Fine-grained module is employed to further improve fine-grained consistency, weighted from the aligned SMPL model.

## 2 Related Work

### 2.1 Avatar With Performance Capture

The reconstruction results can be ambiguous due to the continuous motion of dynamic objects in frame sequences [19,32]. In terms of dynamic object reconstruction, much work [6,8,22,27] has been done to overcome the ambiguity caused by dynamic motion. [13,14,30,39,43,44] attempts to model a dynamic human motion avatar. [26] Learn the set of latent codes of each frame vertex to encode the human poses in motion space. [21] introduces a deformation field to overcome the contradiction of ray intersections. [25] generate novel view synthesis of humans based on the deformation field. [1] jointly optimizes the human pose parameters. [37] Humannerf uses a pose Decoder to obtain non-rigid transform inputs for human body reconstruction and dynamically represents the extraction of features through the decoding of poses. Neuman [12] was proposed at the same time as Humannerf, but Neuman believed that the pose-driven approach based on the encoder-decoder architecture was highly dependent on the accuracy of the neural network, the rigid deformation of SMPL explicit mesh is proposed jointly optimized training phase. These studies emphasize that the implicit representation of neural radiance fields is highly characterized by relying on the accuracy of the neural network. We enhance the effectiveness of explicit constraints during training by incorporating the point mapping representation, aiming to reduce the reliance on the accuracy of the neural network and enhance human performance.

## 2.2 Surface Aligned Human Reconstruction

To better capture the geometric surfaces of humans, many researchers [4,7,9, 16,40] represent the human body as the zero isosurfaces of a signed distance field (SDF). [3] represents the implicit surface with hyper-coordinates in association with camera views and dynamic appearance codes. [39] implemented a dynamic radiance field based on point mapping and pose assistance. [11] represents the human body using a template mesh and an SDF in canonical space, employing a deformation field that consists of rigid forward Linear Blend Skinning (LBS) deformation along with small non-rigid deformations to generate correspondences. [23] introduces a continuous and optimizable intrinsic coordinate for human rendering instead of the original explicit Euclidean coordinate. [41] proposes to model the deformation field by applying bi-directional constraints and strategically using pre-existing keyframe data to analyze and understand feature correlations. These methods focus on optimizing coordinate representation but lack global relation capturing of the human mesh, and neglect the extensibility of dynamic transformations based on point mapping. Recent work [20] proposes using Transformer architecture to capture the global features of explicit constraints, and uses pixel alignment to solve the semantic ambiguity of human pose. However, they ignored the inherent contradiction between the internal pose parameters and the LBS-based deformation.

## 3 Method

Inspired by sequence-based approaches [29,34], we have developed a point registration-based framework called DPhuman, which enables generalizable neural human rendering by translating mapping points into rigid deformations. As shown in Fig. 2, the framework consists of 1) a hybrid learning strategy for neural human rendering, 2) a transformer decoder architecture that integrates a chained mesh codebook and a mesh-based spatial-temporal cross-attention module, and 3) a human representation that enables the transformation of point-based rigid deformation into human deformation.

The hybrid learning strategy initially establishes the human representation using a point mapping method, creating a connection between ray marching and explicit mesh constraints. The point CNN encoder, combined with the hypergraph representation, generates a codebook that associates point features and mesh features, preserving a continuous radiance representation. The transformer decoder first generates a translation matrix using the MLP head, which then instantiates the mapped point features into rigid human motion. Finally, the transformer produces a hybrid human representation by aggregating rigid human motion. We will detail each component below.

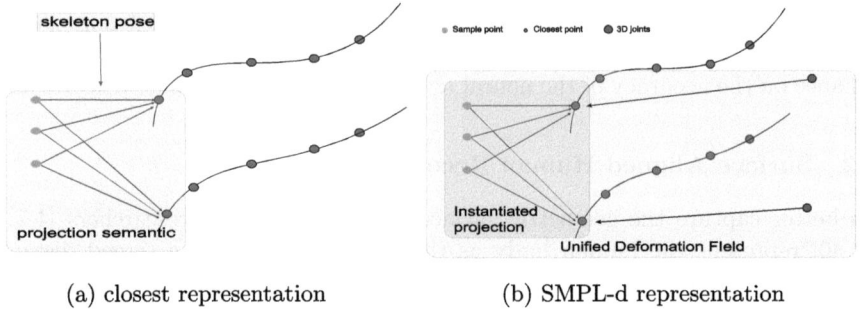

(a) closest representation  (b) SMPL-d representation

**Fig. 3.** Comparison of different projection methods. (a) Dynamic semantic contradiction between the character's pose and explicit constraints imposed by the mesh in LBS-based deformation. Furthermore, to reduce the precision loss caused by the prefitted SMPL, the sample points can be approximated as closely as possible to the surface by using a loss function, which will further exacerbate the semantic contradiction. (b) We integrate point mapping and forward deformation into a unified model, thereby achieving shared rigid body transformations and capturing the global features of pose keypoints through Hypergraph representation.

### 3.1 Representation Initialization

Given a reference image $I$ and its corresponding pre-fitted SMPL model, we denote the template surface as $T$ and the pose as $p$, with $V^o$ representing the template surface geometry. Previous method [12,37] decomposed the motion field into two parts to capture both skeletal and non-rigid deformations. However, a significant challenge arises from the inherent conflict between the character's dynamic pose and the mesh's explicit constraints. This problem arises from the design of the pose parameter $p$, which is intended to accommodate diverse human motions. However, this design frequently collides with the radiance field of alignment with the mesh $V^o$, indicating that the mesh fails to adapt to the continuity driven by the pose deformation, as illustrated in 3a. Consequently, achieving both precise pose accuracy and preserving the prefitted mesh-based mapping becomes challenging. Intuitively, a simple solution is to directly utilize coordinate mapping $F$ as the human representation, i.e., the nearest point, $F_t = \text{map}(F'_t)$, where $F$ denotes the mapped canonical coordinates, $F'$ denotes observation coordinates, and $t$ denotes time. The implicit reconstruction finally directly maps the two-dimensional pixel coordinates to RGB and $\sigma$ value, where $\sigma$ represents voxel density and directly contributes to the rendering process.

**Coordinates-D Based Representation.** Given sample points $x$ at frame $t$, we seek a relative coordinate system that is conditioned on the evolving surface shape $T_t$. This system is designed to dynamically map sample points $x$ in relation to the surface $T$ across different frames, ensuring that corresponding points are consistently represented. As the human body moves, we focus on maintaining the relationship of the nearest surface point $n$ to the sample point $x$, along with its signed distance $d$, to ensure stable feature extraction. We explore two types of relative coordinate systems, XYZ-D and UV-D, each defined by $n$ and $d$, and discuss the rationale behind our preference for the coordinates-d representation in accommodating dynamic human surface interactions in our work. Formally, we compute the Coordinates-D representation as:

$$\rho(x|T_t) = (\mathcal{N}(\text{Coord}(\hat{n})), S(d)) \tag{1}$$

where $\text{Coord}(\cdot)$ extracts the coordinates of point $x$, $S$ represents the data and distance information for a point. These coordinates are normalized by $\mathcal{N}(\cdot)$ and the signed distance $d$ is adjusted by the sigmoid function $S(\cdot)$, focusing on the proximity to the reference surface $T_1$. We initialize the human representation with the coordinate-d representation:

$$\Delta f = \rho(x|T_t) - \rho(x_{t-1}|T_{t-1}) \tag{2}$$

where $\Delta f$ represents the dynamic offsets in the coordinate-D representation from one frame to the next, capturing the evolution of the human motion and geometry effectively.

## 3.2 Mapping-Based Deformable Radiance Fields

The main idea of mapping-based deformation is to bind the varying pre-fitted SMPL mesh with a partial radiance field for a specific semantic part, translating coordinate-based deformation into a shared point mapping based rigid deformation. We follow the original MLP-based vertex positional embedding since the SMPL vertex count does not scale well with transformer architectures, i.e., 6890 [20,29].

We first seek an embedding to represent the relationship between sample points and SMPL mesh. To achieve this, we generate an instantiated mapping relationship $f'$ using per-point embeddings of the sample points and the closest points. Specifically, given a set of sample points $x$ and closest points $p$ on mesh $V$, We denote $X$ and $Y$ as two point sets, where $X = \{x_1, \ldots, x_i, \ldots, x_N\} \subset \mathbb{R}^3$ consists of sample points, and $Y = \{p_1, \ldots, p_j, \ldots, p_M\} \subset \mathbb{R}^3$ consists of the closest points on the mesh corresponding to each point in $x$, with the assumption that $M = N$.

In the rigid alignment problem, we assume $Y$ is to be transformed from $X$ by an unknown rigid deformation. This motion is typically represented by a transformation consisting of a rotation $R_{XY} \in SO(3)$ and a translation $t_{XY} \in \mathbb{R}^3$. Our objective is to find an embedding $E$ that encapsulates this rigid deformation. The embedding $E$ encodes the transformation parameters such that the mean-squared error between the transformed $X$ and $Y$ is minimized. Mathematically, we seek $E$ so that:

$$D_b : X \to (E, Y) \tag{3}$$

the deformation model $D_b$ can be expressed through an enhanced formulation that incorporates the embedding function. The proposed model is represented by the following equation:

$$D_b(x_i, r) = T^b_{NR}(T^b_{mo}(x_i, E(P)), E(P)) \qquad (4)$$

where $r$ is the shared deformation matrix of point mapping and registration. $T^b_{mo}$ is the motion weight which is transformed into the point rigid deformation $E$ and the non-rigid deformation component $T^b_{NR}$.

### 3.3 Hypergraph Construction

Following [38], we employ a 3D Convolutional Neural Network (CNN) to extract point features from the set of sample points $X$. For the SMPL mesh, transformers process each input token in relation to every other token due to their self-attention mechanism, which leads to a computational complexity. To tackle this issue, we propose a Hypergraph representation to reduce dimensionality and enhance feature extraction through graph convolutions. The hypergraph $G$ is defined as $G = (V, E)$, where $V$ is the set of all vertices $v_i$, each being the closest point on the mesh to the sample points $x_i$ is the set of hyperedges, with each $e_j$ containing vertices grouped by their proximity to the joint $Jnt_j$. Each hypernode $h_i$ represents a cluster of vertices $V_i \subset V$, such that $\bigcup_i V_i = V$ and $V_i \cap V_j = \emptyset$ for $i \neq j$.

$$H = \{h_1, h_2, \ldots, h_N\}$$

where $N$ is the number of hypernodes. Hyperedges are defined based on the functional connections between body parts, facilitating the encapsulation of relationships that significantly influence body dynamics.

$$E = \{e_k | e_k \subseteq H\}$$

Formally, the SMPL vertices are grouped into hypernodes based on their anatomical proximity. Let the SMPL mesh be denoted as a set of vertices $V$ where $|V| = 6890$. For each $p_i$ is the closest point on the mesh to $x_i$. We define the vertices (Hypernodes) as $V = \{v_1, v_2, \ldots, v_k\}$, where each $v_i$ corresponds to $p_i$. The 3D joints on the SMPL mesh are represented as $P = \{Jnt_1, Jnt_2, \ldots, Jnt_m\}$. Each vertex $v_i$ is assigned to a hyperedge $e_j$ that corresponds to the nearest joint $Jnt_j$. This is determined by the following formula:

$$e_j = \{v_i \mid \text{dist}(v_i, Jnt_j) \leq \text{dist}(v_i, Jnt_k) \text{ for all } k \neq j\} \qquad (5)$$

where dist() denotes the Euclidean distance.

### 3.4 Fine-Grained Continuous Module

With initialized points pair and Hypergraph representation, we can acheive a deformable human representation $D_b(x_H, r)$. However, deformation-based approaches struggle to model changes in topology [22], despite the coarse continuous relationship we build from mapping embedding from 3.1, we seek fine-grained ways for high-fidelity novel view synthesis.

**Blend Codebook.** To efficiently capture the geometric characteristics of point clouds and meshes, our approach integrates two distinct neural network encoders 3D CNN and DGCNN [35]. Instead of concatenation of two embeddings directly, Given the embedding feature from 3.1, which encapsulates the local and global geometric properties inherent in the point cloud and SMPL mesh, In our network architecture, we employ a unified codebook $C$ to directly quantize point cloud features $P$ and mesh features $M$.

**Cross Attention.** We integrate a cross-attention module to enhance the transformer's focus on mesh features by leveraging human representations derived from a codebook. Specifically, we use the human representation $D_b(x_G, r)$ as the query, and mesh features as the key and value to compute the offset field. This setup allows the transformer to prioritize and integrate mesh features more effectively, producing the integrated offset field $o^{1:N_t} \in \mathbb{R}^{N_t \times d_2}$ shared with $r$. The final offset feature $o$ for a query point $p$ is then derived by applying average pooling across the view dimension, resulting in $o^{(t)} = \phi\left(CNN_Y^{(t)}, DGCNN_G^{(t)}\right)$, where $\phi$ is residual term given by Transformer [33]. This approach ensures that the final representation is in a knowledgeable association in $F_t$, achieving a more continuous radiance field.

### 3.5 Traning Loss

To refine our model's ability to registrate point while ensuring perceptual consistency in reconstructed images, we further adapt mean squared error MSE and perceptual LPIPS loss [42]. The final loss function is defined as:

$$\mathcal{L} = \|t_{xy} - t_{xy}^g\|^2 + \mathcal{L}_{MSE} + \lambda \mathcal{L}_{LPIPS} \tag{6}$$

where $\|t_{xy} - t_{xy}^g\|^2$ quantifies the Euclidean distance between the predicted and ground truth translation vectors, ensuring the spatial alignment of the related points. $\mathcal{L}_{MSE}$ represents the pixel-wise mean squared error, focusing on the accuracy of pixel intensities in the synthesized images compared to the ground truth. $\mathcal{L}_{PER}$, derived from perceptual similarity metrics, aims to maintain structural and textural fidelity against misalignments that may not be captured through pixel-wise differences alone, and the coefficients $\lambda$ is a weight balance coefficient.

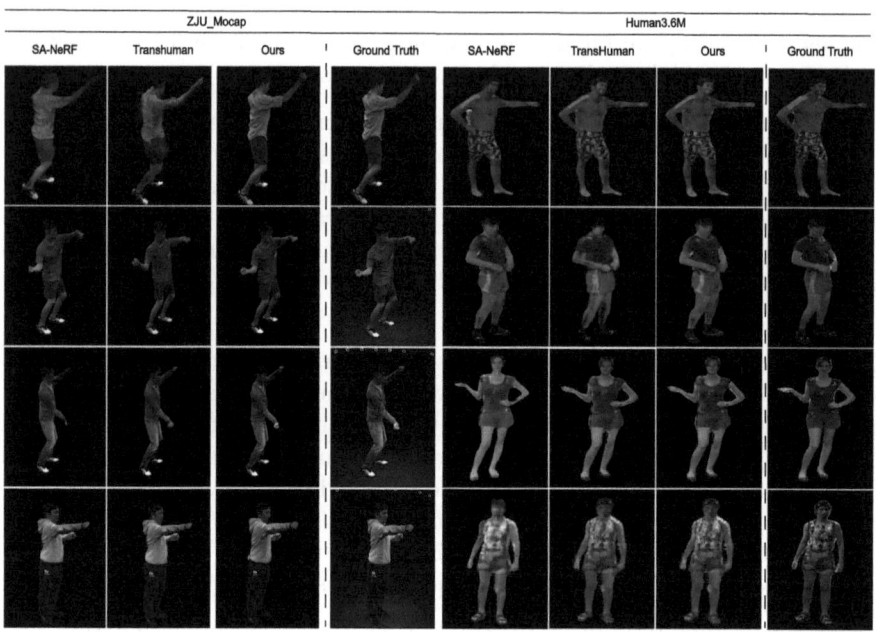

**Fig. 4.** Qualitative result of novel view setting in ZJU-MoCap and Human3.6M. We compare the novel pose synthesis quality with baseline methods in ZJU-MoCap. Result shows that our method synthesizes more realistic images in novel poses

**Table 1.** Comparisons of pose generalization ability with the state-of-the-art methods.

| Method | Train | Test | Pose-independent | Unseen Pose | PSNR | SSIM | LPIPS |
|---|---|---|---|---|---|---|---|
| Surface-aligned generalization | | | | | | | |
| NSR [3] | ZJU-7 | ZJU-7 | × | × | 22.41 | 0.873 | - |
| Hypernerf [22] | ZJU-7 | ZJU-7 | × | × | 23.09 | 0.887 | 0.206 |
| SA-NeRF [39] | ZJU-7 | ZJU-7 | ✓ | ✓ | 23.75 | 0.869 | 0.165 |
| GP-NeRF [5] | ZJU-7 | ZJU-7 | ✓ | × | 25.05 | 0.909 | 0.159 |
| IntrinsicNGP [26] | ZJU-7 | ZJU-7 | ✓ | ✓ | 26.51 | 0.121 | - |
| **Ours** | ZJU-7 | ZJU-7 | ✓ | ✓ | **28.59** | **0.916** | **0.097** |
| Pose Generalization | | | | | | | |
| SA-NeRF [39] | ZJU-3 | ZJU-3 | ✓ | ✓ | 21.84 | 0.861 | 0.173 |
| Neuman [12] | ZJU-3 | ZJU-3 | × | × | 23.03 | 0.885 | 0.193 |
| IntrinsicNGP [23] | ZJU-3 | ZJU-3 | ✓ | ✓ | 25.18 | 0.894 | - |
| GP-NeRF [5] | ZJU-3 | ZJU-3 | ✓ | ✓ | 25.63 | 0.897 | 0.154 |
| Transhuman [20] | ZJU-3 | ZJU-3 | × | ✓ | 26.91 | 0.916 | 0.106 |
| Monohuman [39] | ZJU-3 | ZJU-3 | ✓ | ✓ | 27.31 | 0.879 | 0.124 |
| **Ours** | ZJU-3 | ZJU-3 | ✓ | ✓ | **28.24** | **0.919** | **0.091** |

## 4 Experiment

To validate our method, we conducted comparative experiments on the ZJU-MoCap datasets and Human3.6M datasets.

### 4.1 Experimental Settings

We compare with state-of-the-art methods for implicitly human novel view synthesis from monocular inputs.

1). SA-NeRF [39], represents the implicit surface with hyper-coordinates in association with camera views and dynamic appearance codes.
2). Transhuman [20], combines transformer and implicit-based rendering with painted SMPL for capturing the global relationships between human parts.

We perform this experiment on ZJU-Mocap [26] and Human3.6M [10] data. Specifically, we select 5 subjects from ZJU-Mocap and 3 subjects from Human3.6M datasets with relatively high image quality and use "Camera (1)" for training and other views for evaluation. We use the official open source code of these methods for comparison with our method.

### 4.2 Comparisons with State-of-the-Art Baselines

Following the methodologies established in [19,20], our analysis compares our approach against both per-subject optimization methods [26,31] and generalizable strategies [18,20,41]. Per-subject optimization typically trains individual models on data specific to each subject. In contrast, our emphasis is on generalizable methods, essential for practical and scalable neural human rendering applications. We unify them under the released human split of Surface-Aligned Neural [39], as shown in Fig. 4. Following NeRF [19], we use Three standard metrics to quantify the results of novel view synthesis: peak signal-to-noise ratio (PSNR) and structural similarity index (SSIM) [36]. We also adopt LPIPS to measure the perceived distance between the synthesis image and ground truth image [42], as shown in Table 1.

**Novel Pose Synthesis Evaluation.** We compare the quantitative results with previous state-of-the-art methods in Table 1. Our approach clearly outperforms these methods by significant margins across all settings. Notably, in the pose generalization setting, per-subject methods are directly trained on the target subjects, whereas our model is trained solely on source subjects. Despite this, we surpass them by a large margin, achieving a PSNR increase of +1.93. Compared to methods that are dependent on pose (deformed radiance field with pose assistance), such as MonoHuman [41] and TransHuman [20], our model shows notable gains, including a +0.93 improvement in PSNR and a 26% reduction in LPIPS compared to the second-best approach.

**Surface-aligned Generalization Evaluation.** We sets a new standard in surface-aligned generalization, as shown in Table 1, demonstrating robustness across all evaluated metrics. Specifically, in the surface-aligned generalization setting, our method, which uniquely utilizes shared rigid deformation on human driven, achieves a remarkable PSNR of 28.59, marking an increase of 7.2% over the next best-performing method (26.51). In terms of SSIM, our approach shows a slight enhancement, reaching a value of 0.916. Furthermore, our method achieves a substantial reduction in LPIPS, recording the lowest score of 0.097 among all methods evaluated, indicating improved perceptual quality and alignment.

**Efficiency Analysis.** We compare the efficiency of our method with previous state-of-the-art methods listed in 2 under the pose generalization setting. We have selected SA-Nerf [4] as our baseline model for comparison because it employs an absolute point projection method. Despite using only 27.6% of the parameters and 30.9% of the inference memory compared to SA-NeRF, our method still achieves superior performance. Specifically, our optimized model, outperforms TransHuman significantly in PSNR, with an increase to 28.52, while also showing substantial improvements in SSIM at 0.9424, and the lowest LPIPS at 0.091.

Table 2. Efficiency comparisons under the pose generalization setting. Averages are computed over 100 frames per unseen pose. Inference memory and parameters are in gigabytes (G) and millions (M), respectively our method outperforms both NSR and TransHuman significantly in PSNR albeit requiring fewer parameters and training/inference memory.

|  | PSNR ↑ | SSIM ↑ | LPIPS ↓ | Inference Mem (G) ↓ | Params (M) ↓ |
|---|---|---|---|---|---|
| SA-NeRF [39] | 21.84 | 0.861 | 0.171 | 11 | 8.7 |
| Transhuman [20] | 26.75 | 0.910 | 0.106 | 7.8 | 6.5 |
| **Ours** | **28.52** | **0.9424** | **0.091** | **7.6** | **6.3** |

Table 3. Ablation Study Results on Mapping-based Deformable Radiance Fields. showing the impact of model configurations with and without coordinate offset and Hypergraph structuring.

| Model Configuration | PSNR ↑ | SSIM ↑ | LPIPS ↓ |
|---|---|---|---|
| coordinates offset | 24.31 | 0.6461 | 0.161 |
| w/o Hypergraph Representation | 26.12 | 0.7391 | 0.134 |
| **MDRF(ours)** | **27.59** | **0.9127** | **0.107** |

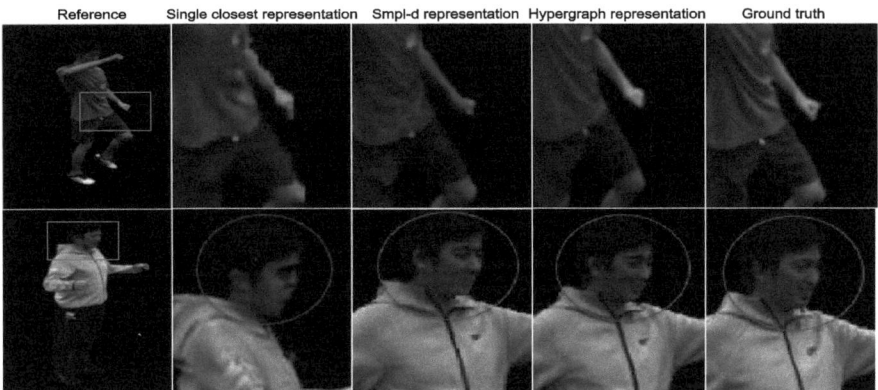

**Fig. 5.** Qualitative results of ablation studies among different representation strategies of the ZJU-MoCap dataset. Single closest representation denotes the closest point representation; SMPL-d representation refers to SMPL-d with an offset field; and Hypergraph representation denotes our method without the fine-grained module.

**Table 4.** Ablation study on ZJU-MoCap in novel view setting. We compute averages over 4 sequences.

|  | PSNR↑ | SSIM↑ | LPIPS↓ |
|---|---|---|---|
| Single closest representation [39] | 17.12 | 0.5611 | 0.197 |
| SMPL-d representation | 23.12 | 0.7611 | 0.149 |
| closest+offsest [11] | 26.74 | 0.9325 | 0.135 |
| **Ours** | **28.52** | **0.9424** | **0.091** |

### 4.3 Ablation Study

We conduct ablation studies for the two key modules in our model, the mapping-based Deformable Radiance Fields and Hypergraph Representation, and particularly explore the effects of human representation.

**Ablation of Representation.** To demonstrate the efficiency of our approach, particularly the Hypergraph Representation, we conducted an ablation study on various point representation methods coupled with a direct offset field as outlined in [11]. We evaluated the following representation settings in a novel pose scenario: 1) Single closest point representation, 2) Smpl-d representation, and 3) Closest point representation with an offset field. We experimented on the novel pose setting, as shown in Table 4. The closest point representation is used to directly associate the sample point with the explicit mesh, and the training process of the closest point representation is simplified, while merely using the closest representation cannot complete the reconstruction task, which is caused by the spatial feature loss in a discontinuous moving space. Thus the evaluation of a single closest representation has poor performance in most evaluation

**Table 5.** Ablation Study Results on Fine-grained. Comparing model configurations with or without codebook and cross-attention components

| Model Configuration | PSNR ↑ | SSIM ↑ | LPIPS ↓ |
|---|---|---|---|
| w/o Codebook | 25.61 | 0.7124 | 0.146 |
| w/o Cross Attention | 27.12 | 0.8391 | 0.109 |
| Full model | **27.59** | **0.9127** | **0.091** |

metrics. Our method outperforms the SMPL-d representation across most metrics. Although the SDF value captures some explicit features, our approach has a distinct advantage in rendering human details as shown in Fig. 5.

**Ablation of MDRF.** To validate the effectiveness of the Mapping-based Deformable Radiance Fields (MDRF), we conducted an ablation study, with results shown in Table 3. The configuration labeled "coordinates offset" uses full mesh coordinates for query points, which includes the exact location information of query points in deformation field, as well as the frame-to-frame offset of the explicit mesh. We use it as a baseline because of its absolute precise representation. The "w/o Hypergraph Representation" configuration, which excludes the Hypergraph structure, achieves a PSNR of 26.12, SSIM of 0.7391, underscoring the Hypergraph's role in enhancing structural and perceptual fidelity as expected. The full MDRF model configuration achieves the best results across all metrics, with a PSNR of 27.59, SSIM of 0.9127, and the lowest LPIPS of 0.107. These results confirm the effectiveness of point registration methods with assistance at Hypergraph representation, despite the fact that the hypergraph structure simplifies the feature space of the explicit mesh.

**Ablation of Fine-grained.** The ablation study assesses the impact of specific components on the performance of our fine-grained module, with results presented in Table 5. Removing the codebook component results in the lowest performance metrics. By excluding the cross-attention mechanism and with the sole assistance of point codebook, the PSNR and SSIM can be elevated to 27.12 and 0.8391, respectively, while significantly increasing the LPIPS to 0.109. The complete model configuration achieves the highest performance across all metrics, with a PSNR of 27.59, an SSIM of 0.9127, and the lowest LPIPS of 0.091, We attribute this to the attention mechanism's ability to capture the global joints of the SMPL model.

## 5 Conclusion

In this study, we introduced DPhuman, a novel framework designed to address the complexities associated with neural human rendering. By innovatively applying Mapping-based Deformable Radiance Fields (MDRF) and Hypergraph Representation, our framework not only overcomes the limitations posed by traditional mesh-based approaches but also enhances the generalizability and efficiency of neural human rendering across varied poses and dynamic meshes. Our extensive experiments, including evaluations on ZJU-MoCap and H36M datasets, demonstrates that DPhuman achieve state-of-the-art results.

## References

1. Alldieck, T., Zanfir, M., Sminchisescu, C.: Photorealistic monocular 3d reconstruction of humans wearing clothing. In: Proceedings of the IEEE/CVF Conference on Computer Vision and Pattern Recognition (2022)
2. Barron, J.T., Mildenhall, B., Verbin, D., Srinivasan, P.P., Hedman, P.: Mipnerf 360: unbounded anti-aliased neural radiance fields. In: Proceedings of the IEEE/CVF Conference on Computer Vision and Pattern Recognition, pp. 5470–5479 (2022)
3. Cai, H., Feng, W., Feng, X., Wang, Y., Zhang, J.: Neural surface reconstruction of dynamic scenes with monocular rgb-d camera. Adv. Neural. Inf. Process. Syst. **35**, 967–981 (2022)
4. Chan, E.R., Monteiro, M., Kellnhofer, P., Wu, J., Wetzstein, G.: pi-gan: periodic implicit generative adversarial networks for 3d-aware image synthesis. In: Proceedings of the IEEE/CVF Conference on Computer Vision and Pattern Recognition, pp. 5799–5809 (2021)
5. Chen, M., et al.: Geometry-guided progressive nerf for generalizable and efficient neural human rendering. In: European Conference on Computer Vision, pp. 222–239. Springer (2022)
6. Garbin, S.J., Kowalski, M., Johnson, M., Shotton, J., Valentin, J.: Fastnerf: high-fidelity neural rendering at 200fps. In: Proceedings of the IEEE/CVF International Conference on Computer Vision, pp. 14346–14355 (2021)
7. Geng, C., Peng, S., Xu, Z., Bao, H., Zhou, X.: Learning neural volumetric representations of dynamic humans in minutes. In: Proceedings of the IEEE/CVF Conference on Computer Vision and Pattern Recognition, pp. 8759–8770 (2023)
8. Gu, J., Liu, L., Wang, P., Theobalt, C.: Stylenerf: a style-based 3d-aware generator for high-resolution image synthesis. arXiv preprint arXiv:2110.08985 (2021)
9. Habermann, M., Xu, W., Zollhoefer, M., Pons-Moll, G., Theobalt, C.: Livecap: real-time human performance capture from monocular video. ACM Trans. Graph. (TOG) **38**(2), 1–17 (2019)
10. Ionescu, C., Papava, D., Olaru, V., Sminchisescu, C.: Human3. 6m: large scale datasets and predictive methods for 3d human sensing in natural environments. IEEE Trans. Pattern Anal. Mach. Intell. **36**(7), 1325–1339 (2013)
11. Jiang, B., Hong, Y., Bao, H., Zhang, J.: Selfrecon: self reconstruction your digital avatar from monocular video. In: Proceedings of the IEEE/CVF Conference on Computer Vision and Pattern Recognition, pp. 5605–5615 (2022)
12. Jiang, W., Yi, K.M., Samei, G., Tuzel, O., Ranjan, A.: Neuman: Neural human radiance field from a single video. In: European Conference on Computer Vision, pp. 402–418 (2022)
13. Kwon, Y., Kim, D., Ceylan, D., Fuchs, H.: Neural human performer: learning generalizable radiance fields for human performance rendering. Adv. Neural. Inf. Process. Syst. **34**, 24741–24752 (2021)
14. Liu, L., Habermann, M., Rudnev, V., Sarkar, K., Gu, J., Theobalt, C.: Neural actor: neural free-view synthesis of human actors with pose control. ACM Trans. Graph. (TOG) **40**(6), 1–16 (2021)

15. Loper, M., Mahmood, N., Romero, J., Pons-Moll, G., Black, M.J.: Smpl: A skinned multi-person linear model. In: Seminal Graphics Papers: Pushing the Boundaries, vol. 2, pp. 851–866 (2023)
16. Ma, Q., Saito, S., Yang, J., Tang, S., Black, M.J.: Scale: modeling clothed humans with a surface codec of articulated local elements. In: Proceedings of the IEEE/CVF Conference on Computer Vision and Pattern Recognition, pp. 16082–16093 (2021)
17. Martin-Brualla, R., Radwan, N., Sajjadi, M.S., Barron, J.T., Dosovitskiy, A., Duckworth, D.: Nerf in the wild: neural radiance fields for unconstrained photo collections. In: Proceedings of the IEEE/CVF Conference on Computer Vision and Pattern Recognition, pp. 7210–7219 (2021)
18. Mihajlovic, M., Bansal, A., Zollhoefer, M., Tang, S., Saito, S.: Keypointnerf: generalizing image-based volumetric avatars using relative spatial encoding of keypoints. In: European Conference on Computer Vision, pp. 179–197. Springer (2022)
19. Mildenhall, B., Srinivasan, P.P., Tancik, M., Barron, J.T., Ramamoorthi, R., Ng, R.: Nerf: representing scenes as neural radiance fields for view synthesis. Commun. ACM **65**(1), 99–106 (2021)
20. Pan, X., Yang, Z., Ma, J., Zhou, C., Yang, Y.: Transhuman: a transformer-based human representation for generalizable neural human rendering. In: Proceedings of the IEEE/CVF International Conference on Computer Vision, pp. 3544–3555 (2023)
21. Park, K., Sinha, U., Barron, J.T., Bouaziz, S., Goldman, D.B., Seitz, S.M., Martin-Brualla, R.: Nerfies: deformable neural radiance fields. In: Proceedings of the IEEE/CVF International Conference on Computer Vision, pp. 5865–5874 (2021)
22. Park, K., et al.: Hypernerf: a higher-dimensional representation for topologically varying neural radiance fields. arXiv preprint arXiv:2106.13228 (2021)
23. Peng, B., Hu, J., Zhou, J., Gao, X., Zhang, J.: Intrinsicngp: intrinsic coordinate based hash encoding for human nerf (2023)
24. Peng, S., et al.: Animatable neural radiance fields for modeling dynamic human bodies. In: Proceedings of the IEEE/CVF International Conference on Computer Vision, pp. 14314–14323 (2021)
25. Peng, S., et al.: Animatable implicit neural representations for creating realistic avatars from videos. arXiv preprint arXiv:2203.08133 (2022)
26. Peng, S., et al.: Neural body: Implicit neural representations with structured latent codes for novel view synthesis of dynamic humans. In: Proceedings of the IEEE/CVF Conference on Computer Vision and Pattern Recognition, pp. 9054–9063 (2021)
27. Pumarola, A., Corona, E., Pons-Moll, G., Moreno-Noguer, F.: D-nerf: neural radiance fields for dynamic scenes. In: Proceedings of the IEEE/CVF Conference on Computer Vision and Pattern Recognition, pp. 10318–10327 (2021)
28. Saito, S., Simon, T., Saragih, J., Joo, H.: Pifuhd: multi-level pixel-aligned implicit function for high-resolution 3d human digitization. In: Proceedings of the IEEE/CVF Conference on Computer Vision and Pattern Recognition, pp. 84–93 (2020)
29. Siddiqui, Y., et al.: Meshgpt: generating triangle meshes with decoder-only transformers. In: Proceedings of the IEEE/CVF Conference on Computer Vision and Pattern Recognition, pp. 19615–19625 (2024)
30. Sigal, L., Balan, A.O., Black, M.J.: Humaneva: synchronized video and motion capture dataset and baseline algorithm for evaluation of articulated human motion. Int. J. Comput. Vision **87**(1), 4–27 (2010)

31. Thies, J., Zollhöfer, M., Nießner, M.: Deferred neural rendering: image synthesis using neural textures. Acm Trans. Graph. (TOG) **38**(4), 1–12 (2019)
32. Tiwari, G., Antić, D., Lenssen, J.E., Sarafianos, N., Tung, T., Pons-Moll, G.: Posendf: modeling human pose manifolds with neural distance fields. In: European Conference on Computer Vision, pp. 572–589. Springer (2022)
33. Vaswani, A.: Attention is all you need. In: Advances in Neural Information Processing Systems (2017)
34. Wang, Y., Solomon, J.M.: Deep closest point: learning representations for point cloud registration. In: Proceedings of the IEEE/CVF International Conference on Computer Vision, pp. 3523–3532 (2019)
35. Wang, Y., Sun, Y., Liu, Z., Sarma, S.E., Bronstein, M.M., Solomon, J.M.: Dynamic graph cnn for learning on point clouds. ACM Trans. Graph. (tog) **38**(5), 1–12 (2019)
36. Wang, Z., Bovik, A.C., Sheikh, H.R., Simoncelli, E.P.: Image quality assessment: from error visibility to structural similarity. IEEE Trans. Image Process. **13**, 600–612 (2004)
37. Weng, C.Y., Curless, B., Srinivasan, P.P., Barron, J.T., Kemelmacher-Shlizerman, I.: Humannerf: free-viewpoint rendering of moving people from monocular video. In: Proceedings of the IEEE/CVF Conference on Computer Vision and Pattern Recognition, pp. 16210–16220 (2022)
38. Xu, Q., et al.: Point-nerf: Point-based neural radiance fields. In: Proceedings of the IEEE/CVF Conference on Computer Vision and Pattern Recognition, pp. 5438–5448 (2022)
39. Xu, T., Fujita, Y., Matsumoto, E.: Surface-aligned neural radiance fields for controllable 3d human synthesis. In: Proceedings of the IEEE/CVF Conference on Computer Vision and Pattern Recognition, pp. 15883–15892 (2022)
40. Xu, W., et al.: Monoperfcap: human performance capture from monocular video. ACM Trans. Graph. (ToG) **37**(2), 1–15 (2018)
41. Yu, Z., Cheng, W., Liu, X., Wu, W., Lin, K.Y.: Monohuman: animatable human neural field from monocular video. In: Proceedings of the IEEE/CVF Conference on Computer Vision and Pattern Recognition, pp. 16943–16953 (2023)
42. Zhang, R., Isola, P., Efros, A.A., Shechtman, E., Wang, O.: The unreasonable effectiveness of deep features as a perceptual metric. In: Proceedings of the IEEE Conference on Computer Vision and Pattern Recognition, pp. 586–595 (2018)
43. Zheng, Z., Huang, H., Yu, T., Zhang, H., Guo, Y., Liu, Y.: Structured local radiance fields for human avatar modeling. In: Proceedings of the IEEE/CVF Conference on Computer Vision and Pattern Recognition, pp. 15893–15903 (2022)
44. Zhi, Y., Qian, S., Yan, X., Gao, S.: Dual-space nerf: Learning animatable avatars and scene lighting in separate spaces. In: 2022 International Conference on 3D Vision (3DV), pp. 1–10. IEEE (2022)

# PSVM-MR: A Parallel Support Vector Machine Algorithm Based on MapReduce

Bin-bin Guo[1], Yimin Mao[1], A Yaser[2], Neelakandan Chandrasekaran[1], Le Kang[1], Wenhao Li[3], and Decheng Miao[1](✉)

[1] School of Information Engineering, Shaoguan University, ShaoguanGuangdong 512005, China
deansgu@163.com
[2] School of Information Engineering, Yancheng Teachers University, Yancheng 224002, Jiangsu, China
[3] School of Information Engineering, Jiangxi University of Science and Technology, Ganzhou 341000, Jiangxi, China

**Abstract.** Big data has become essential in fields such as geospatial analysis and disaster prediction, where it enhances the accuracy and efficiency of predictive models. The Support Vector Machine (SVM) algorithm is widely used for such tasks, but its application to large-scale datasets faces challenges, including excessive deviation in subsets distribution, insufficient parallel training performance, and poor filtering of non-support vectors. To overcome the above limitations, a parallel SVM algorithm based on MapReduce (PSVM-MR) is proposed in this paper, which contains two parts: data partition and parallel SVM training. First, a data partition method based on relative entropy (DP-RE) is proposed, which calculates the relative entropy to avoid excessive deviation of subsets distribution. Next, a redundancy level removing method based on cosine similarity (RLR-CS) is presented to address the insufficient performance of parallel training by removing the redundancy levels in the cascade structure. Finally, a non-support vector filtering method (NSVF) is proposed, which improves the capability of non-support vector filtering by combining rough identification and singular vector identification. Experiment shows that the proposed algorithm has lower training costs and higher parallel efficiency than the general parallel SVM algorithm.

**Keywords:** Parallel SVM · MapReduce · Relative entropy · Cosine similarity

## 1 Introduction

Big data has become a cornerstone of modern technological advancements, driving innovations across diverse domains, including machine learning and data analytics. Among the most influential algorithms in this field is the Support Vector Machine (SVM) [1], a robust supervised learning method widely used for classification and regression tasks. SVM is particularly valued for its strong generalization performance and discriminative power, rendering it highly effective in applications such as pattern recognition [2], handwritten character analysis [3], and other real-world problems [4]. However, as the volume of data continues to grow exponentially in the big data era, SVM faces significant challenges, particularly in terms of computational efficiency. The training process for large-scale datasets and complex problems often becomes prohibitively time-consuming and resource-intensive. This has led to an increasing demand for scalable solutions to enhance the performance of SVM. In response, parallel computing has emerged as a critical approach to accelerate SVM training, enabling its application to the ever-expanding datasets that characterize the big data environment.

Despite its potential, the implementation of parallel computing for SVM presents significant challenges. While parallel SVM algorithms have demonstrated considerable speedups compared to their sequential counterparts, which operates on a single CPU [5], achieving efficient parallelization remains a complex task. Key challenges include communication overhead, computationally dependent steps, and memory limitations, all of which can adversely affect parallel efficiency, particularly when scaling to a large number of samples or processors [6]. These challenges often result in suboptimal performance, limiting the scalability of parallel SVM implementations. To fully exploit the capabilities of parallel computing in SVM, it is essential to thoroughly evaluate the efficiency of existing methods and identify strategies to overcome these limitations. This study aims to address these challenges by analyzing the strengths and limitations of current parallel SVM methods, thereby providing insights for developing more effective and scalable solutions tailored to the demands of large-scale data processing.

In recent years, numerous algorithms have been proposed to improve the efficiency of parallel SVM training. The existing state-of-art approaches applied data partition to the parallel training of SVM in order to obtain higher efficiency. However, random data partitioning can lead to significant deviation among subsets, adversely impacting model performance. Additionally, the layer merging process in parallel SVM training often results in reduced parallel efficiency due to repetitive iterations. Furthermore, non-support vector filtering methods in these algorithms tend to cause substantial accuracy loss. Consequently, these approaches frequently fail to achieve the desired classification accuracy.

The remainder of this paper is organized as follows: Sect. 2. Briefly reviews previous approaches for parallelizing training process of SVM and their strengths and weaknesses are discussed. Section 3. Describes the relative entropy, the cosine similarity measure, and the sequential minimal optimization. Section 4. Introduces the details of the PSVM-MR algorithm and its complexity analysis. Section 5. Discuss the results of experiments. Finally, we draw our conclusions in Sect. 6.

## 2 Related Work

This section provides a concise review of various methods developed for parallelizing Support Vector Machines (SVM), highlighting their strengths as well as the challenges they encounter.

Graf et al. [7] described a cascade SVM algorithm based on early identification of non-support vectors. The data set is split into subsets and optimized separately with multiple SVMs, then the partial results are combined and filtered in SVM 'Cascade' until reaching global optimum. Hsieh et al. [8] proposed a novel Divide-and-Conquer solver for kernel SVMs (DC-SVM). In the division step, they partition the kernel SVM problem into smaller sub-problems by clustering the data, so that each sub-problem can be solved independently and efficiently. In the conquer step, the local solutions from sub-problems are used to initialize a global coordinate descent solver, which converges quickly as suggested by the analysis. The above algorithms have conducted many studies on the computational performance of SVM. However, giant deviation between subsets has not been taken account in data partition.

To mitigate this, Singh et al. [9] proposed an efficient distributed Iterative Reweighted Least Squares SVM by using k-means to choose the centroids of the semiparametric model. Essentially, a divide-and-conquer filter selects the Least Support Vectors and their corresponding Lagrange multipliers from one level to initialize the next level in a cascade SVM, resulting in faster convergence. The partitions are obtained as the clusters resulting from a balanced k-means clustering algorithm. However, partition SVM suffers from repeated iterations, hampering its scalability. Building on this work, Guo et al. [10] designed CSVM, a distributed implementation of kernel support vector machine for large datasets using subspace partitioning. In subspace partitioning, a decision tree is constructed on the projection of data along the direction of maximum variance to obtain smaller partitions of the datasets. On each of these partitions, a kernel SVM is trained independently over a cluster to reduce overall training time. While the tree structure circumvents the necessity of merging subsets in the SVM model, the scale of the leaf node training sets is notably large. Sujitha et al. and Paramasivan proposed Kernel Clustering-Based Support Vector Machine (KCB-SVM) [11], which employs hierarchical clustering to group similar data points into clusters and trains local SVM sub-models within them, mitigates data imbalance and enhances classification accuracy, but may result in insufficient performance of parallel training.

To enhance the parallel efficiency of SVM, Kang et al. [12] proposed a restricted random partition algorithm to avoid the influence of the initial partition on the final model by limiting the proportion of positive and negative samples in each subset to be equal. When two SVMs are combined, a cross-validation merging algorithm is proposed, which considers the special points other than support vectors, that is, the point where the non-support vectors in one subset violate the training results of another subset. The algorithm takes training sets except for support vector and difference points as the non-support vector filtering to avoid filtering support vector. Ramachandran et al. [13] proposed a framework called mutual informative MapReduce and minimum quadrangle classification(MIMR-MQC) algorithm, which uses MapReduce to preprocess and reduce data by removing redundant features, then applies MQC-SVM with optimized classification techniques like Lagrange multipliers and radial basis kernels, enhancing parallel efficiency and scalability for large-scale brain tumor detection. Almaspoor et al. [14] introduced the Distributed Independent Vector Machine (DIVM), which distributes training data across multiple machines, identifies linearly independent samples, and combines local SVM models to form a global solution, improving efficiency and scalability for large-scale datasets. But this method filters out a low proportion of non-support vectors and decreases the accuracy. Li et al. [14] designed an improved parallel SVM algorithm, which can effectively reduce the size of datasets before the training process to accelerate SVM. Meanwhile, in order to maintain the classification accuracy of the final model, they proposed a method to recover effective data from the eliminated samples.

Despite the significant progress in SVM-based machine learning, challenges such as excessive deviation of subsets distribution and insufficient performance of parallel training remain unresolved. These issues hinder the effective utilization of SVM in large-scale datasets and distributed computing environments. The excessive deviation of subsets distribution can lead to imbalanced learning, negatively impacting the model's generalization ability. Meanwhile, insufficient performance in parallel training limits the scalability and efficiency of SVM in handling massive data. These challenges underscore the need for further research into advanced data partitioning strategies, optimized parallel computing frameworks, and enhanced SVM algorithms to fully leverage the potential of distributed machine learning and big data analytics.

In this study, a Parallel Support Vector Machine algorithm based on MapReduce (PSVM-MR) is proposed to address challenges in processing large-scale datasets. The algorithm leverages relative entropy during the data partitioning phase to divide instances into subsets with maximal similarity gain, thereby reducing the distribution gap between subsets compared to random partitioning. After partitioning, local SVMs are trained independently within the MapReduce framework. To enhance the efficiency of parallel training, a Redundancy Level Removal strategy based on Cosine Similarity is introduced, which eliminates redundant hierarchical levels by calculating similarity between consecutive levels. Additionally, a support vector similarity mechanism is implemented to improve the accuracy of filtering non-support vectors. The key contributions of this work are summarized as follows:

1. A novel partitioning approach based on relative entropy is designed to balance the distribution of subsets with the original dataset, minimizing subset deviation.
2. The RLR-CS strategy is employed to calculate similarity between hierarchical levels, enabling early termination of redundant hierarchies and reducing parallel training time.
3. The accuracy of non-support vector filtering is significantly improved by combining rough identification with singular vector identification, ensuring precise retention of support vectors and enhancing classification performance.

## 3 Preliminaries

This section delineates the core theoretical foundations for parallel Support Vector Machine optimization and for clarity and consistency, we summarize the key mathematical notations used throughout this paper in Appendix A (Notation Table).

### 3.1 Relative Entropy

Relative entropy [15, 16] is used in a variety of machine learning algorithms and it reflects the differences of the two information sources with different distributions, the bigger the relative entropy was, the bigger the differences in the information sources were, and vice versa.

The relative entropy, or Kullback-Leibler divergence of two probability distributions P(x) and Q(x) defined over a discrete set X is defined as:

$$RE(P||Q) = \sum_{x}^{X} P(x) \log \frac{P(x)}{Q(x)} \qquad (1)$$

### 3.2 Cosine Similarity Measure

Cosine similarity measure [17] is one of the similarity measures whose range is [−1, 1]. To calculate the similarity between two vectors, the angle between the two vectors is a meaningful measure. If the angle between the two vectors is nearly zero, then the similarity between them is highest (Cos0 = 1).

The cosine similarity measure can be described as follows: given two vectors X and Y,

$$\text{Cos}(X, Y) = \frac{X \cdot Y}{\sqrt{X \cdot X} \times \sqrt{Y \cdot Y}} \qquad (2)$$

### 3.3 Sequential Minimal Optimization

Given training set $D = \{X_i, y_i\}_{i=1}^{n}$ ($X_i$ is the feature vector; $y_i$ is the class labels for $X_i$; $n$ is the number of samples), training an SVM in classification is equivalent to solving the following linearly constrained convex quadratic programming (QP) problem[18]:

$$\min_{\alpha} \frac{1}{2} \sum_{i=1,j=1}^{n} \alpha_i \alpha_j y_i y_j K(X_i, X_j) - \sum_{i=1}^{n} \alpha_i$$
$$\text{s.t.} \sum_{i=1}^{n} a_i y_i = 0, \quad 0 \leq \alpha_i \leq C \qquad (3)$$

where $K$ is the kernel function, $\alpha_i$ is the Lagrange multiplier to be optimized and $C$ is the regularization constant predetermined by users. For each of training data patterns, one $\alpha_i$ is associated. After solving the QP problem (1), the following decision function is used to determine the class label for a new data pattern:

$$f(X) = \sum_{i=1}^{n} \alpha_i y_i K(X_i, X) + b \qquad (4)$$

where $b$ is a bias term. The SMO initially calculates the constraints on all multipliers, and then determines the constrained maximum. When only two multipliers are to be optimized, the constraints can be regarded as defining a 2-D square with a diagonal line segment bounded on a box border.

Without loss of generality, assume two Lagrange multipliers $\{\alpha_1, \alpha_2\}$ from an old set of feasible solutions $\{\alpha_1^{old}, \alpha_2^{old}, \alpha_3......\alpha_n\}$ are to be optimized with the initialization settings $\alpha_1^{old} = \alpha_2^{old} = 0$. From $\sum y_i\alpha_i = 0$, $i = 1, 2, ..., N$, $y_1\alpha_i + y_2\alpha_i = y_1\alpha_i^{old} + y_2\alpha_j^{old} = constant$, where $y \in \{1, -1\}$. This equation will bound the optimization on a line.

Given $t = y_1y_2$, and $y_1\alpha_i + y_2\alpha_i = y_1\alpha_i^{old} + y_2\alpha_j^{old} = constant$, $\alpha_1 = \sigma - t\alpha_2$ is substituted into the objection function (3). Through first and second derivatives by vanishing $\alpha_2$, $\alpha_j^{new}$ is obtained in (5), here $E_i$ is the prediction error

$$\alpha_j^{new} = \alpha_j^{old} + \frac{y_i\left(E_j^{old} - E_i^{old}\right)}{\eta} \quad (5)$$

where $k_{ii} = x_i^T x_i$, $k_{jj} = x_j^T x_j$, $k_{ij} = x_i^T x_j$, $\eta = 2k_{ij} - k_{ii} - k_{jj}$, and $E_i = \omega^T x_i - b - y_i$.

For $\eta < 0$, the unconstrained maximum point $\alpha_j^{new}$ must be checked to determine whether it is in the feasible range. Accordingly, the constrained maximum is determined by clipping the unconstrained maximum to the end of the line segment. Equation (6) is the corresponding clipping function. Eventually, $\alpha_j^{new}$ can be computed from $\alpha^{new,clipped}$ using (6) and (7)

$$\alpha_i^{mew,clipped} = \begin{cases} H, & \text{if } \alpha_j^{new} \geq H \\ \alpha_j^{new}, & \text{if } L < \alpha_j^{new} < H \\ L, & \text{if } \alpha_j^{new} \leq L \end{cases} \quad (6)$$

$$\alpha_i^{new} = \alpha_i^{old} + t\left(\alpha_j^{old} - \alpha_j^{new,clipped}\right), \quad (7)$$

where $t = y_iy_j$.

KKT condition checking is the critical process for SMO algorithm to optimize two multipliers. An optimal point in (3) is obtained if and only if the KKT conditions are satisfied and $Q_{ij} = y_iy_jK(X_i, X_j)$ is positive semi-definite. The KKT optimal conditions require that the product of a Lagrange multiplier and its corresponding constraint vanish. The KKT condition can be summarized as (8), and this representation simplifies the QP problem, making it easier to solve.

$$\begin{aligned} \alpha_i = 0 &\Leftrightarrow y_i \cdot f(X_i) \geq 1 \\ 0 < \alpha_i < C &\Leftrightarrow y_i \cdot f(X_i) = 1 \\ \alpha_i = C &\Leftrightarrow y_i \cdot f(X_i) \leq 1 \end{aligned} \quad (8)$$

$\alpha_2$ depends on $|E_1 - E_2|$ in Eq. (5), thus the selection formula of $\alpha_2$:

$$i = \underset{i}{\operatorname{argmax}}(|E_1 - E_i|) \quad (9)$$

## 4 Algorithm:PSVM-MR

This section provides a detailed description of the proposed PSVM-MR algorithm in detail, which consists of two stages: data partition and parallel training of SVM. The flowchart of the PSVM-MR algorithm is shown in Fig. 1. In the phase of data partition, to reduce the distributed deviation between subsets, the DP-RE strategy is designed, which calculates the relative entropy between current subsets and original set to obtain similar distribution of subsets. In the phase of parallel training, to improve the efficiency of training, the RLR-CS strategy combined with MapReduce framework is presented, which removes the redundant levels during the training process. Subsequently, the NSVF strategy is designed to accelerate the training phase by eliminating non-support vectors from the training set.

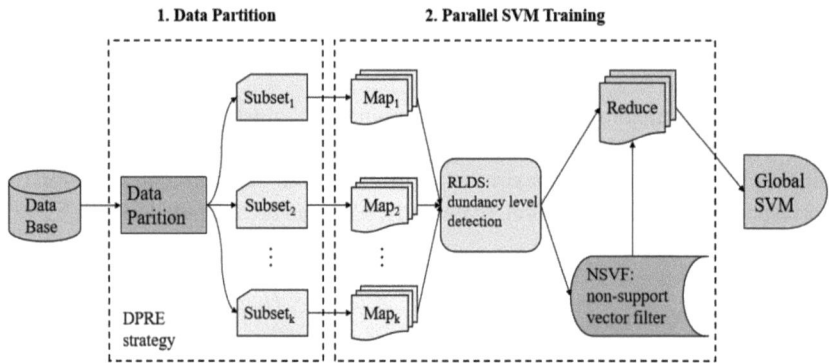

**Fig. 1.** Flowchart of the proposed algorithm (PSVM-MR)

### 4.1 Data Partition

The primary objective of this phase is to reduce the distributed deviation between subsets. To deal with this problem, the DP-RE strategy is proposed, which balances the relative entropy between current subsets and original set. The pseudocode of data partition is shown in Algorithm 1. The procedure of the data partition phase is shown in Fig. 2.

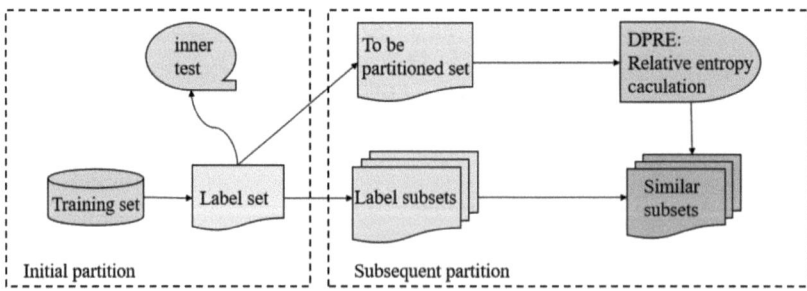

**Fig. 2.** Procedure of data partition

**Initial Partition:** The initial partition aims to roughly partition the original training set into positive subsets and negative subsets. The approach consists of two steps: (1) the original set $D$ is partitioned into positive subset $D^+$ and negative subset $D^-$ according to the label $y$, then the 5% samples of each subset are randomly extracted as the *inner Test* set; (2) the subsets $D^+$ and $D^-$ are partitioned into three parts: $\frac{n^+ - \sqrt{n^+}}{k}$ positive subsets with $k$ samples, $\frac{n^- - \sqrt{n^-}}{k}$ negative subsets with $k$ samples and subset $D^w$ with $\sqrt{n^+ + n^-}$ samples which is used for the subsequent partition.

**Subsequent Partition:** The original set $D$ was roughly divided according to the label $y$ in the previous step, but samples in the subset $D^w$ are left to be partitioned. Thus, it is essential to further partition the samples in the subset $D^w$. To achieve this purpose, the subsequent partition is proposed, which includes four steps: (1) the $k$ relative entropy between $k$ positive subsets and $D^+$ are calculated as $\{re^+\}_{i=1}^{k}$ and the $k$ relative entropy between $k$ positive subsets and $D^+$ are calculated as $\{re^-\}_{i=1}^{k}$; (2) the partition-based similarity ($PS$) is presented, and the partition-based similarity of positive subsets and negative subsets are calculated as $ssf^+$ and $ssf^-$ according to $\{re^+\}_{i=1}^{k}$ and $\{re^-\}_{i=1}^{k}$.

**Theorem 1.** ($PS$) Given the original data set $D$, $\{D_i\}_{i=1}^{k}$ are the $k$ disjoint subsets of $D$, the partition-based similarity between $D$ and subsets $\{D_i\}_{i=1}^{k}$ is shown as follow:

$$PS = \overline{re} + \frac{1}{k}\sum_{i=1}^{k}(re_i - \overline{re})^2 \quad (10)$$

where $re_i$ is the relative entropy between $D_i$ and $D$, $k$ is the number of partitioned subsets, and $\overline{re}$ is the mean value of $\{re_i\}_{i=1}^{k}$.

**Proof:** Suppose the relative entropy represents the degree of similarity between sets, and $\overline{re}$ represents the average relative entropy. Therefore, $\overline{re} \to 0$ implies that the average distribution of $k$ $k$ subsets is similar to the original data set $D$. $\frac{1}{k}\sum_{i=1}^{k}(re_i - \overline{re})^2$ is the second central moment of $\{re_i\}_{i=1}^{k}$, which represents the degree of the gap between $k$ $k$ subsets. $\frac{1}{k}\sum_{i=1}^{k}(re_i - \overline{re})^2 \to 0$ indicates the more similar distribution of $k$ subsets. Consequently, the partition-based similarity between $D$ and the $k$ partitioned subsets is presented by combining $\frac{1}{k}\sum_{i=1}^{k}(re_i - \overline{re})^2$ and $\overline{re}$.

(3) the relative entropy $\{re_i^*\}_{i=1}^{k}$ is calculated after the sample $d$ partitioned into the $k$ initial subsets, and the partition-based similarity $\{ps_i^*\}_{i=1}^{k}$ is calculated using the relative entropy $\{re_i^*\}_{i=1}^{k}$; (4) the partitive formula ($PF$) is presented, and the sample $d$ is partitioned into the optimal subset according to the partition-based similarities $\{ps_i\}_{i=1}^{k}$ and $\{ps_i^*\}_{i=1}^{k}$.

**Theorem 2.** ($PF$) For the given original data set $D$, $\{D_i\}_{i=1}^{k}$ are the $k$ disjoint subsets of $D$, suppose $d \in D$ and $d \notin \{D_i\}_{i=1}^{k}$, the partitive formula of $d$ is shown as follows:

$$PF(d) = \arg\max(\{\frac{ps - ps_i^*}{(n_i - n_{\min} + 1)^2}\}_{i=1}^{k}) \quad (11)$$

where $ps$ represents the partition-based similarity between the original set $D$ and subsets $\{D_i\}_{i=1}^{k}$, $ps_i^*$ represents the partition-based similarity after $d$ is added, and $n_i$ is the number of vectors in $D_i$.

**Proof:** Suppose $ps - ps_i^*$ represents the change of partition-based similarity before and after sample $d$ is added. $(n_i - n_{\min} + 1)^2$ reflects the degree of quantitative difference between subset $D_i$ and the minimal subset. Then $(n_i - n_{\min} + 1)^2$ is adopted as the penalty term which balances the quantitative difference between different subsets. After the sample $d$ is partitioned into subsets $D_i$, the gain can be represented as $\frac{ps-ps_i^*}{(n_i-n_{\min}+1)^2}$. The argmax function is used for obtaining the index $i$ which is corresponded to the maximum gain.

---

Algorithm 1. Data Partition

---

**Input:** Original data set $D = \{X_i, y_i\}_{i=1}^{n}$, number of samples $n$, number of subsets $k$
**Output:** subsets $\{D_i\}_{i=1}^{k}$, *innerTest* set

(1) $D^+, D^- \leftarrow$ Split D by $y$
(2) *innerTest* $\leftarrow$ Choose 5% of $D^+$ and $D^-$ at random
(3) $\{D_i^+\}_{i=1}^{k}, \{D_i^-\}_{i=1}^{k}, D^w \leftarrow$ split $D^+$ and $D^-$
(4) For $\{D_i\}$ in $\{\{D_i^+\}_{i=1}^{k}, \{D_i^-\}_{i=1}^{k}\}$ do
(5)     For $D^s$ in $\{D_i\}_{i=1}^{k}$ do
(6)        Calculate $re_i$ according to eq(1)
(7)     End for
(8)     Calculate $pf$ according to eq(10) by $\{re_i\}_{i=1}^{k}$
(9) End for
(10) For $d$ in $D^w$ do
(11)     If $d.y = 1$ do
(12)        $\{D_i\}_{i=1}^{k} \leftarrow \{D_i^+\}_{i=1}^{k}$
(13)     Else
(14)        $\{D_i\}_{i=1}^{k} \leftarrow \{D_i^-\}_{i=1}^{k}$
(15)     End if
(16)     For $i$ in $\{1, 2, \cdots, k\}$ do
(17)        Push($D_i, d$)
(18)        Calculate $re_i^*$ according to eq(1)
(19)        Calculate $pf_i^*$ according to eq(10) by $re_i^*$
(20)        Pop($D_i, d$)
(21)     End for
(22)     Calculate $j$ according to eq(11) by $pf$ and $\{pf_i^*\}_{i=1}^{k}$
(23)     Push($D_j, d$)
(24)     $re_j \leftarrow re_j^*$
(25) End for
(26) $\{D_i\}_{i=1}^{k} \leftarrow$ Combine $\{D_i^+\}_{i=1}^{k}$ and $\{D_i^-\}_{i=1}^{k}$
(27) Return $\{D_i\}_{i=1}^{k}$ and *innerTest*

## 4.2 Parallel SVM Training

As stated above, the objective of this phase is to improve the efficiency of training SVM. To accomplish this, the RLR-CS strategy is presented to eliminate the redundant layers in the cascade structure to improve parallel efficiency. Meanwhile, the NSVF strategy is designed, which accelerate the training phase by filtering out non-support vectors. The pseudocode of redundant layer detecting is shown in Algorithm 2. The pseudocode of non-support vector filtering is shown in Algorithm 3. The procedure of parallel SVM training is shown in Fig. 3.

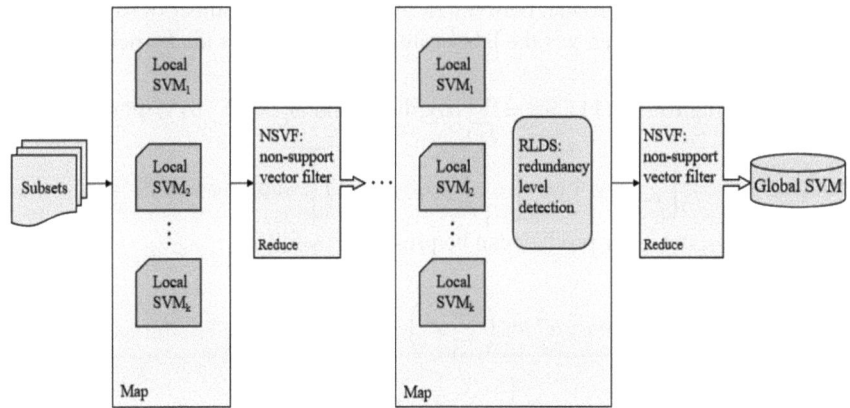

**Fig. 3.** Procedure of parallel SVM training

**Training of Local SVM:** The parallel SVM training phase is initiated by the training of local SVM, which consists of three steps: (1) the $k$ subsets from the data partition phase are transformed into $k$ triples $\{X_i, y_i, \alpha_i\}_{i=1}^n$; (2) the current $k^*$ subsets are distributed into $k^*$ map nodes, and the sequence minimum optimization algorithm (SMO) is adopted during the training process; (3) the trained Lagrange multiplier $\{\alpha^*\}$ is updated to the triples to get $\{X_i, y_i, \alpha_i^*\}_{i=1}^n$.

**Redundant Removement:** The number of cascade levels increases with the number of initial nodes, which leads to inefficiency of parallel training. To handle this problem, the RLR-CS strategy is presented, which consists of the following steps: (1) the normal vector of local SVM in $k$ $k$ map nodes can be represented as $\omega = \sum_{i=1}^{n} \alpha_i y_i \Phi(X_i)$ after the training of local SVM (where $n$ is the number of local SVM support vector, $\alpha_i$ is the Lagrange multiplier, $y_i$ is the label and $X_i$ is the eigenvector) (2) if the kernel function is not used in the training process, the mapping function $\Phi(X) = X$; if the kernel function is $K(X_i, X_j)$, then $\Phi(X_i)\Phi(X_j) = K(X_i, X_j)$, and $\Phi(X)$ is unsolvable in this case; (3) the hierarchical similarity ($HS$) is proposed to measure the degree of cosine similarity between adjacent layers; (4) the $HS$ is compared with the thresholds $\tau$, if $HS \geq \tau$, the parallel training of SVM will stop in advance and the $k$ local SVM will be passed to the global SVM construction. Otherwise, the normal vector $\{\omega_i\}_{i=1}^k$ of current layer will be kept for the following training.

**Theorem 3.** (*HS*): Given the normal vectors $\omega_i$ in the previous and $\omega_j^*$ in the current layers, the hierarchical similarity can be represented as follows:

$$HS = \frac{1}{k \cdot k^*} \sum_{i=1}^{k} \sum_{j=1}^{k^*} \cos(\omega_i, \omega_j^*) \quad (12)$$

$$\omega_i \cdot \omega_j^* = \sum_{l=1}^{ni} \sum_{k=1}^{nj} \alpha_l \alpha_k y_l y_k K(x_l, x_k) \quad (13)$$

where $\omega_i \cdot \omega_j^*$ is the inner product between $\omega_i$ and $\omega_j^*$, $n$ is the number of support vector, $\alpha$ is the Lagrange multiplier, $y$ is the label value and $K(x_l, x_k)$ is the kernel function.

**Proof:** According to Eq. (11), $\omega_i = \sum_{l=1}^{ni} \alpha_l y_l \Phi(x_l)$ and $\omega_j^* = \sum_{k=1}^{nj} \alpha_k y_k \Phi(x_k)$, the inner product $\omega_i \cdot \omega_j^* = \left[\sum_{l=1}^{ni} \alpha_l y_l \Phi(x_l)\right] \cdot \left[\sum_{k=1}^{nj} \alpha_k y_k \Phi(x_k)\right]$, suppose that $Z_l = \alpha_l y_l \Phi(x_l)$, $Z_k^* = \alpha_k y_k \Phi(x_k)$, the inner product can be presented as follow:

$$\begin{aligned}\omega_i \cdot \omega_j^* &= \left(\sum_{l=1}^{ni} Z_l\right) \cdot \left(\sum_{k=1}^{nj} Z_l\right) \\ &= \sum_{l=1}^{ni} \sum_{k=1}^{nj} Z_l \cdot Z_k^* \\ &= \sum_{l=1}^{ni} \sum_{k=1}^{nj} \alpha_l \alpha_k y_l y_k K(x_l, x_k)\end{aligned} \quad (14)$$

the inner product is calculated using $K(x_l, x_k)$ and the cosine similarity is calculated using Eq. (2). $\omega$ is the normal vector of hyperplane and $\cos(\omega_i, \omega_j^*)$ represents the degree of similarity between hyperplane $SVM_i$ and $SVM_j^*$. Therefore, the mean cosine similarity between normal vectors $k$ in adjacent layers represents the similarity degree between adjacent layers.

**Algorithm 2. Redundancy Level Removement**

**Input:** normal vector of previous level $\{\omega_i^*\}_{i=1}^{k^*}$, normal vector of current level $\{\omega_i\}_{i=1}^{k}$, threshold $\tau$
**Output:** *isStopped* {True or False}

(1) For $\omega^*$ in $\{\omega_i^*\}_i^{k^*}$ do
(2)     For $\omega$ in $\{\omega\}_i^k$ do
(3)         $\{\{\cos(\omega_i^*, \omega_j)\}_{i=1}^{k^*}\}_{j=1}^{k}$
(4)     If $hs \geq \tau$ do
(5)         *isStopped* ← True
(6)     Else
(7)         *isStopped* ← False
(8)     End if
(9) Return *isStopped*

**Filtering of Non-Support Vector:** This stage aims to filter out non-support vector efficiently, which includes rough identification and singular vector identification. The samples are roughly identified as non-support vectors, support vectors and singular vectors in rough identification, which consists of three steps: (1) the prediction $\{f_i(d)\}_{i=1}^k$ in the $k$ local SVM is calculated using Eqs. (3); (2) the rough identification (RI) is proposed, which identify training samples according to $\{f_i(d)\}_{i=1}^k$; (3) the non-support vectors are filtered, the support vectors are retained as the reduced training set and the singular vectors are kept for the following identification.

**Theorem 3.4.** (*RI*): Given the $k$ local SVM model $SVM_1, SVM_2, ...SVM_k$, the result of rough identification can be presented as follow:

$$RI(d) = \begin{cases} \text{Support vector}, & f_{\max}(d) > 1 \\ \text{Non-support vector}, & f_{\min}(d) \leq 1 \\ \text{Singular vector}, & \text{other} \end{cases} \quad (15)$$

$$f_{\max}(d) = \max\left(\{f_i(d) \cdot y\}_{i=1}^k\right) \quad (16)$$

$$f_{\min}(d) = \min\left(\{f_i(d) \cdot y\}_{i=1}^k\right) \quad (17)$$

where $d$ is the sample and $f_i(d)$ is obtained using Eq. (3).

**Proof:** According to Eq. (3), $f_i(d)$ is the predictive value of sample $d$ in $SVM_i$, $y = \pm 1$ is the label of $d$. Consequently, $f_i(d) \cdot y$ represents both the label of the prediction and the distance to the separating hyperplane. When $f_i(d) \cdot y > 1$, sample $d$ is correctly classified and the distance is more than 1, which means sample $d$ is the support vector; when $f_i(d) \cdot y \leq 1$, sample $d$ is correctly classified and the distance is less than 1, which means sample $d$ is the non-support vector; when $f_i(d) \cdot y \leq 0$, sample $d$ is misclassified, which also means sample $d$ is the non-support vector. According to Eqs. (16) and (17), $f_{\max}(d)$ and $f_{\min}(d)$ is the maximal and minimal value of $\{f_i(d)\}_{i=1}^k$, respectively. When $f_{\max}(d) \leq 1$, $\forall f_i(d) \cdot y \leq 1$, sample $d$ is identified as the non-support vector in local SVMs; when $f_{\min}(d) > 1$, $\forall f_i(d) \cdot y > 1$, sample $d$ is identified as the support vector in local SVMs; when $f_{\max}(d) \not\leq 1 \& f_{\min}(d) \not\leq 1$, $\exists f_i(d) \leq 1 \& f_j(d) > 1$, sample $d$ is identified as both support vector and non-support vector in local SVMs. To sum up, the RI can roughly identify the support vector based on the performance in multiple local SVM models.

After the rough identification, the singular vectors are left for the following identification. The specific steps are: (1) the prediction accuracy of $k$ local SVMs is evaluated by the cross-training set:

$$p = \frac{1}{m} \sum_{i=1}^{ni} \max\left(sign\left(y_j\left[\sum_{j=1}^{nj} \alpha_j y_i K(X_i, X_j) + b\right]\right), 0\right) \quad (18)$$

where $nj$ is the number of support vectors, $\alpha_j$ is the corresponded Lagrange multiplier, $y_j$ is the label, $X_j$ is the eigenvector, $X_i$ is the eigenvalue and $b$ is the intercepts.

(2) for each singular vector $d$ and local SVM model, $\{h_i(d)\}_{i=1}^k$ is calculated using Eqs. (9) and (10); (3) the $k$ local SVM models are divided into two groups according to $h(d)$, where singular vector $d$ is identified as support vector in group $\{SVM^s\}_{i=1}^a$ and $d$ is identified as non-support vector in group $\{SVM^s\}_{i=1}^b$; (4) once the $k$ local SVMs are grouped, the distance between sample $d$ and corresponded decision boundaries in SVMs is given by

$$h = \left| \sum_{i=1}^n \alpha_i y_i K(X_i, X) + b - y \right| \quad (19)$$

(5) the support vector similarity (*SVS*) is proposed, which calculates the support vector similarity of singular vector based on the above performance in SVMs; (6) if the similarity is less than the threshold $\mu$, the singular vector will be identified as non-support vector, otherwise, the vectors will be merged into the reduced training set which is used for the following training.

**Theorem 5.** (*SVS*): Know as sample $d$ is support vector in $SVM^s$, and non-support vector in $SVM^{ns}$, then the support vector similarity of $d$ can be represented as follow:

$$SVSF(d) = \frac{\sum_{i=1}^b p_i^{ns}}{\sum_{i=1}^a p_i^s} [p_1^s \; p_2^s \; \cdots \; p_a^s] \begin{bmatrix} h_{11} & h_{12} & \cdots & h_{1b} \\ h_{21} & h_{22} & \cdots & h_{2b} \\ \vdots & \vdots & \ddots & \vdots \\ h_{a1} & h_{a2} & \cdots & h_{ab} \end{bmatrix} \left[ \frac{1}{p_1^{ns}} \; \frac{1}{p_2^{ns}} \; \cdots \; \frac{1}{p_b^{ns}} \right] \quad (20)$$

$$h_{ij} = \frac{h_i^s}{h_i^s + h_j^{ns}} \; i = 1, 2, \cdots, a \; j = 1, 2, \cdots, b \quad (21)$$

where $p_i^s$ and $p_i^{ns}$ is the accuracy of $i$th $SVM^s$ and $SVM^{ns}$, respectively, $h_i^s$ and $h_i^{ns}$ is the distance between $d$ and the decision boundaries corresponding to $SVM^s$, $SVM^{ns}$, respectively.

**Proof:** Suppose $SVM_i^s$ and $SVM_j^{ns}$ are constructed by different subsets, sample $d$ is identified as support vector in $SVM_i^s$ and sample $d$ is identified as non-support vector in $SVM_j^{ns}$. Thus, $\frac{h_i^s}{h_i^s + h_j^{ns}}$ can represent the distance between sample $d$ and the corresponded decisions in global model. $\frac{h_i^s}{h_i^s + h_j^{ns}} \to 1$ implies the higher probability of being support vector in global model. Conversely, $\frac{h_i^s}{h_i^s + h_j^{ns}} \to 0$ implies the lower probability of being support vector in global model. Then the corresponding decision distances between $d$ and SVMs are combined to get $[h_{ij}]^{a \times b}$. Probability vector $[p_1^s \; p_2^s \; \cdots \; p_a^s]$ of $SVM^s$ is used as the weight vector of $[h_{1j} \; h_{2j} \; \cdots \; h_{aj}]^T$, reciprocal probability vector $\left[ \frac{1}{p_1^{ns}} \; \frac{1}{p_2^{ns}} \; \cdots \; \frac{1}{p_b^{ns}} \right]^T$ of $SVM^{ns}$ is used as the penalty term of $[h_{1j} \; h_{2j} \; \cdots \; h_{bj}]$ and $\sum_{i=1}^b p_i^{ns} / \sum_{i=1}^a p_i^s$ is used as the normalization factor. Therefore Eq. (20) is able to measure the probability of becoming a support vector in global SVM model.

**Algorithm 3.** Non-support Vector Filtering

---
**Input:** subsets $\{d_i\}_{i=1}^n$, $k$ local SVM models $\{SVM_i\}_{i=1}^k$
**Output:** non-support vector set $NSV$, Reduced vector set $RSV$
---
(1)　For $i$ in $[1,\cdots,k]$ do
(2)　　Calculate $p_i$ according to eq(18)
(3)　End for
(4)　For $d$ in $\{d_i\}_{i=1}^n$ do
(5)　　Calculate $\{h_i(d)\}_{i=1}^k$ according to eq(19) and eq(13)
(6)　　Calculate $RI(d)$ according to eq(15) by $\{h_i(d)\}_{i=1}^k$
(7)　　If $RI(d)$ = support vector do
(8)　　　Push( $RSV$, $d$ )
(9)　　Else if RI(d) = non-support vector do
(10)　　　Push( $NSV$, $d$ )
(11)　　Else
(12)　　　For $i$ in $[0,\cdots,k]$ do
(13)　　　　If $h_i(d) \leq 1$ do
(14)　　　　　Push( $\{SVM^s\}$, $SVM_i$ )
(15)　　　　Else
(16)　　　　　Push( $\{SVM^{ns}\}$, $SVM_i$ )
(17)　　　　End if
(18)　　　End for
(19)　　　Calculate $svsf$ according to eq(20) and eq(21) by $\{SVM^s\}$ and $\{SVM^{ns}\}$
(20)　　　If $svsf \geq \mu$ do
(21)　　　　Push( $RSV$, $d$ )
(22)　　　Else
(23)　　　　Push( $NSV$, $d$ )
(24)　　　End if
(25)　　End if
(26)　End for
(27)　Return $NSV$ and $RSV$
---

**Global SVM Model Construction:** As previously stated, the RLR-CS strategy is used to improve the efficiency of parallel training. In this case, redundant levels will stop in advance, which means not all support vectors converge to the same node. Then, global SVM model is constructed based on the cascade layers which stopped in advance. The specific steps are: (1) the number of local SVM models is summarized as $n$ once the cascade structure terminates; (2) if $n = 1$, the local SVM will be outputted as the global SVM model, otherwise, the *innerTest* set from the data partition phase is used to test the $n$ local SVMs; (3) the obtained accuracies $p_i(i = 1, 2, \cdots, n)$ are taken as the weights of each local SVM; (4) the weighted voting method is used to construct the integrated model and the it will be outputted as the global SVM model.

### 4.3 Time Complexity

In order to analyze the time complexity of PSVM-MR algorithm, DP-SVM [11], MIMR-MQC [13] and DIVM [14] were selected as the comparison.

The time complexity of PSVM-MR is composed of two parts: data partition and training of parallel SVM, which are denoted as $T_1$, $T_2$, respectively.

(1) Data Partition: The time taken in data partition includes the time taken in initially partitioning most samples, calculating the relative entropy and partitioning the remaining samples using relative entropy. Assuming the number of original samples is $n$, the number of partitioned subsets is $k$, the total time is:

$$T_1 = O(k \cdot n) \tag{22}$$

(2) Parallel SVM Training: In this stage, the first step is the training of local SVM, and the corresponding time complexity is expressed as $O(n_i^2)$. Assuming that the nodes in the first layer is $k_1$, and $k_i$ $(i < j \Rightarrow k_i < k_j)$ in the $i$th layer, the number of samples in each nodes of $i$ $i$ layer is $n_i(k_i \cdot n_i \leq n)$, and the number of layers is $i$. The time complexity of redundant removement is expressed as $O(k_{i-1} \cdot n_s^2)$. In the third step, the non-support vectors are roughly filtered and the distance matrix between samples in two local SVM is constructed to calculate the similarity of support vectors, the time complexity is: $O(k_i \cdot n_i^c + k_i^2 \cdot n_i^{nc})$. The time complexity of each layer is expressed as $O(n_i^2 + k_{i-1} \cdot n_s^2 + k_i \cdot n_i^c + k_i^2 \cdot n_i^{nc})$

Thus, the total time of parallel SVM training is:

$$T_2 = O\left(m \cdot \left(n_i^2 + k_{i-1} \cdot n_s^2 + k_i \cdot n_i^c + k_i^2 \cdot n_i^{nc}\right)\right) \tag{23}$$

The total time of PSVM-MR is : $T = O(k \cdot n + m \cdot (n_i^2 + k_{i-1} \cdot n_s^2 + k_i \cdot n_i^c + k_i^2 \cdot (n_i - n_i^{nc})))$, $n_i$ is the number of training set in $i$ layer, $n_i^c$ is the number of roughly filter sample in $i$ layer and $n_s$ is the average number of support vectors in nodes. Since $n_i \leq \frac{n}{k_i}, n_i^c \leq n, n_i^{cn} < n, n_s \leq \frac{n}{k_i}$ and $\forall i > j \Rightarrow k_i > k_j$, the time complexity of PSVM-MR algorithm can be approximated as:

$$T_{PSVM-MR} = O\left(k^2 \cdot n + m \cdot \frac{n^2}{k^2}\right) \tag{24}$$

In the MIMR-MQC algorithm, the Mutual Informative MapReduce is adopted i k n the data preprocessing phase, which removes redundant attributes and extracts relevant features in parallel. Assuming the number of original samples is $n$, the feature dimension is $d$, and the number of nodes for parallel processing is $k$, the total time of feature extraction and reduction in the MIMR phase is $O\left(\frac{n \cdot d}{k} + \frac{n \cdot \log N}{k}\right)$. After preprocessing, Assuming the sample after preprocessing is $n_s(n_s < n)$, the Minimum Quadrangle Classification based on Support Vector Machine is used for classification, the total time is $O(n_s^2)$.

The total time complexity of the MIMR-MQC algorithm is

$$T_{MIMR-MQC} = \frac{n \cdot d}{k} + \frac{n \cdot \log n}{k} + n_s^2 \tag{25}$$

In the DIVM algorithm, the Distributed Independent Vector Machine identifies linearly independent samples and performs SVM training through distributed processing. Assuming the number of original samples is $n$ and the number of parallel nodes is $k$, the time complexity of identifying linearly independent samples is $O\left(\frac{n_s^2}{k^2}\right)$. Next, the SVM model is trained on local nodes using the Sequential Minimal Optimization algorithm, with a time complexity of $O\left(\frac{n_s^2}{k}\right)$, where $n_s$ is the size of the subset.

The total time complexity of the DIVM algorithm is:

$$T_{DIVM} = O\left(\frac{n^2 + n_s^2}{k^2}\right) \tag{26}$$

In the DP-SVM algorithm, the Parallel Support Vector Machine is adopted in the data processing phase, where the Map phase calculates the kernel function values for each sample, and the Reduce phase trains the SVM model using these values. Assuming the number of original samples is $n$, the feature dimension is $d$, and the number of nodes for parallel processing is $k$, the total time of calculating kernel function values in the Map phase is $O\left(\frac{n \cdot d^2}{k}\right)$ In the Reduce phase, the SVM model is trained using the kernel values, with a time complexity of $O(\frac{n^2}{k^2})$.

The total time complexity of the DP-SVM algorithm is:

$$T_{DP-SVM} = O\left(\frac{n \cdot d^2}{k} + \frac{n^2}{k^2}\right) \tag{27}$$

In Support Vector Machines, since the number of support vectors $n$ is generally much smaller than the total number of samples $N$, $\frac{n \cdot d}{k} + \frac{n \cdot \log n}{k} + n_s^2 > \frac{n^2 + n_s^2}{k^2} > \frac{n \cdot d^2}{k} + \frac{n^2}{k^2} > k^2 \cdot n + m \cdot \frac{n^2}{k^2}$, the time complexity of proposed PSVM-MR algorithm is the smallest compared with the above algorithms.

## 5 Experimental Evaluation

This section explains the experimental environment and verifies the proposed PSVM-MR algorithm's performance by comparing it with other parallel SVM algorithms.

### 5.1 Experimental Settings

The specific configuration of the cluster nodes is presented in Table 1. Each node contains an Intel Core i9-10900K, 16 GB RAM, ten processing units, and a GPU of NVIDIA RTX 3070 8G, which is connected via 1 Gb/s Ethernet. One of the machines is designated as the master node, and the others are designated as slave nodes. The algorithm is implemented in Java and runs on CentOS 7.6. The JDK version is 16.0.2. The software packages include JDK 16.0.2 and Hadoop 3.2.3.

**Table 1.** The specific configuration of each node

| Node type | Node No. | IP | Role |
|---|---|---|---|
| Master | 1 | 192.168.10.103 | Master/JobTracker/NameNode |
| Slaver | 2,3,4,5,6,7,8 | 192.168.10.111 ~ 192.168.10.117 | Slaver/TaskTracker/DataNode |

### 5.2 Experimental Dataset

To evaluate the performance of the proposed PSVM-MR algorithm, experiments were conducted on the following four datasets from different application domains. The Ijcnn1 dataset [19] is used in the machine learning challenge during IJCNN 2001(Prokhorov, 2001). The Adult dataset [20] is used to predict whether income exceeds $50K/year based on census data. The Webspam dataset [21] is a data collection which includes 350,000 Web spam pages. The Kddcup99 dataset [22] is from UCI machine learning repository. The detailed information of these datasets is shown in Table 2.

**Table 2.** Description of the four datasets

|  | Ijcnn1 | Adult | Webspam | Kddcup99 |
|---|---|---|---|---|
| Training samples | 49,990 | 32,561 | 280,000 | 4,898,431 |
| Testing samples | 91,701 | 16,281 | 70,000 | 311,029 |
| Features | 22 | 14 | 254 | 41 |

### 5.3 Experimental Metrics

(1) **Speed-up ratio**

The speed-up ratio [23] represents the runtime ratio that the same task cost in serial and parallel systems. It can be used to measure the performance of parallel algorithms and it is defined as follow:

$$Speed - up = T_s/T_n \tag{28}$$

where $T_s$ and $T_n$ represents the running time of the algorithm in the case of serial and parallel respectively.

(2) **F-measure**

F-measure [24] is the harmonic mean of precision and recall, which is used for evaluating the accuracy of classification algorithm. The F-measure is defined as follow:

$$F - Measure = \frac{(\beta^2 + 1) precision \times recall}{\beta^2 \cdot precision + recall} \tag{29}$$

where $\beta$ is 1.

(3) **Accuracy**

Accuracy measures the overall correctness of a classifier by calculating the ratio of correct predictions to total predictions:

$$Accuracy = \frac{TP + TN}{TP + TN + FP + FN} \tag{30}$$

where TP, TN, FP, and FN represent true positives, true negatives, false positives, and false negatives, respectively.

(4) **Kappa**

Kappa (Cohen's Kappa) measures the agreement between two raters (or a classifier and ground truth) while accounting for chance agreement. It is calculated as:

$$k = \frac{p_o - p_e}{1 - p_e} \tag{31}$$

where $p_o$ is the observed agreement (equivalent to accuracy), and $p_e$ is the expected agreement by chance. A $k$ value of 1 indicates perfect agreement, while 0 means no agreement beyond chance.

Alternatively, in terms of the confusion matrix:

$$\begin{array}{l} p_o = \frac{TP+TN}{TP+TN+FP+FN} \\ p_e = \frac{(TP+FP)(TP+FN)+(FN+TN)(FP+TN)}{(TP+TN+FP+FN)^2} \end{array} \tag{32}$$

where TP, TN, FP, and FN denote true positives, true negatives, false positives, and false negatives, respectively.

## 5.4 Experimental Results and Analysis

To verify the feasibility of the proposed PSVM-MR algorithm, the experiments were conducted based on the four datasets, namely ijcnn1, webspam, adult and kddcup99. The speed-up ratio of PSVM-MR algorithm on the four datasets is shown in Fig. 5. It can be seen in Fig. 5, the speed-up ratio in the four datasets increases dramatically with the number of computing nodes, which shows the good performance in the parallel framework. Moreover, the results indicated that the proposed PSVM-MR algorithm is adaptable to the big data environment.

The reason that the PSVM-MR algorithm achieves accelerating speed-up ratios across ijcnn1, web spam, adult, and kddcup99 datasets as computing nodes increase is threefold: first, the RLR-CS mechanism's targeted elimination of redundant computational layers substantially reduces training overhead; second, the NSVF method's dual-stage filtration of non-support vectors minimizes inter-node communication burdens; third, the DP-RE approach maintains balanced subset distributions to prevent computational skew. This synergistic optimization enables near-linear scalability in distributed environments, confirming the algorithm's superior adaptability to large-scale geospatial and disaster prediction datasets where conventional SVMs exhibit performance degradation.

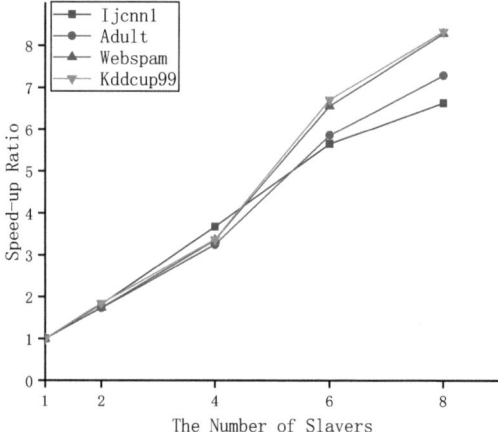

**Fig. 5.** Validation of Speed-up ratio

(1) **Running time**

The running time is shown in Fig. 6, which contains the implementation of our proposed DP-SVM [11], MIMR-MQC [13] and DIVM [14] on the Ijcnn1, Adult, Webspam, and Kddcup99 datasets.

From Figure 6, it can be observed that compared to the DP-SVM, MIMR-MQC, and DIVM algorithms, the PSVM-MR algorithm consistently consumes the least running time across all datasets. Specifically, compared to the DP-SVM, MIMR-MQC, and DIVM algorithms, the running time of the PSVM-MR algorithm on the Ijcnn1 dataset is reduced by 12.96%, 20.92%, and 29.93%, respectively; on the Adult dataset, the running time is reduced by 14.85%, 8.78%, and 25.65%, respectively; on the Webspam dataset, the running time is reduced by 17.34%, 9.66%, and 35.26%, respectively; and on the Kddcup99 dataset, the running time is reduced by 11.47%, 1.88%, and 24.63%, respectively.

The reason for the substantially reduced running time is the systematic elimination of redundant computational layers during training, which directly alleviates the computational burden through optimized resource utilization; moreover, the proportion of structurally expendable components in SVM architectures escalates disproportionately when processing large-scale datasets, severely impeding computational efficiency; consequently, the proposed algorithm achieves demonstrably superior execution speeds compared to conventional methods on large-scale data, as empirically verified across diverse experimental configurations.

(2) **Speed-up ratio**

The speed-up ratio of PSVM-MR algorithm is compared with other algorithms in Fig. 7, namely DP-SVM, MIMR-MQC and DIVM, using datasets of different scales.

From Fig. 7, it is obvious that the speed-up ratio of each algorithm showed an upward trend with the increase of slave nodes. This is expected because the computing speed can be improved by increasing the number of slave nodes. When the number of computing nodes is small, the speed-up ratio of the PSVM-MR algorithm is close to other algorithms on the four datasets. For instance, when the number of slave nodes is 2, the speed-up ratio of the PSVM-MR algorithm is 1.82 on the ijcnn1 dataset. It is only higher than DP-SVM, MIMR-MQC, and DIVM by 0.1, 0.05, and 0.14, respectively. This is due to the fact that the proposed algorithm has time overhead in task scheduling and node storage when there are fewer slave nodes, which results in a lower speed-up ratio. However, when the number of slave nodes increases to 8, the speed-up ratio of the PSVM-MR algorithm is higher than DP-SVM, MIMR-MQC, and DIVM by 0.67, 1.15, and 1.58, respectively, on the ijcnn1 dataset, respectively. Moreover, the gap between the proposed algorithm and other algorithms becomes more remarkable with the increment in data size.

The main reason is that the CLRS mechanism strategically eliminates redundant computational layers through structured pruning, directly reducing model complexity and accelerating the training process, while simultaneously, the NSVF technique systematically identifies and eliminates non-support vectors via discriminative filtering, which minimizes communication overhead and optimizes resource utilization during parallel training; this dual optimization framework synergistically enhances distributed computing efficiency, as evidenced by experimental results demonstrating that the PSVM-MR algorithm achieves superior scalability on large-scale datasets—with parallel performance exhibiting near-linear improvement as slave nodes increase—due to effective mitigation of computational bottlenecks and communication latency inherent in conventional distributed SVM implementations.

(3) **F-measure**

The F-measure of PSVM-MR and other algorithms, namely DP-SVM, MIMR-MQC and DIVM on four datasets is shown in Fig. 8.

It can be observed from Fig. 8 that the F-measure of PSVM-MR algorithm is higher than the other algorithms on the four datasets. For instance, when processing the Adult dataset, the F-measure of the PSVM-MR algorithm increased by 1.23%, 1.61%, and 3.07% compared with the DP-SVM, MIMR-MQC and DIVM, respectively. Especially when dealing with the complicated datasets such as adult and kddcup99 datasets, the F-measure of the proposed algorithm is even more pronounced compared with other algorithms.

The reason is that distributed deviation across data subsets is fundamentally minimized through systematic relative entropy balancing between the original dataset and its partitions, which actively preserves statistical representativeness during parallelization and thereby prevents accuracy degradation caused by skewed data distributions, while simultaneously, non-support vectors are efficiently identified and eliminated via a dual-stage NSVF (Non-Support Vector Filtering) mechanism that discriminatively isolates noise-inducing feature vectors without compromising critical decision boundaries, consequently enhancing classification precision and computational efficiency; this synergistic integration of distributional alignment and targeted vector refinement collectively optimizes the model's discriminative power, mitigates representation bias and feature redundancy inherent in high-dimensional data processing, and ultimately establishes the algorithm's consistent performance superiority over conventional approaches across diverse testing scenarios.

(4) **Accuracy**

The classification accuracy comparison between PSVM-MR and others methods (DP-SVM, MIMR-MQC, and DIVM) across four benchmark datasets is illustrated in Figure 9. Experimental results demonstrate that PSVM-MR consistently achieves superior accuracy performance on all evaluated datasets. Specifically, for the Adult dataset, PSVM-MR exhibits accuracy improvements of 0.82%, 1.33%, and 2.15% over DP-SVM, MIMR-MQC, and DIVM respectively. The performance advantage becomes more significant when processing complex datasets with high-dimensional features, such as adult and kddcup99.

The reason is that relative entropy balancing minimizes distributional divergence between data subsets during partitioning to maintain statistical representativeness across parallel processing nodes, thereby preventing accuracy degradation from skewed data distributions, while non-support vector filtering employs a dual-stage identification process to eliminate irrelevant feature vectors and reduce noise while preserving discriminative features, thus enhancing classification precision; these complementary innovations synergistically optimize decision boundaries by simultaneously addressing representation bias through distribution alignment and feature redundancy through vector refinement, which overcomes fundamental limitations in existing parallel SVM implementations and consequently establishes a consistent accuracy advantage across diverse testing scenarios, particularly with complex, high-dimensional datasets where traditional approaches typically underperform.

(5) **Kappa**

The inter-rater reliability comparison measured by Cohen's kappa coefficient between PSVM-MR and others methods (DP-SVM, MIMR-MQC, DIVM) across four datasets reveals PSVM-MR's consistent superiority. Experimental results demonstrate significantly higher kappa values for PSVM-MR on all evaluated datasets. Specifically for the Kddcup99 dataset, PSVM-MR achieves kappa improvements of 0.034 0.0083, and 0.0513 points over DP-SVM, MIMR-MQC, and DIVM respectively. This performance advantage amplifies when processing complex, high-dimensional datasets like Adult and KDDCup99, where PSVM-MR maintains superior agreement consistency amidst label distribution challenges, as further corroborated by the divergence patterns in Figure 10.

The reason is that relative entropy-based data partitioning (DP-RE) minimizes distributional divergence between subsets to maintain statistical representativeness across computing nodes, thereby preventing accuracy degradation from skewed data distributions; cosine similarity-driven redundancy removal (RLR-CS) eliminates computationally redundant layers through cascade structure optimization to accelerate training efficiency; and dual-stage non-support vector filtering (NSVF) combines rough identification with singular vector analysis to eliminate noise-inducing features while preserving discriminative vectors, thus enhancing classification precision. These integrated innovations synergistically overcome fundamental limitations in distributed SVM implementations by simultaneously addressing data skew through entropy alignment, computational bottlenecks through structural pruning, and feature redundancy through intelligent filtration, which collectively establish superior scalability and reduced training costs across diverse large-scale datasets where conventional methods exhibit performance degradation.

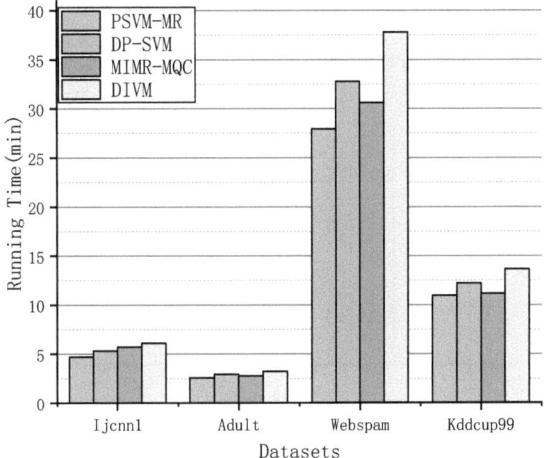

**Fig. 6.** The running time of each algorithm on four datasets

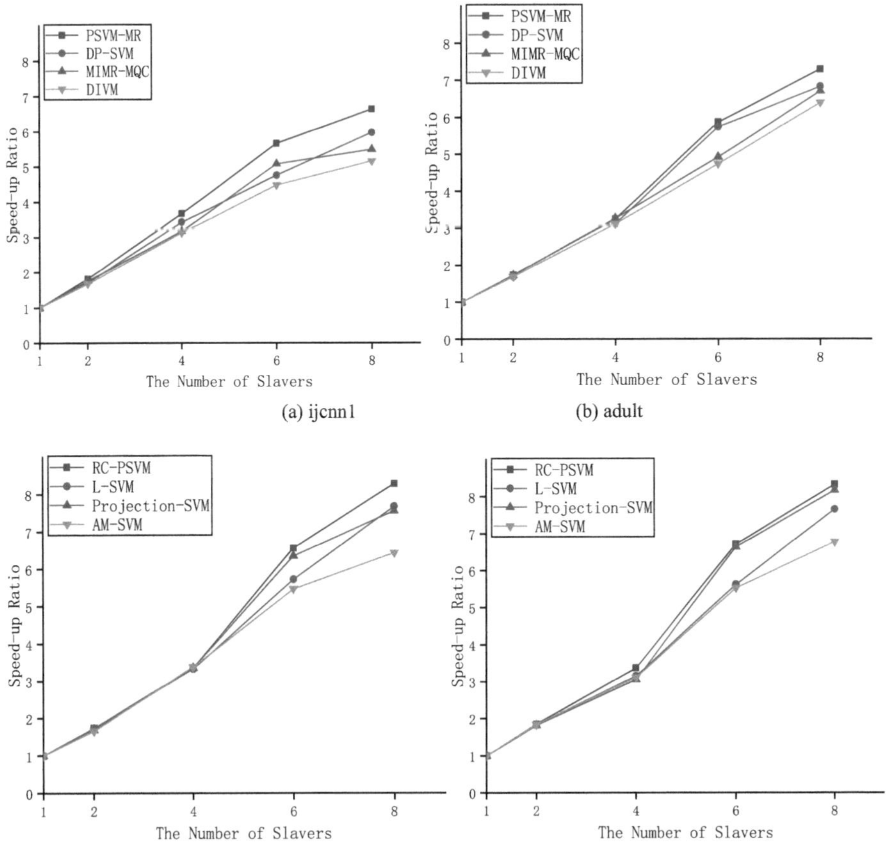

(a) ijcnn1

(b) adult

(c) webspam

(d) kddcup99

**Fig. 7.** The speed-up ratio of each algorithm on four datasets

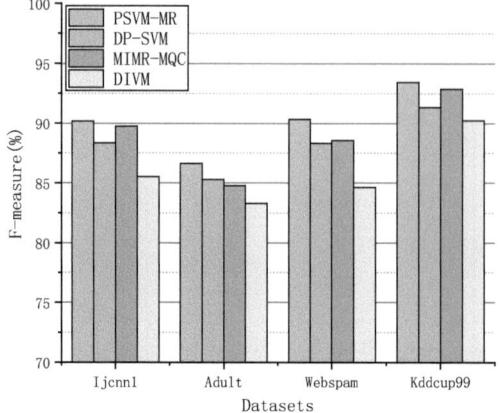

**Fig. 8.** The F-measure of each algorithm on four datasets

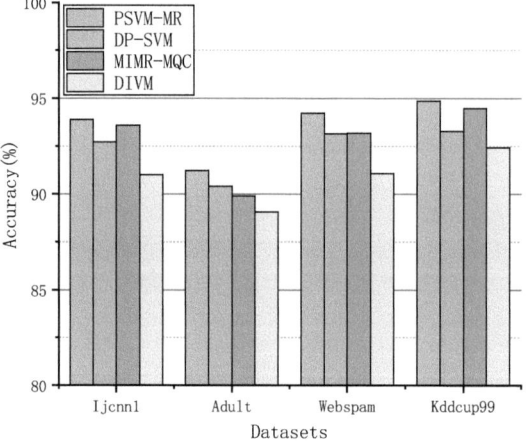

**Fig. 9.** The accuracy of each algorithm on four datasets

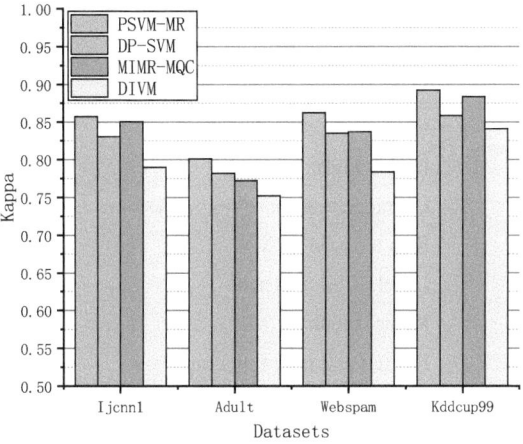

**Fig. 10.** The kappa of each algorithm on four datasets

## 6 Conclusion

This paper proposes PSVM-MR algorithm designed to overcome limitations of general parallel SVM approaches in big data environments. The algorithm consists of two primary stages: data partitioning via the DP-RE strategy, which effectively minimizes distributional deviation among subsets, and parallel SVM training enhanced by the RLR-CS strategy for removing hierarchical redundancies and the NSVF strategy for filtering non-support vectors to accelerate training. Experimental results demonstrate that PSVM-MR consistently outperforms existing methods in running time, speed-up ratio, and classification accuracy across multiple benchmark datasets.

**Funding:.** This research was funded by the Key Improvement Projects of Guangdong Province(2022ZDJS048,SZ2022KJ06)and Education Department Science and Technology ProjectG in Jiangxi (GJJ218505, GJJ218504, GJJ209406).

## Appendix

**Notation Table**

To ensure symbols rigor notation table is provided in Table 3. All symbols follow standard machine learning conventions unless otherwise specified. The table provides both mathematical definitions and brief explanations to facilitate interpretation.

**Table 3.** Summary of Mathematical Notations

| Symbol | Meaning |
|---|---|
| $X$ | Feature vector/Instance |
| $x_i$ | i-th component of feature vector |

(*continued*)

**Table 3.** (*continued*)

| Symbol | Meaning |
|---|---|
| $D$ | Dataset (unlabeled) |
| $d$ | Labeled instance |
| $\alpha$ | Lagrange multiplier (in SVM) |
| $b$ | Bias term (in SVM) |
| $y_i$ | Label of i-th instance |
| $K(X_i, X_j)$ | Kernel function |
| $\Phi(x)$ | Feature mapping function |
| $n_+$ | Number of positive samples |
| $n_-$ | Number of negative samples |
| $k$ | Number of subsets/parallel nodes |
| $re_i$ | Relative entropy of i-th subset |
| $RE()$ | Relative entropy function |
| *Map* | Map procedure |
| *Reduce* | Reduce procedure |
| $\omega$ | Normal vector (of SVM decision boundary) |
| $\tau$ | User-defined threshold |
| $h_i$ | Distance from i-th sample to decision boundary |
| $\max()$ | Maximization function |
| $\min()$ | Minimization function |
| $sign()$ | Absolute value function |
| $\arg\max()$ | Argmax function |

# References

1. Lou, C., Xijiong, X.: Intuitionistic fuzzy multi-view support vector machines with universum data. Appl. Intell. **32**(2), 1365–1385 (2024)
2. Hadi, D.M., Niaki, S.T.A.: Pattern recognition in financial surveillance with the ARMA-GARCH time series model using support vector machine. Exp. Syst. Appl. **65**(5), 122–144 (2021)
3. Kumar, S.S., Chaturvedi, A.: Leveraging deep feature learning for wearable sensors based handwritten character recognition. Biomed. Sig. Process. Control **161**(2), 104–198 (2023)
4. Saeed, A.I.M., Hariprasad, D.: Hyper-heuristic salp swarm optimization of multi-kernel support vector machines for big data classification. Int. J. Inf. Technol. **55**(2), 651–663 (2023)
5. Shirin, T.: Parallel computing of support vector machines: a survey. ACM Comput. Surv. **78**(4), 123–155 (2019)
6. Mahmudul, H., Bansal, S.: S3QLRDF: distributed SPARQL query processing using Apache Spark—a comparative performance study. Distrib. Parall. Databases **121**(2), 1–41 (2023)

7. Hans, G., Cosatto, E.: Parallel support vector machines: the cascade SVM. Adv. Neural. Inf. Process. Syst. **55**(5), 1040–1066 (2004)
8. Hsieh, C.-J., Si, S., Dhillon, I.: A divide-and-conquer solver for kernel support vector machines. In: International Conference on Machine Learning, vol. 87, no. 4, pp. 54–72 (2014)
9. Singh, D., Roy, D., Mohan, C.K.: DiP-SVM : distribution preserving kernel support vector machine for big data. IEEE Int. Conf. Big Data (big data) **145**(2), 88–95 (2017)
10. Penghui, G.: Optimization and parallelization of the Cascade SVM. School of Information Science and Engineering, Lanzhou University, Lanzhou, vol. 132, no. 4, pp. 45–67 (2018)
11. Sujitha, R., Paramasivan, B.: Distributed healthcare framework using MMSM-SVM and P-SVM classification. CMC-Comput. Mater. Continua **70**(1), 1557–1572 (2022)
12. Zelu, K., Xiao, N.: An improved parallel SVM algorithm on distributed system. In: 2020 International Conference on Cyber-Enabled Distributed Computing and Knowledge Discovery (CyberC), vol. 56, no. 4, pp.55–75 (2020)
13. Ramachandran, M., Patan, R., Kumar, A., et al.: Mutual informative MapReduce and minimum quadrangle classification for brain tumor big data. IEEE Trans. Eng. Manage. **70**(8), 2644–2655 (2021)
14. Almaspoor, M.H., Safaei, A.A., Salajegheh, A., et al.: Distributed independent vector machine for big data classification problems. J. Supercomput. **80**(6), 7207–7244 (2024)
15. Fariba, S., Keyvanpour, M.R., Sharifi, A.: SMKFC-ER: Semi-supervised multiple kernel fuzzy clustering based on entropy and relative entropy. Inf. Sci. **76**(7), 667–688 (2021)
16. Chandrasekaran, V., Shah, P.: Relative entropy optimization and its applications. Math. Program. **161**(1–2), 1–32 (2016). https://doi.org/10.1007/s10107-016-0998-2
17. Xia, P., Li, Z., Li, F.: Learning similarity with cosine similarity ensemble. Inf. Sci. **25**(4), 39–52 (2015)
18. Alberto, T.-B., Alaíz, C.M., Dorronsoro, J.R.: Faster SVM training via conjugate SMO. Pattern Recogn. **55**(4), 107–144 (2021)
19. Prokhorov D.: Ijcnn 2001 neural network competition" Slide presentation In IJCNN. In: 2020, International Conference on Cyber-Enabled Distributed Computing and Knowledge Discovery (CyberC). (2020)
20. Deepajothi, S., Selvarajan, S.: A comparative study of classification techniques on adult data set. Int. J. Eng. Res. Technol. (IJERT) **34**(6), 204–209 (2020)
21. Webb, S., Caverlee, J., Pu, C.: Introducing the webb spam corpus: using email spam to identify web spam automatically. In: CEAS (2020)
22. Mahbod, T., Bagheri, E.: A detailed analysis of the KDD CUP 99 data set. In: 2009 IEEE Symposium on Computational Intelligence for Security and Defense Applications, vol. 35, no. 5, pp. 122–155 (2009)
23. Juan, C.L., Sathiya Keerthi, S: Parallel sequential minimal optimization for the training of support vector machines. IEEE Trans. Neural Networks **144**(5), 139–149 (2006)
24. Yueh, C.T., Kuo, F.-C., Merkel, R.: On the statistical properties of the f-measure. In: Fourth International Conference on Quality Software, 2004. QSIC 2004, Proceedings, vol. 76, no. 4, pp.155–167 (2004)

# Algorithm Application

# A Novel Homogenization-Based Method for Population Initialization of Improved Chaotic Artificial Bee Colonies and Convergence Analysis

Haiyan Yang[1], Liyong Bao[1(✉)], Dongming Zhou[2], and Yonghui Si[1]

[1] School of Information Science and Engineering, Yunnan University, Kunming 650504, China
bly.yx@163.com
[2] School of Electronic Science and Engineering, Hunan University of Information Technology, Changsha 410100, China

**Abstract.** Chaos possesses outstanding pseudo - random properties. The chaotic time series fits well for the initialization of food sources in the artificial bee colony algorithm. However, the distribution of most chaotic mappings is not homogenized, which lowers the search efficiency and accuracy of the traversal algorithm. Hence, this paper puts forward a novel homogenization-based optimization method for population initialization of improved chaotic artificial bee colonies. According to the principle of maximum entropy, Logistic chaotic mapping is optimized to achieve homogenization. Subsequently, the randomness of the generated homogenized time series is checked through entropy spectrum analysis and NIST randomness test. Moreover, a dynamic grouping strategy based on fitness is designed to balance the exploration and development phases of the algorithm. Furthermore, experimental simulations are conducted on 18 standard test functions. It is also compared with other optimization algorithms in terms of convergence curve and optimization result. And related algorithms are appropriately introduced into the material flow distribution to seek the shortest path. The results indicate that the proposed algorithm enables the initial value to be more homogeneously distributed in the search space, thus improving the global pioneering of the algorithm. Through dynamic grouping of the population, the fine - grained search ability is enhanced.

**Keywords:** Artificial Bee Colony Algorithm · Chaotic System · Population Distribution · Dynamic Grouping Strategy

## 1 Introduction

Artificial bee colony (ABC) [1] algorithm is a bio - inspired swarm intelligence optimization algorithm developed by Turkish researcher Karaba based on the process where bee colonies search for superior food sources. The ABC algorithm possesses remarkable advantages such as strong global optimization capability, simple implementation process, and wide range of applications. However, when the distribution of the initial food sources is not homogenizing, the convergence speed of the algorithm shows a slower trend, and the search accuracy and population diversity also decrease [2].

Considering the limitations of the ABC algorithm, many scholars have put forward corresponding improvement measures after in-depth research. Sally proposed a hybrid genetic ABC algorithm. It improves the search probability by introducing genetic operators, thereby improving the global optimization ability [3]. Kai Li et al. proposed an ABC algorithm based on the modified nearest neighbor sequence (MNN). By introducing MNN and a dynamic strategy pool, this approach enhances the global search efficiency of ABC and its adaptability to complex problems [4]. Tingyu Ye et al. proposed RNSABC, an ABC algorithm based on random neighborhood structure (RNS). By constructing RNS with independent random neighborhood sizes, designing improved search strategies, and introducing depth-first search to enhance the onlooker bee phase, it boosts ABC's performance on classical, complex, and polynomial problems [5]. Fusing Zhao et al. proposed the MEEABC, an ABC algorithm incorporating maximum entropic epistasis (MEE). By introducing dimension interaction information computed via MEE to guide the search process and combining adaptive mutation with dynamic population size reduction, this approach enhances ABC's convergence speed and local exploitation capability for continuous optimization problems [6]. Song Xiaoyu used different search strategies and appropriate mixing ratios to achieve the balance between exploration and development of ABC algorithms [7].

In summary, although the improvement measures have enhanced the algorithm's optimization ability, they have not thoroughly studied the influence of distribution of initial food sources. And there are deficiencies in search accuracy and convergence speed. In view of this, this paper fuses the time series generated by the homogenizing Logistic mapping into the initial food sources and search strategy. The homogenizing dynamic grouping artificial bee colony (HDABC) algorithm is proposed. Firstly, this paper employs homogenized time series for initializing food sources, aiming to make the food sources tend to exhibit global randomness and homogeneous distribution as much as possible. Then, according to the differences in population division of labor, the population is dynamically grouped, and their search formulas are designed. Finally, 18 standard test functions featuring diverse characteristics undergo simulation based on the analysis of initial food source distribution. 6 algorithms are applied to address the shortest path in logistics distribution. The results indicate that the HDABC algorithm demonstrates superiority in both convergence speed and accuracy.

## 2 Characteristic Analysis of Homogenizing Logistic Mapping

### 2.1 Construction of Homogenizing Logistic Mapping

In the initialization stage, in order to simulate the process of employed bees releasing pheromone at the food sources after collecting food, to guide other individuals to collect and expand the search area, a strategy of food source initialization based on time series generated by the homogenizing Logistic mapping is proposed, which makes the food sources tend to be globally random and homogenizing distribution, and has correlation with the increase of iteration times. The expression of Logistic mapping is as follows:

$$x_{n+1} = \mu x_n (1 - x_n) \tag{1}$$

Within this framework, the parameters satisfy $\mu \in [0,4]$ and $x_n \in [0,1]$. The Logistic mapping exhibits chaotic behavior when $\mu$ lies in the interval (3.57,4] [8].

We know the probability density function of random variable $x$ in Logistic mapping when $\mu = 4$, so according to the distribution theorem of random variable function in probability theory [9], the random variable $Y = G(X)$ is constructed, which is on (0,1) Obey the homogenizing distribution, and further mathematically derive the homogenization shaping function of the mapping [10], as presented in formula (2). This shaping method is a classical optimization method of homogenization in probability theory. It is complete and universal. It is still applicable to other typical chaotic mappings, that is, when the probability density function of a chaotic map is known, a time series conforming to a homogenizing distribution can be constructed based on this formula.

$$y = \frac{2\arcsin(\sqrt{x})}{\pi} \qquad (2)$$

Combine Eqs. (1) and (2) together to get the homogenizing Logistic mapping expression:

$$\begin{cases} x_{n+1} = 4x_n(1-x_n), 0 \le x_n \le 1 \\ y_n = x_{n+1} \\ y_{n+1} = \frac{2}{\pi}\arcsin(\sqrt{y_n}), 0 \le y_n \le 1 \end{cases} \qquad (3)$$

## 2.2 Homogenization Analysis

### (1) Information entropy

Information entropy can represent the average uncertainty about the likelihood of analog signals occurring, serving as a key metric to evaluate the uniformity of information distribution [11]. In this section, the principle of maximum entropy is used to analyze the time series generated. If the sources have N values and are independent of each other, then the information entropy will be the statistical average value of the symbol uncertainty of each source $(-log_2 P_i)$, that is:

$$H = E[-log_2 P_i] = -\sum_{i=1}^{N} P_i log_2 P_i \qquad (4)$$

Among them, $P_i$ is the probability of taking values in different intervals.

Subsequently, 50,000 runs are configured with an initial value of 0.33. For different M values, the information entropy of the three functions is calculated, and the results are shown in Table 1.

As shown in Table 1, under the same statistical interval M, the Homogenizing Logistic sequence exhibits the highest information entropy and is closest to the theoretical maximum entropy corresponding to M. This indicates that the sequence is the most uniformly distributed within this interval, demonstrating the effectiveness of the homogenization processing of the Logistic map proposed in this paper.

**Table 1.** Information entropy and theoretical maximum entropy of three functions.

| Number of intervals | Rand | Logistic | Homogenizing Logistic | Maximum information entropy |
|---|---|---|---|---|
| 10 | 3.2839 | 3.1458 | 3.3189 | 3.3219 |
| 100 | 6.5383 | 6.3436 | 6.6352 | 6.6439 |
| 200 | 7.5167 | 7.3254 | 7.6335 | 7.6439 |
| 400 | 8.4937 | 8.3117 | 8.6316 | 8.6439 |
| 600 | 9.0648 | 8.8903 | 9.2154 | 9.2288 |

(2) **Frequency graph, ergodic graph and probability distribution**

In order to verify the homogenization of the mapping, this section draws the frequency histogram and the traversal distribution diagram for comparison. Figure 1 shows the frequency histogram before and after the Logistic mapping homogenization, and Fig. 2 shows the traversal distribution diagram before and after the Logistic mapping homogenization. And from a numerical point of view, the number of sequence values in the distribution interval after 500,000 iterations before and after Logistic homogenization is calculated, the initial value is 0.33, and the probability distribution of the number of sequence values in different intervals in the total number of sequence values is calculated. The situation is shown in Table 2.

The distribution of the traditional Logistic map, as shown in Fig. 1, exhibits a bimodal distribution at both ends. The probability of values in [0,0.1] and [0.9,1] is significantly higher than the probability of values in other segments, but the sequence generated by homogenizing Logistic mapping are approximately linearly distributed, and the probability of taking values in each segment of the feasible region is relatively equal. Although the traditional logistic mapping time series in Fig. 2 traverses the entire space, it is more concentrated in the two ends of 0 and 1. Compared with the traditional logistic sequence, the homogenized Logistic sequence exhibits a more uniform distribution.

The statistical results of Table 2 show that the distribution of sequence values generated by Logistic mapping is not homogenizing. The values of the two intervals [0,0.1] and [0.9,1] account for 41.02% of the global value probability, and the probability of the other eight intervals is below 10%, but the distribution of the sequence values generated by homogenizing Logistic mapping is relatively homogenizing. The value probabilities of the ten intervals are all about 10%, and the maximum value probability and the minimum value probability are only 0.05%.

It can be seen that according to the analysis result of the combination of number and shape, the uniformity of the homogenizing Logistic sequence is significantly better than that of the Logistic sequence, and its homogenizing distribution characteristics are more prominent.

# A Novel Homogenization-Based Method for Population Initialization 127

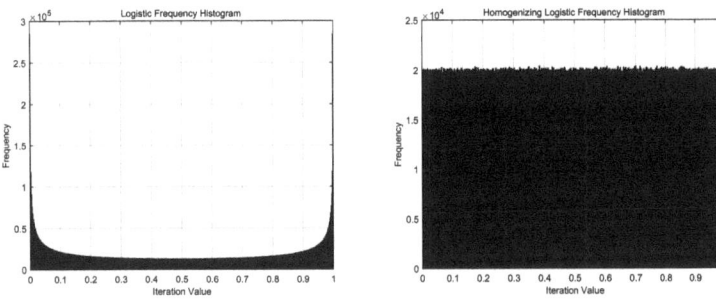

**Fig. 1.** Frequency histogram before and after Logistic mapping homogenization

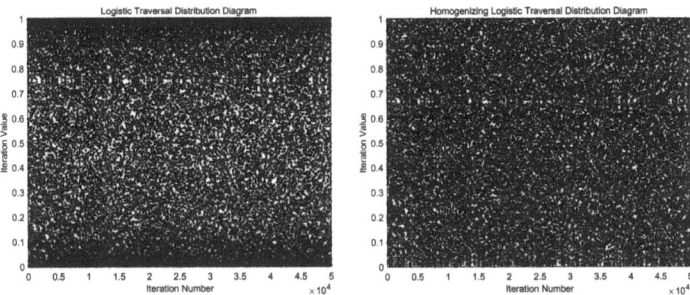

**Fig. 2.** Traversal distribution diagram before and after Logistic mapping homogenization

**Table 2.** Probability distribution before and after logistic homogenization

| Interval | Number before homogenization | Probability | Number after homogenization | Probability |
|---|---|---|---|---|
| 0–0.1 | 102577 | 20.52% | 50079 | 10.02% |
| 0.1–0.2 | 45283 | 9.06% | 50011 | 10.00% |
| 0.2–0.3 | 36748 | 7.35% | 50132 | 10.03% |
| 0.3–0.4 | 33586 | 6.72% | 49904 | 9.98% |
| 0.4–0.5 | 31807 | 6.36% | 49875 | 9.98% |
| 0.5–0.6 | 32314 | 6.46% | 50160 | 10.03% |
| 0.6–0.7 | 33192 | 6.64% | 49901 | 9.98% |
| 0.7–0.8 | 36975 | 7.40% | 49903 | 9.98% |
| 0.8–0.9 | 45035 | 9.01% | 50025 | 10.01% |
| 0.9–1 | 102483 | 20.50% | 50010 | 10.00% |

## 2.3 Complexity Analysis

Complexity is a quantitative indicator to evaluate how closely a system-generated time series approximates a random sequence, comprising two main categories, behavioral complexity and structural complexity. Behavioral complexity focuses on analyzing the time series itself—specifically, the higher the probability of generating novel patterns within the sequence, the greater its complexity. It is commonly expressed by Kolmogorov entropy and approximate entropy. In contrast, structural complexity examines the energy characteristics within the transform domain, emphasizing the global properties of the sequence rather than local features. It has global statistical significance and is often expressed by spectral entropy.

### (1) Kolmogorov entropy

Kolmogorov entropy serves to quantify the average rate of information loss during the system's iterative process, acting as a global measure to evaluate the system's degree of chaos [12]. Kolmogorov entropy can be defined as:

$$K = -\lim_{\tau \to 0}\lim_{\varepsilon \to 0}\lim_{d \to 0}\frac{1}{d\tau}\sum_{n-0}^{d} P(i_0, \ldots, i_n)\ln P(i_0, \ldots, i_n) \tag{5}$$

Among them, $P$ is the joint probability at different moments.

$K$ value is an important indicator for judging the nature of motion: $K = 0$ indicates that the system exhibits a state of regular motion, the amount of information does not change over time, which is completely predictable; $K = \infty$ indicates that the system exhibits a state of purely random motion, which is completely unpredictable; the process of increasing the $K$ value is the process of increasing disorder of the system. The greater the value of $K$, the higher the level of chaos in the system. And for one-dimensional mapping, the $K$ value is exactly the positive Lyapunov exponent [13]. As illustrated in Fig. 3, comparison results of Kolmogorov entropy before and after Logistic homogenization are given. Among them, the value range of the horizontal coordinate $\mu$ is [1.5,4], and the ordinate is the positive Lyapunov exponent of Logistic expression.

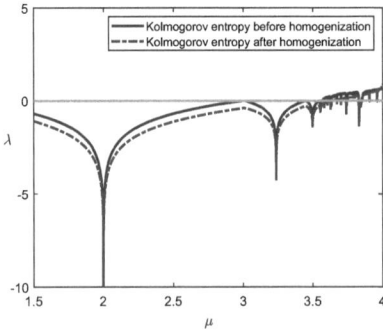

**Fig. 3.** Comparison of $K$ entropy before and after Logistic homogenization

It can be seen from Fig. 3 that the Kolmogorov entropy of the time series generated by homogenizing Logistic mapping shows a downward shift, and the behavioral complexity is also reduced. However, at $\mu = 4$, the change of Kolmogorov entropy is extremely small and basically maintained random characteristics of the original system.

(2) **Approximate entropy**

Approximate entropy represents the possibility of new information emerging within the time series. It uses statistical edge condition probabilities to calculate the degree of randomness of the sequence, thereby reflecting the inherent complexity of the entire sequence. The more complex the time series, the greater the approximate entropy [14]. Approximate entropy ($ApEn$) can be defined as:

$$ApEn = \varphi^P(r) - \varphi^{P+1}(r) \qquad (6)$$

Among them, $P$ is the dimension of the vector, and $r$ is the threshold of the distance.

Then, in this section, we respectively count the approximate entropy of different time series lengths L = 500, 1000, 2000, 3000, and the initial value is 0.33. The results of the calculations are displayed in Table 3.

Table 3. Comparison approximate entropy of three functions

| Sequence length | Rand | Logistic | Homogenizing Logistic |
| --- | --- | --- | --- |
| 500 | Inf | 0.6922 | 0.6600 |
| 1000 | Inf | 0.6809 | 0.6519 |
| 2000 | Inf | 0.6717 | 0.6480 |
| 3000 | Inf | 0.6657 | 0.6479 |

In Table 3, when calculating the approximate entropy of different sequence lengths L, the approximate entropy of the Rand function is Inf (infinite), which has high complexity and good randomness. The *ApEn* of Logistic sequence and homogenizing Logistic sequence decreases with the increase of sequence length. The *ApEn* of the homogenizing Logistic sequence is overall smaller than the other two functions, This leads to a reduction in the behavioral complexity of the series.

(3) **Spectral entropy**

Spectral entropy measures the degree of dispersion or uniformity of energy in the frequency domain by analyzing the distribution of the signal power spectrum. A more uniform power spectrum corresponds to higher spectral entropy, reflecting greater complexity; conversely, less uniform distributions result in lower spectral entropy and reduced complexity. The spectral entropy adopts Fourier transform and combines with Shannon entropy to obtain the corresponding value of spectral entropy [15], the spectral entropy ($se$) can be defined as:

$$se = -\sum_{k=0}^{\frac{n}{2}-1} P_k \ln P_k \qquad (7)$$

Among them, $n$ represents the sequence length, and $P_k$ is the probability of the relative power spectrum.

Then, in this section, we respectively count the *se* of different time series lengths L = 500, 1000, 2000, 3000, and the initial value is 0.33. The calculation results are shown in Table 4 below.

Table 4. Spectral entropy of three functions

| Sequence length | Rand | Logistic | Homogenizing Logistic |
|---|---|---|---|
| 500 | 0.9226 | 0.9231 | 0.9232 |
| 1000 | 0.9318 | 0.9314 | 0.9320 |
| 2000 | 0.9386 | 0.9384 | 0.9388 |
| 3000 | 0.9419 | 0.9419 | 0.9421 |

Table 4 demonstrates that when calculating the *se* for different sequence lengths L, the *se* of the three functions increases as L grows. Overall, the *se* of time series of homogenizing Logistic mapping is greater than other two functions, and the structural complexity of the sequence increases.

In summary, the complexity of the three functions is compared. The Kolmogorov entropy and approximate entropy of the time series generated by homogenizing Logistic mapping are reduced, and the behavioral complexity is reduced. However, the spectral entropy is increased, and the structural complexity is increased. This is because the homogenized Logistic mapping enhances the uniform distribution characteristics of the generated time series, sequence values become more evenly distributed, and behavioral complexity decreases, demonstrating the effectiveness of the Logistic system's time series homogenization proposed in this study. And the increase in structural complexity shows that from the global statistics, the random characteristics of the system are improved.

## 3 NIST Randomness Test

To further validate the good randomness of time series generated by the homogenized Logistic mapping, this section performs the NIST randomness test. This test evaluates the degree of deviation from ideal randomness for the tested sequence across multiple perspectives [16]. So mainly uses NIST sts-2.1.2 to conduct 14 tests on it. Each index does not affect each other and is independent of each other, so as to accurately reflect the random characteristics of the sequence. The results are shown in Table 5.

According to the above table, the P-value of homogenizing Logistic mapping is all greater than 0.0001, and all of them pass the test. All 8 indicators exceed 0.4, indicating that the homogenized Logistic mapping-generated time series exhibit a high level of chaos and retain excellent random properties.

**Table 5.** NIST randomness test results of homogenizing Logistic mapping

| Test index | P-value | Whether to pass | Test index | P-value | Whether to pass |
|---|---|---|---|---|---|
| Frequency test | 0.122325 | Pass | Overlapping module matching test | 0.804337 | Pass |
| In-block frequency test | 0.253551 | Pass | General Statistical Test | 0.100508 | Pass |
| Cumulative test | 0.462665 | Pass | Approximate entropy test | 0.739918 | Pass |
| Run test | 0.407091 | Pass | Random deviation test | 0.475562 | Pass |
| Longest run test | 0.804337 | Pass | Random deviation variable test | 0.585209 | Pass |
| Binary matrix order test | 0.804337 | Pass | Serial test | 0.095920 | Pass |
| Discrete Fourier Transform Spectral Test | 0.082177 | Pass | Linear complexity test | 0.066882 | Pass |

## 4 Chaotic ABC Algorithm Integrating Homogenization and Dynamic Distribution Optimization

### 4.1 SABC Algorithm

The Standard Artificial Bee Colony (SABC) algorithm is a swarm intelligence optimization algorithm inspired by the food-collecting behavior of bees. By simulating the division of labor and collaboration mechanism in bee colonies, the algorithm abstracts the food collection process of bees into a function optimization problem and classifies the colony members into three categories based on their roles: employed bees, onlooker bees, and scout bees. The employed bee is responsible for determining the position of the food sources and sharing the information of food sources with the onlooker bee in the dance area according to a certain probability. The onlooker bees perform local search optimization on candidate solutions corresponding to high-quality food sources based on the quality information transmitted by employed bees, and the scout bees explore unexplored regions in the solution space through random search strategies, avoiding the algorithm from falling into premature convergence [17]. Details are as follows:

(1) **Initialization stage**

In the SABC algorithm, firstly, SN food sources are created in the search space according to formula (8) (number of employed bees = number of onlooker bees = SN/2), and every food source serves as a representation of a feasible solution.

$$X_i^j = X_{min}^j + rand(0,1)(X_{max}^j - X_{min}^j) \tag{8}$$

Among them, $X_i^j$ signifies the current food source position, $i \in \{1,2,\ldots,SN\}, j \in \{1,2,\ldots,D\}$, D denoting the optimization problem's dimension, $X_{max}^j$ is the maximum boundary of the jth dimension, and $X_{min}^j$ is the minimum boundary of the jth dimension.

(2) **The employed bee stage**

The employed bee searches near food sources according to the formula (9), and when a new food source is found, it compares and selects the current optimal food source according to the greed rule.

$$new\_X_i^j = X_i^j + rand()(X_i^j - X_k^j) \qquad (9)$$

Among them, $new\_X_i^j$ denotes the new food source position, $X_i^j$ represents the current food source position, $X_k^j$ signifies a nearby food source position, where $j \in \{1,2,\ldots,D\}$, $K \in \{1,2,\ldots,SN\}$ and $K \neq i$.

(3) **The onlooker bee stage**

Using the food source information shared by employed bees in the dance area, the onlooker bee randomly select a food source to collect in a roulette way. The selection probability is given by:

$$P_i = \frac{fit_i}{\sum_{i=1}^{SN} fit_i} \qquad (10)$$

Among them, $P_i$ is the probability of selecting the ith food source, $fit_i$ is the fitness value of the ith food source, and $fit_i$ is given by formula (11)

$$fit_i = \begin{cases} \frac{1}{1+f_i}, f_i \geq 0 \\ 1 + abs(f_i), f_i < 0 \end{cases} \qquad (11)$$

Among them, $f_i$ is the objective function value of $new\_X_i^j$.

(4) **The scout bee stage**

If the employed bee searches for more than the limited number of times and continues to fail in discovering a superior food source, the employed bee will turn into a scout bee and discard the food source that has been found. Then, a new food source will be randomly selected by the scout bee via formula (8) to replace the original one.

## 4.2 Improvement of SABC Algorithm

The SABC algorithm tends to fall into local optima and exhibits slow convergence when handling high-dimensional complex optimization problems. To address these limitations, this paper proposes HDABC algorithm based on chaotic mapping, dynamic grouping strategy, and hybrid optimization mechanisms. The core improvements include:

**Improvement of initial population**: The initial population is generated by homogenized logistic chaotic mapping, and more diverse solutions are obtained.

**Dynamic grouping adaptive search strategy:** A dynamic grouping mechanism divides the swarm into mining groups, balanced groups, and exploration groups, each adopting differentiated search strategies. To balance exploration and exploitation.

(1) **Improvement of initial population**

Whether the initial population is homogenizing in the swarm intelligence optimization algorithm has an important impact on the search performance of the algorithm [18]. In the initialization stage of the SABC algorithm, the method of generating random numbers by the Rand function is generally used to initialize food sources, but this method is easy to cause the food sources to be missing and cannot guarantee that the food sources is homogenizing and stable throughout the entire feasible region, thereby reducing the search accuracy. Therefore, this paper proposes a method to initialize the food sources by using the homogenizing Logistic mapping, and updates the initialization formula to:

$$\begin{cases} X_{i+1}^j = 4X_i^j\left(1 - X_i^j\right), 0 \leq X_i^j \leq 1 \\ Y_i^j = X_{i+1}^j \\ Y_{i+1}^j = \frac{2}{\pi}\arcsin\left(\sqrt{Y_i^j}\right), 0 \leq Y_i^j \leq 1 \end{cases} \quad (12)$$

Among them, $Y_i^j$ is the current food source position, where $i \in \{1,2,\ldots,SN\}$, $j \in \{1,2,\ldots,D\}$.

To verify whether the initialization method promotes a homogeneous distribution of food sources and lay a solid foundation for global optimization, this paper uses Rand function, Logistic mapping and homogenizing Logistic mapping to generate 10000 time series values each time, which are distributed in 50 intervals of the range, and count the average number of each confidence interval with the number of food sources of 200 and the confidence level of 0.975. After running 10,000 times, the average distribution is shown in Table 6.

**Table 6.** Three random number generation methods produce an average distribution of 200 values

| Function | Proportion of intervals less than 195 | Proportion of intervals between 195–205 | Proportion of intervals greater than 205 |
|---|---|---|---|
| Logistic mapping | 72% | 3% | 25% |
| Rand function | 36% | 29% | 35% |
| Homogenizing Logistic mapping | 27% | 36% | 37% |

In Table 6, the interval probability of 200 values generated by the homogenizing Logistic mapping is 36%, which is greater than the interval probability of the other two functions. This indicates that the time series generated by it has a low missed detection rate, strong randomness and good uniformity. This method of initialization effectively enhances the global pioneering and provides a greater possibility for searching for the best food source.

(2) **Dynamic grouping adaptive search strategy**

The SABC algorithm is a classic swarm intelligence optimization algorithm. By simulating the information-sharing mechanism in bees' foraging behavior and combining local search strategies, it can find the global optimal solution in a short time and has high robustness and reliability. However, when dealing with complex optimization problems such as high-dimensional and multi-modal ones, the SABC algorithm has the risk of imbalance between exploration and exploitation: the single search strategy adopted in the employed bee stage leads to a rapid loss of population diversity, eventually resulting in premature convergence. Therefore, this paper proposes an adaptive dynamic grouping strategy. This strategy achieves synergistic optimization of global exploration and local exploitation by quantifying the population state and differentially assigning search roles. Based on the fitness values of the population during initialization, the population is divided into Group $\alpha$ (exploitation group), Group $\beta$ (balance group), and Group $\gamma$ (exploration group) [19]. Different search strategies are applied to different groups to guide the swarm in optimizing and avoid falling into local optima. The specific process is as follows:

(1) Population diversity measurement

The diversity index $D_t$ is defined as the ratio of the degree of dispersion to the central tendency of the fitness distribution:

$$D_t = \frac{\sigma(f_t)}{\mu(f_t)} \tag{13}$$

where $\sigma(f_t)$ is the standard deviation of the population fitness in the $t$-th generation, and $\mu(f_t)$ is the mean value. A larger $D_t$ indicates higher population diversity, calling for enhanced exploration; conversely, a smaller $D_t$ requires a focus on exploitation.

(2) Dynamic grouping adaptive search strategy

Based on $D_t$ and the iteration process, the population is dynamically adjusted into Groups $\alpha$, $\beta$, and $\gamma$, where Group $\alpha$ is responsible for the exploitation stage, Group $\beta$ for the balance stage, Group $\gamma$ for the exploration stage and *expl* represents the exploration rate. As shown in the following formula. In the high-diversity early stage, *expl* increases, and the proportion of Group $\gamma$ rises to enhance the algorithm's exploration ability. As population diversity decreases in the later stage, *expl* decreases, and the proportion of Group $\alpha$ increases to boost the algorithm's exploitation ability.

$$expl = \min(0.5, \frac{D_t}{0.5} * e^{-iter/maxCycle}) \tag{14}$$

$$\begin{cases} \alpha = pop * (1 - expl) * 0.3 \\ \beta = pop - \alpha - \gamma \\ \gamma = pop * expl \end{cases} \tag{15}$$

where *iter* is the current iteration number, *maxCycle* is the total number of iterations, and *pop* represents the total population size of employed bees.

The three population groups adopt different search strategies according to their distinct roles, thereby achieving the goal of balancing the algorithm's exploration and exploitation phases. Their main functions are shown in Table 7.

Individuals in Group $\alpha$ adopt the following update formula:

$$v_{i,j} = x_{i,j} + \varepsilon\left(gbest_j - x_{i,j}\right) + \varepsilon * rand * (x_{i,j} - x_{k,j}) \tag{16}$$

$$\varepsilon = \max(0.1, \frac{maxCycle - iter}{maxCycle}) \tag{17}$$

where $x_i^j$ is the position of the current food source, $i \in \{1,2,\ldots,SN\}, j \in \{1,2,\ldots,D\}.\varepsilon$ is a dynamic decay coefficient, and $gbest_j$ denotes the $j$-th dimension of the global optimal solution, $k \in \{1,2,\ldots,SN\} and k \neq i$.

Individuals in Group $\beta$ adopt the following update formula:

$$v_{i,j} = \begin{cases} x_{i,j} + \varepsilon\left(x_{elite,j} - x_{i,j}\right) + \varepsilon * rand * \left(x_{r1,j} - x_{r2,j}\right), if rand < cr \\ x_{i,j}, otherwise \end{cases} \tag{18}$$

where $x_{elite,j}$ is the value of the $j$-th dimension of an elite individual (randomly selected from Group $\alpha$, and $x_{r1,j}, x_{r2,j}$ are values of random individuals, with $r1, r2 \in \{1, 2, \ldots, SN\}$ and $r1, r2 \neq i$.

Individuals in Group $\gamma$ adopt the following update formula:

$$v_{i,j} = x_{i,j} + y(iter) * (ub - lb) * (rand - 0.5) * \varepsilon \tag{19}$$

where $y$ is the homogenized logistic sequence generated by Eq. (2), $ub$ and $lb$ are the upper and lower bounds of the solution space, and $(rand - 0.5)$ is a directional random number.

### 4.3 Steps of HDABC Algorithm

The flowchart of this algorithm is as follows (Fig. 4).

**Table 7.** The characteristics of different search strategies

| Group | Search strategy | Characteristics |
| --- | --- | --- |
| Group $\alpha$ | Elite-guided exploitation | This formula guides current individuals toward the global optimal solution through the best solution to enhance the algorithm's exploitation capability. Meanwhile, random perturbations are introduced to maintain population diversity, with the weights of the two components dynamically adjusted by the $\varepsilon$ parameter. |
| Group $\beta$ | Differential crossover evolution | The elite term dominates local search, the random term provides global perturbation, and the crossover probability $cr$ regulates the update frequency, thereby maintaining population diversity. |
| Group $\gamma$ | Chaotic perturbation exploration | Leverage the ergodicity of chaos to enhance the algorithm's exploitation capabilities and prevent it from getting trapped in local optima. |

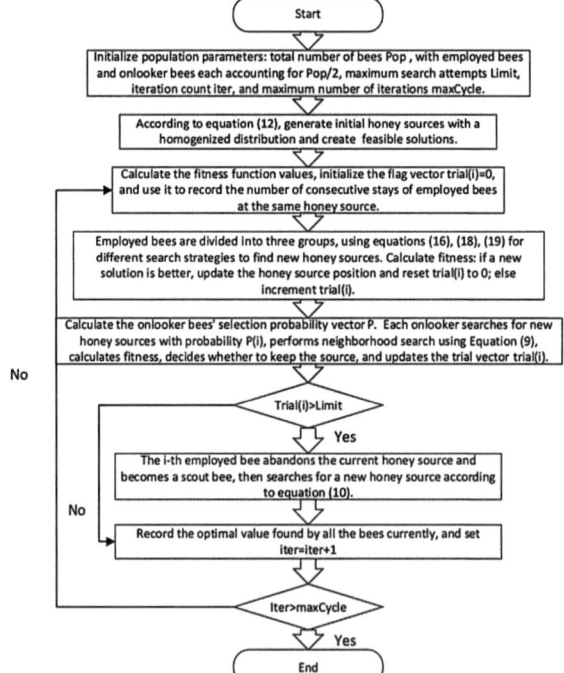

**Fig. 4.** HDABC algorithm flow chart.

### 4.4 Complexity Analysis of HDABC Algorithm

For the time complexity, the time complexity of the ABC algorithm is $O(maxcycle*NP)$. In contrast, the HDABC algorithm proposed in this paper uses a homogenizing time series for traversal search, and its time complexity depends on the length of the generated time series $M$, So the time complexity of the HDABC algorithm is $O(maxcycle * NP + maxcycle * M)$, Among them, maxcycle is the maximum number of iterations, and $NP$ is the number of bee colonies. However, according to the content of the algorithm, there is a linear relationship between the time series $M$ and the number of bees $NP$, that is, $M = NP$. After simplification, the time complexity of the HDABC algorithm is still $O(maxcycle * NP)$, which is consistent with the ABC algorithm.

For the space complexity, the space complexity of the ABC algorithm is $O(NP * D)$, and the number of bee colonies $NP$ and the dimension $D$ in the HDABC algorithm are unchanged, so its space complexity is still $O(NP * D)$.

## 5 Experimental Simulation and Analysis

### 5.1 Selection of Standard Test Function

In order to verify the feasibility and superiority of the improved ABC algorithm, 18 standard test functions (see Table 8) are selected for testing in this paper [20]. Covering unimodal (F1-F4, F13, F17) and multimodal (F5-F11, F14-F16, F18) problems, with the characteristics of smooth, nonsmooth, variable coupling and constraints. The robustness and efficiency of the algorithms are tested through the scenarios of local optimal traps, flat regions, and high-dimensional coupling. And the dimensionality is set to 100 to fully test the advantage of the algorithm in facing the high-dimensional complex problems. Figure 5 is a three-dimensional model diagram of the standard test function (F3, F7, F11).

**Table 8.** Standard test functions

| Function name | Equation | Search range | fmin |
|---|---|---|---|
| Sphere | $f_1(x) = \sum_{i=1}^{n} x_i^2$ | [−100,100] | 0 |
| Schwefel 2.22 | $f_2(x) = \sum_{i=1}^{D} |x_i| + \prod_{i=1}^{D} x_i$ | [−10,10] | 0 |
| Schwefel 2.21 | $f_3(x) = \max\{|x_i|, 1 \le i \le D\}$ | [−100,100] | 0 |
| Step | $f_4(x) = \sum_{i=1}^{D} [x_i + 0.5]^2$ | [−100,100] | 0 |
| Generalized Rastrigin | $f_5(x) = \sum_{i=1}^{D} [x_i^2 - 10\cos(2\pi x_i) + 10]$ | [−5.12,5.12] | 0 |
| Ackley1 | $f_6(x) = -20\exp\left(-0.2\sqrt{\frac{1}{D}\sum_{i=1}^{D} x_i^2}\right) - \exp\left(\frac{1}{D}\sum_{i=1}^{D} \cos 2\pi x_i\right) + 20 + e$ | [−32,32] | 0 |
| Generalized Griewank | $f_7(x) = \frac{1}{4000}\sum_{i=1}^{D} x_i^2 - \prod_{i=1}^{D} \cos\left(\frac{x_i}{\sqrt{i}}\right) + 1$ | [−600,600] | 0 |
| Generalized Penalized 1 | $f_8(x) = \frac{\pi}{D}\left\{10\sin^2(\pi y_1) + \sum_{i}^{D-1} (y_i - 1)^2[1 + 10\sin^2(\pi y_{i+1})] + (y_D - 1)^2\right\} + \sum_{i=1}^{D} u(x_i, 10, 100, 4)$ | [−50,50] | 0 |
| Generalized Penalized 2 | $f_9(x) = 0.1\left\{\sin^2(\pi 3x_1) + \sum_{i}^{D-1} (x_i - 1)^2[1 + \sin^2(3\pi x_{i+1})] + (x_D - 1)^2[1 + \sin^2(2\pi x_D)]\right\} + \sum_{i=1}^{D} u(x_i, 5, 100, 4)$ | [−50,50] | 0 |
| Rastrigin | $f_{10}(x) = 10D + \sum_{i=1}^{D} [x_i^2 - 10\cos(2\pi x_i)]$ | [−5.12,5.12] | 0 |

(continued)

**Table 8.** (*continued*)

| Function name | Equation | Search range | fmin |
|---|---|---|---|
| Schwefel | $f_{11}(x) = 418.9829D - \sum_{i=1}^{D} x_i \sin(\sqrt{|x_i|})$ | [−500,500] | 0 |
| Rotated Hyper-Ellipsoid | $f_{12}(x) = \sum_{i=1}^{D} \sum_{j=1}^{i} x_j^2$ | [-65.536,65.536] | 0 |
| Sum of Different Powers | $f_{13}(x) = \sum_{i=1}^{D} |x_i|^{i+1}$ | [−1,1] | 0 |
| Zakharov | $f_{14}(x) = \sum_{i=1}^{D} x_i^2 + (\sum_{i=1}^{D} 0.5ix_i)^2 + (\sum_{i=1}^{D} 0.5ix_i)^4$ | [−5,10] | 0 |
| Dixon-Price | $f_{15}(x) = (x_1 - 1)^2 + \sum_{i=2}^{D} i(2x_i^2 - x_{i-1})^2$ | [−10,10] | 0 |
| Powell | $f_{16}(x) = \sum_{i=1}^{D/4}[(x_{4i-3} + 10x_{4i-2})^2 + 5(x_{4i-1} - x_{4i})^2 + (x_{4i-2} - 2x_{4i-1})^4 + 10(x_{4i-3} - x_{4i})^4]$ | [−4,5] | 0 |
| Rosenbrock | $f_{17}(x) = \sum_{i=1}^{D-1}[100(x_{i+1} - x_i^2)^2 + (x_i - 1)^2]$ | [−2.048,2.048] | 0 |
| Trid | $f_{18}(x) = \sum_{i=1}^{D}(x_i - 1)^2 - \sum_{i=2}^{D} x_i x_{i-1}$ | [$-D^2, D^2$] | $-D(D+4)(D-1)/6$ |

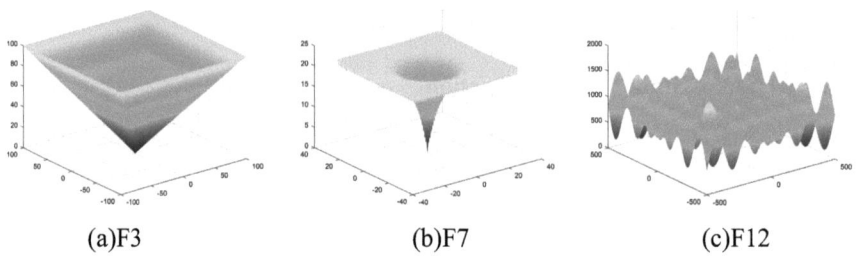

(a)F3  (b)F7  (c)F12

**Fig. 5.** Three-dimensional model diagram of the standard test function

### 5.2 Effectiveness Analysis of Improvement Strategies

In order to systematically evaluate the impact of different improvement strategies on the optimization performance of ABC algorithm, the following three algorithms are selected for comparative analysis: standard ABC (SABC), improved ABC algorithm based on single homogenized logistic initial population distribution (HABC), and ABC algorithm based on improved dynamic grouping strategy on the basis of HABC algorithm (HDABC). The experiments were based on 18 standard test functions with uniform parameter settings of $Pop = 100$ for population size, $MaxCycle = 1000$ for maximum number of iterations, and $Dim = 100$ for search space. To eliminate the randomness interference, all algorithms were run independently 51 times, and the optimal value, worst value, mean value, and standard deviation were recorded. The experimental results are shown in Table 9. To further quantify the specific degree of improvement of the algorithm, the method proposed by Bolufé - Röhler et al. in the literature [21] is introduced, by which the relative performance improvement of the algorithms before and after the application of the improved strategy is calculate. The specific calculation formula is as follows:

$$\mu = \frac{a - b}{\max(a, b)} * 100\% \qquad (20)$$

A Novel Homogenization-Based Method for Population Initialization 139

where $a$ denotes the optimization result of the original algorithm and $b$ denotes the optimization result of the improved algorithm. The calculation results are shown in Table 9.

**Table 9.** Optimization performance improvement rate based on different strategies

| Func | SABC | HABC | %-diff | HABC | HDABC | %-diff |
|---|---|---|---|---|---|---|
| 1 | 3.74E-03 | 1.04E-13 | 100% | 1.04E-13 | 2.89E-16 | 99.7% |
| 2 | 5.62E-02 | 3.92E-08 | 100% | 3.92E-08 | 3.98E-13 | 100% |
| 3 | 8.29E+01 | 6.74E+01 | 18.8% | 6.74E+01 | 34.70244 | 48.5% |
| 4 | 3.79E-03 | 8.04E-02 | -95.3% | 8.04E-02 | 1.106294 | -92.7% |
| 5 | 6.30E+01 | 5.55E-13 | 100% | 5.55E-13 | 0 | 100% |
| 6 | 2.53E+00 | 4.27E-08 | 100% | 4.27E-08 | 1.42E-11 | 100% |
| 7 | 4.76E-01 | 4.34E-04 | 99.9% | 4.34E-04 | 1.98E-16 | 100% |
| 8 | 1.42E-03 | 8.12E-04 | 42.8% | 8.12E-04 | 0.006925 | -88.3% |
| 9 | 2.31E-03 | 5.05E-02 | -95.4% | 5.05E-02 | 0.575319 | -91.2% |
| 10 | 7.10E+01 | 6.43E-01 | 99.1% | 6.43E-01 | 0 | 100% |
| 11 | 7.07E+03 | 1.06E+04 | -33.3% | 1.06E+04 | 23854.83 | -55.6% |
| 12 | 1.14E-01 | 1.05E-12 | 100% | 1.05E-12 | 3.16E-16 | 100% |
| 13 | 1.01E-09 | 7.59E-17 | 100% | 7.59E-17 | 6.95E-17 | 8.42% |
| 14 | 1.39E+03 | 1.02E+03 | 26.4% | 1.02E+03 | 484.6462 | 52.6% |
| 15 | 2.93E+01 | 9.24E-01 | 96.8% | 9.24E-01 | 0.667461 | 27.8% |
| 16 | 1.37E+01 | 1.22E+01 | 11.1% | 1.22E+01 | 20.07716 | -39.3% |
| 17 | 2.80E+02 | 9.71E+01 | 65.3% | 9.71E+01 | 96.97681 | 0.125% |
| 18 | 1.37E+07 | 3.35E+06 | 75.6% | 3.35E+06 | 602902 | 82% |

From the above experimental results, it can be seen that in the performance comparison of the three algorithms, SABC, HABC and HDABC, the improvement strategy has a significant impact on the performance of the algorithms. For most of the test functions, HABC shows an outstanding performance improvement compared to SABC. For example, for Func 1, the optimization result of SABC is 3.74E - 03, while that of HABC is 1.04E - 13, which is a 100% improvement, demonstrating the effectiveness of improving the population optimization performance by improving the initial population distribution.

Further observation of the HDABC algorithm, which is continuously optimized on the basis of HABC, shows very impressive performance in several function tests. In Func 2, 5, 6, 7, 10 and 12, HDABC achieves 100% improvement over HABC, and finds the theoretical optimal solution in Func 5 and Func 10. Although in some of the function tests, the percentage of performance improvement is negative, which indicates that the improvement effect is not good or even performance degradation occurs in certain cases, in general, HDABC achieves performance improvement in most of the 18 tested functions, which fully demonstrates the effectiveness and potential of the improvement strategy in most of the scenarios. In summary, by improving the initial distribution and search strategy, HABC and HDABC optimize the performance of the algorithms to different degrees, and significantly improve the convergence accuracy and robustness of the algorithms in most scenarios.

## 6 Algorithm Convergence and Optimization Results

### 6.1 Convergence Analysis of the Algorithm

This section uses the method of drawing the convergence curve to compare HDABC algorithm, HABC algorithm, SABC algorithm, Particle Swarm Optimization algorithm (PSO) [22], Snow Ablation Optimizer algorithm (SAO) [23] and Ant Colony Optimization algorithm (ACO) [24] in 18 standard test functions. The specific settings are as follows: the population size of the all algorithms $Pop = 100$, the dimension $Dim = 100$, the number of iterations $MaxCycle = 1000$, the upper limit of neighborhood search is $limit = 300$, and the initial values of the HDABC algorithm and the HABC algorithm are 0.75. In the ACO algorithm, the pheromone play coefficient is 0.85. In the PSO algorithm, the maximum particle velocity $Vmax = 6$, the inertia weight $wMax = 0.5$ and $wMin = 0.2$. Through experimental simulation, six functions were selected for analysis, and the convergence curve comparison diagram of Fig. 6(a) ~ (f) was obtained. The horizontal coordinate is the number of iterations of the test function, the upper limit is set to 1000, and the vertical coordinate is the average fitness value of 51 experiments.

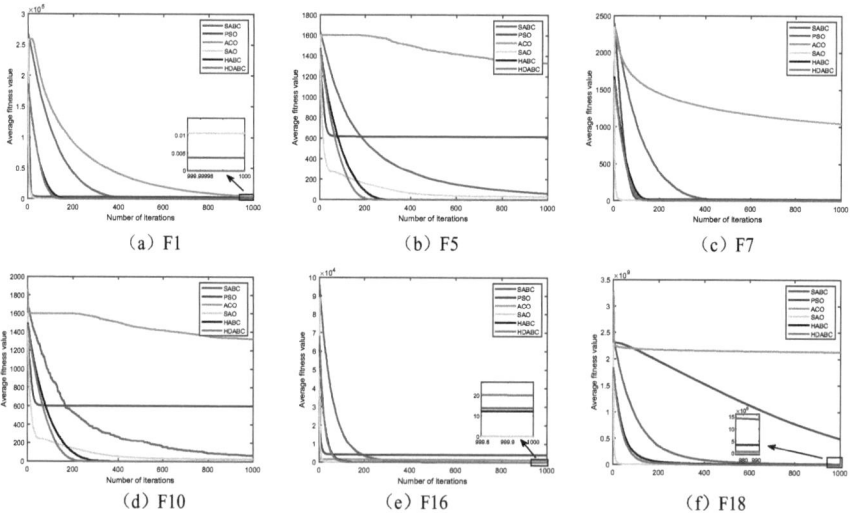

**Fig. 6.** Comparison of convergence curves of six algorithms

As shown in Fig. 6, the improved HABC and HDABC algorithms demonstrate significant competitiveness in most of the test functions. In the single-peak function F1,

SAO and PSO achieve the fastest fitness decrease at the beginning of the iteration, while HABC and HDABC perform second but better than SABC, as the iteration enters the middle stage, the HABC and HDABC algorithms make the fitness values significantly lower than the comparison algorithms through efficient local development, and finally HDABC reaches the lowest fitness value. In the multi-peak functions (F5, F7, F10), SAO maintains the lead at the beginning of the iteration, but HDABC and HABC begin to show their advantages in the middle of the iteration: In F5, where there are multiple local optima, they successfully jump out of the trap of the local optima, and HDABC converges to the theoretical optimum eventually; For F7, where there is strong coupling between variables, HDABC achieves efficient convergence by virtue of its outstanding local search accuracy; and in F10, HDABC also achieves the global optimum with the lowest fitness value. For high-dimensional complex functions F16 and F18, the overall convergence of the improved algorithm is slightly inferior to that of SAO, but still significantly better than SABC and other comparative algorithms. The experimental results show that HABC and HDABC achieve an effective balance between global exploration and local exploitation in six types of test functions, and their optimization accuracies are significantly better than those of the traditional SABC algorithm and most of the comparative algorithms, and they are only slightly inferior to SAO in two test functions.

## 6.2 Analysis of Algorithm Optimization Results

This section selects four measurement indicators: optimal value, worst value, average value, and variance. Through experimental simulation, the optimization results of HDABC algorithm, HABC algorithm, SABC algorithm, PSO algorithm, SAO algorithm and ACO algorithm are comprehensively compared to fully verify the search performance of HDABC algorithm. The parameter settings are the same as those in Sect. 6.1. After each test function is run 51 times, the corresponding measurement indicators are obtained. The optimization results of HDABC algorithm, HABC algorithm, SABC algorithm, PSO algorithm, SAO algorithm and ACO algorithm are shown in Table 10. The comparison of statistical results of different algorithms under optimal value, worst value, average value and variance index are presented in Fig. 7. For the performance comparison of different optimization algorithms on standard test functions, the radar chart is depicted in Fig. 8. Given the significant order-of-magnitude differences in the experimental results of each algorithm on the test functions, the data in the figure are standardized by taking the logarithm base 10 of the original results ($y = \log_{10} x$) to facilitate multi-indicator visual comparison. The box plots of the four test functions are shown in Fig. 9.

**Table 10.** Comparison of optimization results of standard test functions

| Function | Algorithms | Optimum value | Worst value | Average value | Variance |
|---|---|---|---|---|---|
| F1 | SABC | 1.37E-03 | 1.23E-02 | 3.74E-03 | 2.07E-03 |
| | PSO | 2.36E + 03 | 5.37E + 03 | 3.42E + 03 | 6.58E + 02 |
| | ACO | 2.69E + 03 | 6.31E + 03 | 4.34E + 03 | 8.17E + 02 |

(continued)

**Table 10.** (*continued*)

| Function | Algorithms | Optimum value | Worst value | Average value | Variance |
|---|---|---|---|---|---|
| | SAO | 2.86E-04 | 4.67E-02 | 1.06E-02 | 8.71E-03 |
| | HABC | 2.32E-15 | 7.50E-13 | 1.04E-13 | 1.51E-13 |
| | HDABC | 9.83E-17 | 5.51E-16 | **2.89E-16** | 8.89E-17 |
| F2 | SABC | 3.63E-02 | 8.59E-02 | 5.62E-02 | 1.10E-02 |
| | PSO | 1.45E + 02 | 2.70E + 02 | 1.97E + 02 | 3.03E + 01 |
| | ACO | 4.59E + 13 | 9.67E + 24 | 2.93E + 23 | 1.41E + 24 |
| | SAO | 2.05E-03 | 3.05E-02 | 7.93E-03 | 4.51E-03 |
| | HABC | 5.37E-09 | 1.29E-07 | 3.92E-08 | 2.89E-08 |
| | HDABC | 3.14E-15 | 8.31E-12 | **3.98E-13** | 1.17E-12 |
| F3 | SABC | 7.48E + 01 | 8.82E + 01 | 8.29E + 01 | 2.88E + 00 |
| | PSO | 1.31E + 01 | 2.14E + 01 | 1.72E + 01 | 1.73E + 00 |
| | ACO | 6.38E + 01 | 7.58E + 01 | 7.15E + 01 | 2.12E + 00 |
| | SAO | 2.07E + 00 | 3.37E + 01 | **1.26E + 01** | 5.14E + 00 |
| | HABC | 4.88E + 01 | 7.79E + 01 | 6.74E + 01 | 8.20E + 00 |
| | HDABC | 26.24487 | 54.71222 | 34.70244 | 4.913596 |
| F4 | SABC | 6.78E-04 | 1.58E-02 | **3.79E-03** | 2.98E-03 |
| | PSO | 2.36E + 03 | 4.70E + 03 | 3.58E + 03 | 6.34E + 02 |
| | ACO | 2.22E + 03 | 6.46E + 03 | 4.09E + 03 | 9.06E + 02 |
| | SAO | 3.56E-04 | 5.90E-02 | 1.09E-02 | 1.08E-02 |
| | HABC | 3.96E-02 | 1.65E-01 | 8.04E-02 | 2.56E-02 |
| | HDABC | 7.27E-01 | 1.66E + 00 | 1.11E + 00 | 2.02E-01 |
| F5 | SABC | 4.24E + 01 | 8.35E + 01 | 6.30E + 01 | 7.46E + 00 |
| | PSO | 4.93E + 02 | 7.22E + 02 | 6.16E + 02 | 5.03E + 01 |
| | ACO | 1.22E + 03 | 1.39E + 03 | 1.33E + 03 | 3.53E + 01 |
| | SAO | 2.77E-04 | 1.20E + 02 | 3.38E + 01 | 2.66E + 01 |
| | HABC | 2.27E-13 | 1.14E-12 | 5.55E-13 | 1.91E-13 |
| | HDABC | 0.00E + 00 | 0.00E + 00 | **0.00E + 00** | 0.00E + 00 |
| F6 | SABC | 1.73E + 00 | 3.10E + 00 | 2.53E + 00 | 3.21E-01 |
| | PSO | 1.12E + 01 | 1.40E + 01 | 1.24E + 01 | 6.31E-01 |
| | ACO | 2.00E + 01 | 2.00E + 01 | 2.00E + 01 | 5.28E-04 |
| | SAO | 2.67E-03 | 2.30E-02 | 8.88E-03 | 4.91E-03 |
| | HABC | 7.50E-09 | 1.77E-07 | 4.27E-08 | 3.02E-08 |
| | HDABC | 2.69E-12 | 3.36E-11 | **1.42E-11** | 7.92E-12 |
| F7 | SABC | 1.32E-01 | 8.63E-01 | 4.76E-01 | 2.11E-01 |

(*continued*)

**Table 10.** (*continued*)

| Function | Algorithms | Optimum value | Worst value | Average value | Variance |
|---|---|---|---|---|---|
| | PSO | 1.40E + 01 | 2.77E + 01 | 2.03E + 01 | 3.32E + 00 |
| | ACO | 8.89E + 02 | 1.17E + 03 | 1.04E + 03 | 7.08E + 01 |
| | SAO | 2.91E-02 | 9.98E-01 | 3.04E-01 | 2.40E-01 |
| | HABC | 2.96E-13 | 1.65E-02 | 4.34E-04 | 2.42E-03 |
| | HDABC | 0.00E + 00 | 1.44E-15 | **1.98E-16** | 2.67E-16 |
| F8 | SABC | 1.09E-05 | 3.13E-02 | 1.42E-03 | 6.12E-03 |
| | PSO | 1.59E + 01 | 1.59E + 04 | 6.27E + 02 | 2.35E + 03 |
| | ACO | 6.41E + 03 | 1.32E + 05 | 5.75E + 04 | 3.25E + 04 |
| | SAO | 2.50E-06 | 1.87E-01 | 1.81E-02 | 3.91E-02 |
| | HABC | 3.53E-04 | 2.10E-03 | **8.12E-04** | 4.09E-04 |
| | HDABC | 3.79E-03 | 1.72E-02 | 6.93E-03 | 2.45E-03 |
| F9 | SABC | 2.76E-04 | 1.24E-02 | **2.31E-03** | 3.68E-03 |
| | PSO | 5.65E + 04 | 1.27E + 06 | 4.41E + 05 | 2.58E + 05 |
| | ACO | 2.65E + 05 | 1.39E + 06 | 8.30E + 05 | 2.53E + 05 |
| | SAO | 2.47E-04 | 2.35E + 01 | 1.94E + 00 | 4.78E + 00 |
| | HABC | 1.93E-02 | 9.56E-02 | 5.05E-02 | 1.74E-02 |
| | HDABC | 2.82E-01 | 9.70E-01 | 5.75E-01 | 1.11E-01 |
| F10 | SABC | 3.77E + 01 | 1.29E + 02 | 7.10E + 01 | 2.06E + 01 |
| | PSO | 5.05E + 02 | 6.69E + 02 | 6.00E + 02 | 3.89E + 01 |
| | ACO | 1.22E + 03 | 1.36E + 03 | 1.32E + 03 | 2.74E + 01 |
| | SAO | 4.55E-03 | 7.96E + 01 | 2.74E + 01 | 1.81E + 01 |
| | HABC | 0.00E + 00 | 1.41E + 01 | 6.43E-01 | 2.46E + 00 |
| | HDABC | 0.00E + 00 | 0.00E + 00 | **0.00E + 00** | 0.00E + 00 |
| F11 | SABC | 5.20E + 03 | 1.08E + 04 | **7.07E + 03** | 1.38E + 03 |
| | PSO | 2.83E + 04 | 3.66E + 04 | 3.38E + 04 | 1.72E + 03 |
| | ACO | 1.52E + 04 | 1.86E + 04 | 1.67E + 04 | 8.73E + 02 |
| | SAO | 7.57E + 03 | 1.34E + 04 | 1.05E + 04 | 1.28E + 03 |
| | HABC | 7.62E + 03 | 4.06E + 04 | 1.06E + 04 | 4.87E + 03 |
| | HDABC | 1.43E + 04 | 2.44E + 04 | 2.39E + 04 | 1.38E + 03 |
| F12 | SABC | 2.78E-02 | 6.36E-01 | 1.14E-01 | 1.14E-01 |
| | PSO | 6.84E + 04 | 1.44E + 05 | 1.01E + 05 | 1.63E + 04 |
| | ACO | 7.18E + 04 | 1.13E + 05 | 9.10E + 04 | 1.02E + 04 |
| | SAO | 1.63E-02 | 7.08E-01 | 1.49E-01 | 1.51E-01 |
| | HABC | 2.27E-14 | 4.95E-12 | 1.05E-12 | 1.05E-12 |

(*continued*)

**Table 10.** (*continued*)

| Function | Algorithms | Optimum value | Worst value | Average value | Variance |
|---|---|---|---|---|---|
| F13 | HDABC | 8.37E-17 | 7.66E-16 | **3.16E-16** | 1.10E-16 |
|  | SABC | 3.77E-13 | 1.99E-08 | 1.01E-09 | 2.92E-09 |
|  | PSO | 1.24E-08 | 3.28E-06 | 6.85E-07 | 7.66E-07 |
|  | ACO | 5.87E-01 | 1.89E + 00 | 1.16E + 00 | 2.98E-01 |
|  | SAO | 4.84E-19 | 6.29E-13 | 1.82E-14 | 8.94E-14 |
|  | HABC | 6.73E-18 | 1.11E-16 | 7.59E-17 | 2.73E-17 |
| F14 | HDABC | 4.20E-18 | 1.11E-16 | **6.95E-17** | 3.27E-17 |
|  | SABC | 1.17E + 03 | 1.50E + 03 | 1.39E + 03 | 6.89E + 01 |
|  | PSO | 1.16E + 03 | 3.36E + 03 | 2.00E + 03 | 5.46E + 02 |
|  | ACO | 1.43E + 03 | 1.76E + 03 | 1.62E + 03 | 7.55E + 01 |
|  | SAO | 7.41E + 01 | 6.48E + 02 | **3.24E + 02** | 1.38E + 02 |
|  | HABC | 8.52E + 02 | 1.20E + 03 | 1.02E + 03 | 9.95E + 01 |
| F15 | HDABC | 3.15E + 02 | 6.70E + 02 | 4.84E + 02 | 9.34E + 01 |
|  | SABC | 1.03E + 01 | 5.08E + 01 | 2.93E + 01 | 1.02E + 01 |
|  | PSO | 3.38E + 05 | 1.16E + 06 | 7.03E + 05 | 2.07E + 05 |
|  | ACO | 6.14E + 05 | 1.07E + 06 | 8.69E + 05 | 1.02E + 05 |
|  | SAO | 6.68E-01 | 1.33E + 01 | 1.09E + 00 | 1.78E + 00 |
|  | HABC | 6.67E-01 | 4.64E + 00 | 9.24E-01 | 6.60E-01 |
| F16 | HDABC | 6.67E-01 | 6.89E-01 | **6.67E-01** | 3.22E-03 |
|  | SABC | 1.59E + 00 | 5.28E + 01 | 1.37E + 01 | 1.21E + 01 |
|  | PSO | 1.46E + 03 | 5.72E + 03 | 4.01E + 03 | 8.63E + 02 |
|  | ACO | 1.15E + 03 | 1.28E + 03 | 1.23E + 03 | 2.92E + 01 |
|  | SAO | 2.74E-03 | 9.48E-02 | **2.76E-02** | 1.89E-02 |
|  | HABC | 1.12E-01 | 4.26E + 01 | 1.22E + 01 | 1.25E + 01 |
| F17 | HDABC | 3.67E-01 | 5.39E + 01 | 2.01E + 01 | 1.31E + 01 |
|  | SABC | 1.49E + 02 | 3.73E + 02 | 2.80E + 02 | 4.57E + 01 |
|  | PSO | 1.28E + 03 | 2.79E + 03 | 1.99E + 03 | 3.48E + 02 |
|  | ACO | 1.80E + 04 | 2.83E + 04 | 2.40E + 04 | 1.84E + 03 |
|  | SAO | 9.59E + 01 | 9.68E + 01 | **9.63E + 01** | 1.98E-01 |
|  | HABC | 9.51E + 01 | 9.88E + 01 | 9.71E + 01 | 7.55E-01 |
| F18 | HDABC | 9.55E + 01 | 9.77E + 01 | 9.70E + 01 | 5.50E-01 |
|  | SABC | 6.96E + 06 | 2.19E + 07 | 1.37E + 07 | 3.48E + 06 |
|  | PSO | 4.41E + 08 | 5.58E + 08 | 4.95E + 08 | 2.24E + 07 |
|  | ACO | 1.80E + 09 | 2.35E + 09 | 2.13E + 09 | 1.29E + 08 |

(*continued*)

**Table 10.** (*continued*)

| Function | Algorithms | Optimum value | Worst value | Average value | Variance |
|---|---|---|---|---|---|
| | SAO | 4.55E + 03 | 7.59E + 04 | **1.66E + 04** | 1.69E + 04 |
| | HABC | 3.26E + 05 | 9.29E + 06 | 3.35E + 06 | 1.95E + 06 |
| | HDABC | 4.28E + 03 | 3.28E + 06 | 6.03E + 05 | 7.61E + 05 |

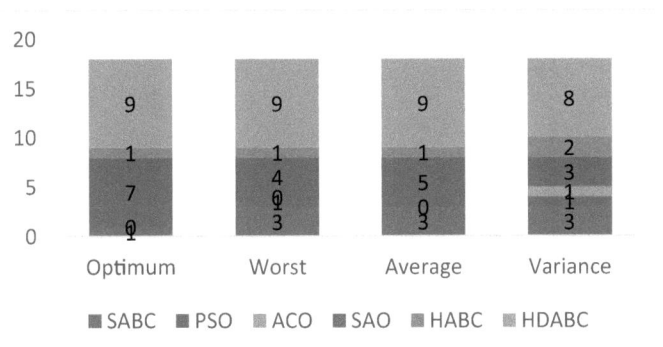

**Fig. 7.** The comparison of statistical results of different algorithms under optimal value, worst value, average value and variance index.

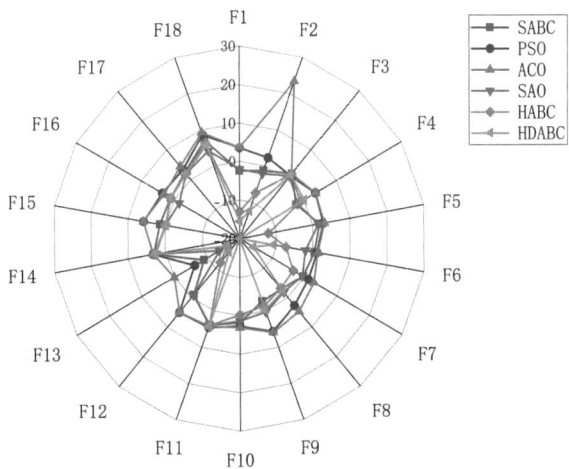

**Fig. 8.** Radar chart for performance comparison of different optimization algorithms on standard test functions.

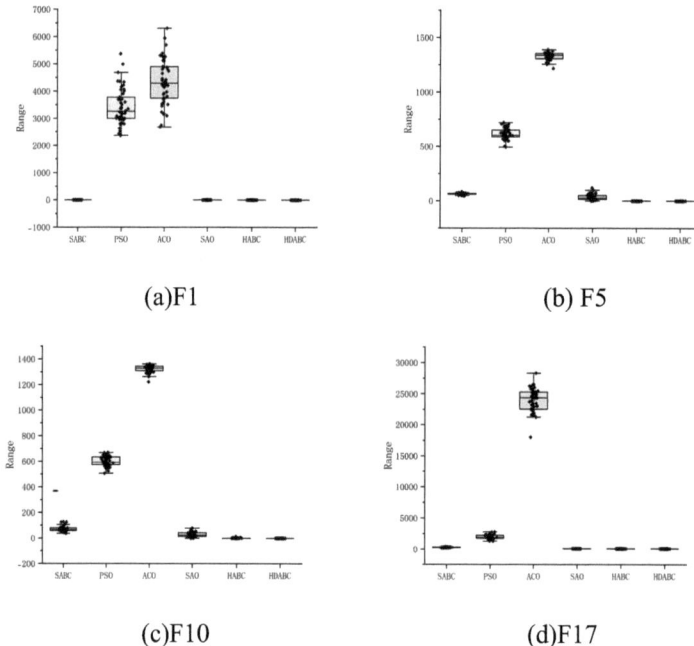

**Fig. 9.** Box plots of four test functions.

From Table 10, it can be seen that the improved algorithm HDABC shows a significant advantage over the other compared algorithms on the standard test set. It can reach the theoretical optimal value on both F5 and F10. In many test function scenarios, such as F1, F2, F6, F7, F12, etc., the optimization results of HDABC algorithm are infinitely close to the theoretical optimal value compared with other algorithms, and the optimization accuracy of HDABC algorithm is improved by more than ten times compared with SABC algorithm, and the stability of HDABC algorithm is also better, and the worst and variance of HDABC algorithm is significantly lower than that of other algorithms in most of test functions. Especially in complex scenarios, HDABC algorithm is less volatile and more robust. In terms of comprehensive performance, HDABC algorithm also performs well. When facing high-dimensional complex multi-peak problems, such as F16 and F18 functions, it can effectively break the strong coupling relationship between variables, and not only locate the potential region by global search, but also accurately optimize through the local development ability, and the optimization result is only second to the SAO algorithm proposed in 2023.

When we further consider the statistical charts of the optimal value, worst value, average value, and variance in Fig. 7, it can be seen that the HDABC algorithm has a relatively large number of advantages in these four key indicators and shows stable performance. This further and fully demonstrates that the algorithm can maintain good performance in different test scenarios and has strong robustness. As for the SAO algorithm, although its optimal value statistic reaches 7, indicating a certain advantage in finding the optimal value, it can be seen from the worst value statistic and the variance statistic that the SAO algorithm has poor stability and a relatively high probability of obtaining inferior results. From Fig. 8, it is evident that HDABC is closer to the center of the radar chart across multiple test functions. Compared with other algorithms, it exhibits better values in these functions and has the smallest comprehensive area. This indicates that HDABC conducts optimization more efficiently in corresponding test scenarios, demonstrates outstanding performance in terms of convergence speed or accuracy, possesses stronger adaptability to different optimization scenarios, and highlights its performance advantages. As can be seen from the box plot in Fig. 9, the box range of the box plot of the improved algorithm is relatively narrow, which indicates that the data dispersion degree is low, that is, the variance is relatively small. Moreover, from the position of the optimized value in the box plot and the overall distribution trend, the optimized values obtained by the improved algorithm in multiple experiments are relatively concentrated, with a small fluctuation range, showing a relatively stable performance. In conclusion, the HDABC algorithm obtained by improving the initial population and the search strategy is effective. Through the reasonable allocation of the population distribution, a full balance is achieved between the two stages of global search and local development, thereby significantly enhancing the optimization performance of the algorithm.

## 7 Example of Logistics Distribution

### 7.1 Model Description

With the continuous development of today's major logistics companies, the logistics and distribution business has also improved. How to reduce transportation costs, increase service revenue, and rationally optimize the company's distribution routes on the premise of ensuring distribution efficiency, so as to save time and effort, increase income and reduce expenditure, which has become a problem that my country's logistics companies urgently need to solve.

The essence of the logistics distribution problem is the TSP problem [25], that is, given the distance between every two points in n distribution points, a delivery person starts from the distribution center and visits each distribution point only once, and finally returns to the distribution center, making the distribution route is the shortest. It is worth noting that the delivery person starts from the distribution center to the end of returning to the distribution center, the route taken by the delivery person cannot be repeated. The final distribution plan should be the shortest distance, that is, the cost is the smallest.

From the mathematical model: The demand point is set to n. In order to achieve the minimum distance traversing each demand point, each demand point is set to $X = \{v_1, v_2, \ldots, v_n\}$. Among them, the distance between demand points can be expressed as $d = (v_i, v_j), i, j \in n$ and $i \neq j$. the objective function is $T = \sum_{i=1}^{n-1} d(v_i, v_{i+1}) + d(v_i, v_n)$, which finds the shortest path $T_{min}$ after traversing all demand points[26].

### 7.2 Analysis of Example

Take 14 distribution points in a certain city as an example. Their location coordinates are shown in Table 11. In a 100x100 area, the model of TSP logistics distribution is established. And this section uses the HDABC algorithm, SABC algorithm, HABC algorithm, PSO algorithm, SAO algorithm and ACO algorithm mentioned in this article to solve the relevant distribution routes, which gets the optimized path of each algorithm. The operating environment and setting parameters are the same as in the previous section. The original route diagram is shown in Fig. 10, and the optimized route diagram is shown in Fig. 11. The optimal total path length, the worst total path length, the mean value of the total path length and the mean square error of the total path length are obtained after 30 independent optimization of the six algorithms. As shown in Table 12.

**Table 11.** The coordinates of 14 nodes

| nodal | 1 | 2 | 3 | 4 | 5 | 6 | 7 |
|---|---|---|---|---|---|---|---|
| X | 16.47 | 16.47 | 20.09 | 22.39 | 25.23 | 22.00 | 20.47 |
| Y | 96.10 | 94.44 | 92.54 | 93.37 | 97.24 | 96.05 | 97.02 |
| nodal | 8 | 9 | 10 | 11 | 12 | 13 | 14 |
| X | 17.20 | 16.30 | 14.05 | 16.53 | 21.52 | 19.41 | 20.09 |
| Y | 96.29 | 97.38 | 98.12 | 97.38 | 95.59 | 97.13 | 94.55 |

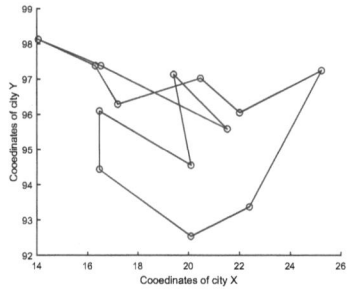

**Fig. 10.** The original route diagram for TSP problem.

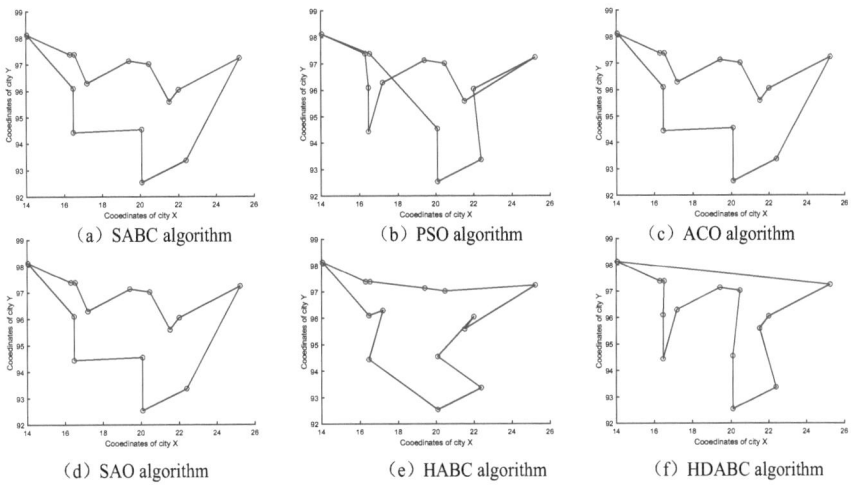

Fig. 11. The optimized route diagram for TSP problem.

Table 12. The optimized length of 14 nodes

| Algorithm | Optimal value | Worst value | Average value | Mean square error |
| --- | --- | --- | --- | --- |
| SABC | 3.09E + 01 | 3.09E + 01 | 3.09E + 01 | 1.19E-14 |
| PSO | 3.43E + 01 | 3.77E + 01 | 3.57E + 01 | 9.26E-01 |
| ACO | 3.09E + 01 | 3.12E + 01 | 3.09E + 01 | 1.38E-01 |
| SAO | 3.41E + 01 | 3.73E + 01 | 3.60E + 01 | 8.54E-01 |
| HABC | 2.44E + 01 | 2.56E + 01 | 2.45E + 01 | 3.10E-01 |
| HDABC | **2.44E + 01** | 2.50E + 01 | **2.44E + 01** | 1.22E-01 |

Through six different algorithms to solve the shortest path of the logistics distribution problem, Figs. 10 and 11 respectively show the path diagrams of the distribution points before and after optimization. It can be clearly seen from the figures that the optimized paths found by the HDABC algorithm and the HABC algorithm are the simplest and have the shortest distances. As can be seen from Table 12, the four algorithms, namely SABC, PSO, ACO, and SAO, have not found the theoretical optimal path, and there is a certain gap in terms of path length compared with the HDABC algorithm and the HABC algorithm. However, both the HABC and HDABC algorithms have successfully found the theoretical optimal path. Among them, the path length found by the HDABC algorithm is superior to that of the HABC algorithm in terms of indicators such as the worst value, average value, and variance. The above data fully illustrate the algorithm stability and robustness of the HDABC algorithm in solving the logistics distribution problem. Therefore, the HDABC algorithm proposed in this paper effectively solves the path planning problem of logistics distribution, significantly optimizes the distribution routes, and thus reduces the freight cost.

## 8 Conclusion

This paper studies a novel homogenization-based optimization method for population initialization of improved chaotic ABC. Firstly, according to the maximum entropy principle and the results of the NIST randomness test, it is ensured that the distribution of the time series generated by the homogenizing Logistic mapping is homogenizing and random. The homogenizing time series is introduced in the initialization stage of the ABC algorithm, Ensuring that feasible solutions are uniformly and randomly distributed across the entire solution space as iterations progress. The global pioneering is increased. Secondly, a dynamic grouping strategy was designed. By grouping the population according to requirements and designing corresponding search formulas, the convergence speed and accuracy of the algorithm are ensured. Finally, after analyzing the distribution of the initial food sources and the advantages of the traversal search strategy, the feasibility of the algorithm in this paper is verified through the convergence curve, iterative value and optimization results. This algorithm is introduced into the path optimization of logistics distribution. It shows the superiority of the algorithm in the path planning.

In short, HDABC algorithm is compared with HABC algorithm, SABC algorithm, SAO algorithm, PSO algorithm and ACO algorithm. It improves the problem of uneven distribution of initial food sources and imbalance between exploitation and exploration phases. While strengthening the random and homogenizing distribution of the initial food sources, the accuracy of search and the speed of convergence have been significantly improved.

**Acknowledgement.** We sincerely thank the National Natural Science Foundation of China (No. 62066047) for providing great support for the research.

## References

1. Karaboga, D., Basturk, B.: Artificial bee colony (ABC) optimization algorithm for solving constrained optimization problems. In: International Fuzzy Systems Association World Congress. Springer, Berlin, Heidelberg (2007). https://doi.org/10.1007/978-3-540-72950-1_77
2. Brajević, I., Ignjatović, J.: Multilevel thresholding of color images using globally informed artificial bee colony algorithm. Sci. Rep. **15**, 22041 (2025). https://doi.org/10.1038/s41598-025-05238-z
3. Sally, M.E.: Security in cognitive radio network: defense against primary user emulation attacks using genetic artificial bee colony (GABC) algorithm. Future Gener. Comput. Syst. **109**(2020), 479–487 (2018). https://doi.org/10.1016/j.future.2018.08.022
4. Li, K., Wang, H., Wang, W., et al.: Improving artificial bee colony algorithm using modified nearest neighbor sequence. J. King Saud Univ.-Comput. Inf. Sci. **34**(10), 8807–8824 (2022). https://api.semanticscholar.org/CorpusID:261287141
5. Ye, T., et al.: Artificial bee colony algorithm with efficient search strategy based on random neighborhood structure. Knowl.-Based Syst. **241**, 108306 (2022). https://doi.org/10.1016/j.knosys.2022.108306

6. Zhao, F., et al.: An exploratory landscape analysis driven artificial bee colony algorithm with maximum entropic epistasis. Appl. Soft Comput. **137**, 110139 (2023). https://doi.org/10.1016/j.asoc.2023.110139
7. Song, X.Y., Zhao, Y., Zhao, M.: Artificial bee colony algorithm based on multi-strategy hybrid search. Comput. Eng. Design **41**(9), 2530–2537 (2020)
8. Mai, X., Zhong, Y., Li, L.: The crossover strategy integrated secretary bird optimization algorithm and its application in engineering design problems. Electron. Res. Arch. **33**(1), 471–512 (2025). https://doi.org/10.3934/era.2025023
9. Sheng, Z., Xie, S.Q., Pan, C.Y.: Probability Theory and Mathematical Statistics, pp. 42–50. Higher Education Press, Beijing (2008)
10. Cao, G.H., Hu, K., Tong, W.: Image scrambling method based on Logistic uniform distribution. Acta Phys. Sinica **60**(11), 1502–1509 (2011). https://doi.org/10.7498/aps.60.110508
11. Li, F.P., Liu, J.B., Wang, G.Y., et al.: An image encryption algorithm based on chaotic set. J. Electron. Inf. Technol. **42**(4), 981–987 (2020). https://doi.org/10.11999/JEIT190344
12. Hongzhong, M.A., Yan, Y.A.N.: Analysis and calculation method of on-load tap changers state characteristics based on chaos theory and grasshopper optimization algorithm-K-means algorithm. Trans. China Electrotechnical Soc. **36**(7), 1399–1406 (2021)
13. Bao, L., Tang, J., Ding, H., et al.: The N-level ($N \geq 4$) logistic cascade homogenized mapping for image encryption. Nonlinear Dyn. **105**, 1911–1935 (2021). https://doi.org/10.1007/s11071-021-06688-6
14. Diabi, L., Ouannas, A., Momani, S., et al.: On chaos in fractional discrete financial risk model and its control approaches. Asian J. Control (2025). https://doi.org/10.1002/asjc.3748
15. Wang, W., Hu, X., Wang, B., Sun, D.J.: Performance degradation GG clustering based on spectral entropy and bending time features. Chin. J. Construct. Mach. **18**(02), 95–100 (2020)
16. Huang, L.-L., Ma, Y.-H., Li, C.: Characteristic analysis of 5D symmetric Hamiltonian conservative hyperchaotic system with hidden multiple stability. Chin. Phys. B **33**(1), 010503 (2024). https://doi.org/10.1088/1674-1056/acf9e7
17. Sha, Y., Chen, H.: Permanent magnet motor control system based on fuzzy PID control. Int. J. Adv. Comput. Sci. Appl. (IJACSA) **15**(4) (2024)
18. Zhang, J.P., Ni, Z.W., Ni, L.P., et al.: Scheduling optimization of homogeneous machines based on improved discrete artificial bee colony algorithm. J. Comput. Appl. **40**(3), 689–697 (2020)
19. Zhou, X., Hu, J., Wu, Y., Zhong, M., Wang, M.: A multi-strategy artificial bee colony algorithm based on fitness grouping. Pattern Recogn. Artif. Intell. **35**(8), 688–700 (2022)
20. Yao, X., Liu, Y., Lin, G.: Evolutionary programming made faster, **3**(2), 0–102 (1999). https://doi.org/10.1109/4235.771163
21. Bolufé-Röhler, A., Chen, S., Tamayo-Vera, D.: An analysis of minimum population search on large scale global optimization. In: 2019 IEEE Congress on Evolutionary Computation (CEC), pp. 1228–1235. IEEE (2019). https://doi.org/10.1109/CEC.2019.8789978
22. Kennedy, J., Eberhart, R.: Particle swarm optimization. In: Proceedings of ICNN'95-International Conference on Neural Networks, vol. 4. IEEE (1995). https://doi.org/10.1109/ICNN.1995.488968
23. Deng, L., Liu, S.: Snow ablation optimizer: a novel metaheuristic technique for numerical optimization and engineering design. Expert Syst. Appl. **225**, 120069 (2023). https://doi.org/10.1016/j.eswa.2023.120069
24. Dorigo, M., Birattari, M., Stutzle, T.: Ant colony optimization. IEEE Comput. Intell. Mag. **1**(4), 28–39 (2006). https://doi.org/10.1109/MCI.2006.329691

25. Manthey, B., van Rhijn, J.: Performance of efficient variants of the 2-Opt heuristic for the traveling salesperson problem. Discret. Appl. Math. **375**, 7–16 (2025). https://doi.org/10.1016/j.dam.2025.05.034
26. Hu, R., Bao, L., Ding, H., Zhou, D., Kong, Y.: Analysis of the influence of population distribution characteristics on swarm intelligence optimization algorithms. Inf. Sci. **645**, 119340 (2023). https://doi.org/10.1016/j.ins.2023.119340

# A Truthful Resource Allocation and Task Offloading Mechanism of Internet of Vehicles Edge Computing Based on Joint Optimization

Xing He[1], Hongyu Pi[1], Xi Liu[2], and Xutao Yang[1](✉)

[1] Yunnan University, Kunming 650500, Yunnan, China
hexing@stu.ynu.edu.cn
[2] Qujing Normal University, Qujing 6555011, Yunnan, China

**Abstract.** Vehicular Edge Computing (VEC) integrates edge computing with the Internet of Vehicles (IoV) to provide low-latency, high-reliability data processing near vehicles. While existing VEC resource allocation research often maximizes social welfare or minimizes delay, the critical aspect of energy consumption, which significantly impacts user Quality of Experience (QoE), is frequently overlooked. This paper addresses the joint resource allocation and task offloading problem in VEC, aiming to simultaneously optimize social welfare and minimize energy consumption. We formulate this as a mechanism design problem and decompose it into two sub-problems: Winner Determination (selecting which Vehicle Devices (VDs) offload tasks) and Offloading Decision (assigning tasks to specific Mobile Edge Computing (MEC) servers). For winner determination, we propose a truthful greedy algorithm that ranks VDs based on a weighted combination of their bid (representing social welfare contribution) and potential energy savings. For the offloading decision, we employ an approximation algorithm based on local search to minimize energy usage among selected VDs. The proposed overall mechanism is truthful, guaranteeing that VDs are incentivized to report their true valuations. Simulation results demonstrate that, compared to recent algorithms, our approach improves energy savings by 8%-12% in high-competition scenarios with only a minor (1%-2.5%) reduction in social welfare. In low-competition environments, our mechanism enhances energy savings by approximately 6% while concurrently increasing social welfare by about 2%.

**Keywords:** mechanism design · Internet of vehicles · edge computing

## 1 Introduction

The Internet of Vehicles (IoV), as an important part of the Intelligent Transportation System (ITS), utilizes technologies like vehicle-based self-organized networks (VANETs) to enhance traffic efficiency and safety. VANETs equip vehicles with on-board units (OBUs) that provide small-scale computing resources and storage capacity. However, for large-scale services such as image processing, media applications, and video games, the computing and storage capabilities of OBUs are insufficient [1].

Emerging applications like the Mobile Digital Twin (MDT) in transportation further highlight this challenge. MDT aims to create persistent digital replicas of drivers or connected and automated vehicles (CAVs) using real-world data, demanding substantial computational resources for continuous data collection, modeling, and processing [2–4]. Even a small number of CAVs generate extremely large data volumes from sensors (cameras, lidar, radar), necessitating efficient collection and processing methods.

The introduction of edge computing in IoV offers an effective solution. Mobile Edge Computing (MEC), often combined with the Internet of Things (IoT) and applied in fields like transportation and manufacturing, has become a research hotspot [2]. MEC shifts computation from the cloud closer to the end-users (vehicles), ensuring real-time responsiveness, security, and reliability. IoV naturally benefits from MEC due to the wide distribution of vehicles. Furthermore, vehicles can often generate sufficient power to offload tasks to MEC servers [3], significantly improving the Quality of Experience (QoE) for demanding computational tasks [4].

Auction mechanisms provide a method for effective resource allocation via market behavior [5]. In simple auctions, users submit demands and bids, and the provider allocates resources and determines payments. However, users' self-interest can lead to untruthful bidding, necessitating mechanisms that are truthful (incentive-compatible or strategy-proof), where users maximize their benefit by being honest. Auction mechanism design involves creating both an allocation algorithm and a payment algorithm. The issues examined in this paper, however, are more complex, involving heterogeneous resources and deployment constraints across different edge servers, which presents significant design challenges.

Currently, many studies employ auction mechanisms for edge computing resource allocation [6], often translating the problem into maximizing social welfare under multi-server, multi-dimensional resource, and deployment constraints, while ensuring authenticity and individual rationality. Existing designs include optimal approaches using Vickery-Clark-Groves (VCG) payments [7] and various approximation methods [8]. However, most existing studies prioritize social welfare maximization and neglect energy consumption requirements.

While research exists on minimizing energy consumption in edge computing, such as jointly optimizing power and computing resources [9] or minimizing total user energy consumption in MIMO-NOMA systems through offloading and resource optimization [10], there is a gap in addressing both social welfare and energy consumption simultaneously. Current research predominantly focuses on either energy/delay optimization or social welfare maximization. Therefore, the main challenge addressed in this paper is to devise a reasonable and truthful mechanism that jointly optimizes for social welfare maximization and energy consumption minimization under task delay constraints.

Main contribution

This paper tackles the critical challenge of efficient resource allocation and task offloading in Vehicular Edge Computing (VEC) environments. Our primary contribution is the design and analysis of a novel mechanism that uniquely optimizes for both social welfare maximization and energy consumption minimization simultaneously. The main contributions of this paper are as follows.

1. We explicitly formulate and address the joint optimization of social welfare and energy savings within a truthful mechanism design framework for IoV edge computing. This tackles a significant limitation in prior work, which often focuses on only one of these objectives. The problem is methodically decomposed into Winner Determination and Offloading Decision sub-problems.
2. For the Winner Determination sub-problem, we develop an efficient greedy algorithm. It strategically selects winning VDs based on a novel metric combining their economic value (bid) and potential energy efficiency gains. Crucially, this algorithm is proven to be truthful, encouraging honest participation from VDs.
3. For the Offloading Decision sub-problem, we propose an approximation algorithm using local search techniques, specifically designed to assign the tasks of the determined winners to MEC servers in a way that maximizes overall energy savings (Es), subject to resource constraints.
4. The integrated mechanism is rigorously analyzed and demonstrated to satisfy essential properties: truthfulness (incentive compatibility), individual rationality (VDs benefit from participating), and polynomial-time computational efficiency, making it practical for deployment.

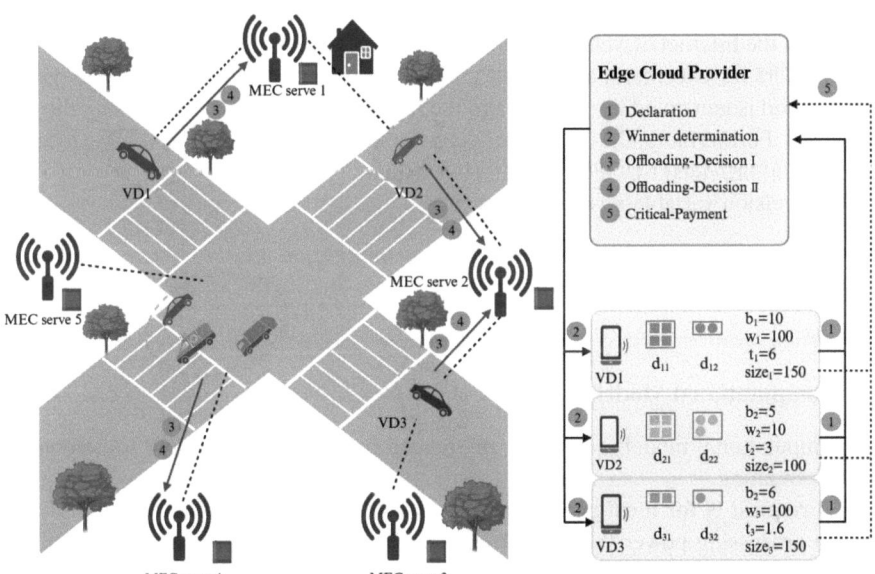

**Fig. 1.** Typical IoV application scenarios with deployment constraint

## 2 System Model and Problem Formulation

### 2.1 Basic Model

We consider an edge computing system consisting of multiple MEC and multiple VDs. Suppose the IoV edge computing service provider has M MEC servers, denoted as the set $\mathcal{M} = \{1, 2, \cdots, M\}$,, and each MEC servers has R resources (e.g., memory, external memory), such that m, $m \in \mathcal{M}$, provides the resource vector $c_m = (c_{m1}, \ldots, c_{mR})$. Let $F_m$ be the number of CPU cycles per second of the MEC server $m \in \mathcal{M}$.

There are N VDs, let the set $\mathcal{N} = \{1, \ldots, N\}$ denote a set of VDs, whose connectivity is indicated by the matrix $S_i = (S_{i1}, S_{i2}, \cdots, S_{iM})$ ($S_{ij} = 1$ denotes that the $VD_i$ and $MEC_j$ are associated, and 0 otherwise ), and the connectivity matrix $S = (\delta_1, \ldots, \delta_N)$. In reality, $S_{ij}$ is influenced by many factors, such as communication power, bandwidth, noise and obstacles. In this model, $S_{ij}$ is reduced to a 0 or 1 constant, and this simplification is beneficial for focusing on our problem model.

The VD request $\theta_i = (b_i, w_i, d_i, t_i^{req}, size)$, the bid is $b_i$, $w_i$ is the number of CPU cycles required by the task, the resource requirement is $d_i = (d_{i1}, \ldots, d_{iR})$, and $t_i^{req}$ is the deadline. Please note that we assume that VDs might falsely report their bids, such that $\hat{b}_i > b_i$ or $\hat{b}_i < b_i$. We do not discuss the situation where VDs falsely report resource requirements and deployment constraints $\delta_{ij}$,, because in the edge computing services of the Internet of Vehicles, data must be offloaded to edge computing servers or cloud servers for execution, and VDs cannot forge resource requirements - the data to be processed is generated by sensors, and the resources required for processing the data are pre-set. Furthermore, the deployment constraints originate from the vehicle location information (provided by GPS) and are also difficult to forge.

The decision variable x is defined as

$$x_{im} = \begin{cases} 1, & \text{if } VD_i \text{ wins in } m, S_{im} = 1 \\ 0, & \text{otherwise} \end{cases} \quad (1)$$

### 2.2 Computational Model

The computational model is partially referenced from [11] and adapted to Telematics Edge Computing.

**VD request $\theta_i$ for local processing**

The processing power (i.e. CPU frequency in cycles/second) allocated by the VD for local computing is denoted as $f_i$, then the power of the VD to process the data locally is denoted as

$$p_i = \kappa_1 (f_i)^3 \quad (2)$$

where $\kappa_1$ is the energy efficiency factor of the terminal equipment, set $\kappa_1 = 10^{-28}$.

Local processing time delay

$$t^1 = w_i / f_i \quad (3)$$

$w_i$ is the number of CPU cycles required for the task and $f_i$ is the VD's own CPU processing power.

Local energy consumption

$$E_i^l = p_i t^l = \kappa_1 (f_i)^2 w_i \qquad (4)$$

**MEC Processing of VD Requests** $.\theta_i$

The total MEC transmission time delay consists of three components: the VD transmission delay, the MEC processing delay and the MEC return delay:

$$t_{im}^a = t_{im}^{tra} + t_{im}^{pro} + t_{im}^{down} \qquad (5)$$

MEC transmission time

$$t_{im}^{tra} = size_i / r_{im} \qquad (6)$$

where transfer rate

$$r_{im} = E\left\{ Blog2\left(1 + \rho_1 |h|^2 / \sigma^2 d^{-\vartheta}\right) \right\} \approx Blog2\left(1 + \rho_1 / \sigma^2 d^{-\vartheta}\right)_{[12]} \qquad (7)$$

where d denotes the distance from the VD to the edge, and $\vartheta$ denotes the path loss exponent. h denotes the channel fading coefficient, which obeys a complex Gaussian distribution with zero-mean-unit variance. The transmission bandwidth B is 20 MHz. The variance of Gaussian white noise $\sigma^2$ is $3 \times 10^{-13}$. The transmission power of the VD $\rho_1$ is 0.5W.

MEC Transmission Energy Consumption

$$E_{im}^r = \rho_1 t_{im}^{tra} = \rho_1 size_i / r_{im} \qquad (8)$$

Terminal Transmission Power $\rho_1$ for 0.5W.

MEC processing time

$$t_{im}^{pro} = w_i / f_{im} \qquad (9)$$

where $f_{im}$ is the remote CPU processing power per second that the $VD_i$ receives from the MEC server $m \in \mathcal{M}$.

MEC Processing Power:

$$p_{im} = \kappa_2 (f_{im})^3 \qquad (10)$$

$\kappa_2$ is the energy efficiency factor for MEC equipment, set $\kappa_2 = 10^{-29}$.

MEC Processing Energy Consumption

$$E_{lm}^e = p_{im} t_{im}^{pro} = \kappa_2 (f_{lm})^2 w_i \qquad (11)$$

MEC return delay

$$t_{im}^{down} = size_i / r_{2im} \qquad (12)$$

where the downlink transmission rate

$$r_{2im} = B\log_2\left(1 + \rho_2/\sigma^2 d^{-\vartheta}\right) \tag{13}$$

The return transmission power of the MEC server is $\rho_2 = 10W$.
MEC return energy consumption

$$E_{im}^{down} = \rho_2 t_{im}^{down} = \rho_2 size_i/r_{2im} \tag{14}$$

Remote calculation of energy consumption

$$E_{im}^a = E_{im}^r + E_{im}^e + E_{im}^{down} = \rho_1 size_i/r_{im} + \kappa_2(f_{im})^2 w_i + \rho_2 size_i/r_{2im} \tag{15}$$

We define the energy savings as

$$E_{im}^s = E_i^l - E_{im}^a \tag{16}$$

The task per VD can be achieved by one server and is limited to a single bid. The valuation function of the VD is defined as

$$v_i = \begin{cases} \hat{b}_i, & \text{if } t_{im}^a \le t_i^{req},\ S_{im} = 1 \\ 0, & \text{otherwise} \end{cases} \tag{17}$$

where $\hat{b}_i$ is the true valuation of $VD_i$. A VD wins if it can obtain the required resources from any of the connected MEC servers, otherwise it is a loser.

The goal of this problem is to maximize the social welfare, that is, the total valuation of all winners.

$VD_i \in \mathcal{N}$ There is a quasi-linear utility function that can be obtained from the following equation:

$$u_i = \begin{cases} v_i - pay_i, & \text{if } VD_i\ wins \\ 0, & \text{otherwise} \end{cases} \tag{18}$$

And the total utility U can be given by: $U = \sum_{i \in \mathcal{N}} u_i$.

Where $pay_i$ is the cost it needs to pay, as calculated by the mechanism. Note that VD's bid is privately known, and it can declare different bids to maximize its utility.

For example, $VD_i(\forall i \in \mathcal{N})$ declares a bundle $\theta_i(10, 2000, (5, 20), 1, 200)$, which means that the bid is 10, the number of CPU cycles required is 2000, the vector of remote resources requested is $(5, 20)$, the deadline is 1 s, and the size of the task is 200 KB. we assume that the true bid $\hat{b}_i$ is 10, and the payment is 5. If its task completes within the deadline, it wins and $u_i = 10 - 5 = 5$, otherwise it fails and $u_i = 0$. Without loss of generality, we assume $b_i > 0$, $w_i > 0$, $t_i^{req} > 0$, $size_i > 0$, $c_{mr} > 0$, and $F_m > 0, \forall i \in \mathcal{N}, m \in \mathcal{M}$.

## 2.3 Mathematical Formula

The integer planning formulation of the ROTA problem (IP - RATO) can be expressed as:

$$\max \sum_{i \in \mathcal{N}} \sum_{m \in \mathcal{M}} x_{im} b_i \quad (19)$$

$$\text{s.t.} : \sum_{i \in \mathcal{N}} x_{im} d_{ir} \leq c_{mr}, \forall m \in \mathcal{M}, r \in \mathcal{R} \quad (20)$$

$$\sum_{i \in \mathcal{N}} f_{im} x_{im} \leq F_m, \forall m \in \mathcal{M} \quad (21)$$

$$t_{im}^a x_{im} \leq t_i^{req}, \forall i \in \mathcal{N}, m \in \mathcal{M} \quad (22)$$

$$\sum_{m \in \mathcal{M}} x_{im} \leq 1, \forall i \in \mathcal{N} \quad (23)$$

$$x_{im} = 0, \forall i \in \mathcal{N}, m \in \mathcal{M} \text{ where } S_{im} = 0 \quad (24)$$

$$x_{im} \in \{0, 1\}, \forall i \in \mathcal{N}, m \in \mathcal{M} \quad (25)$$

Goal (19) is to maximize social welfare. Constraint (20) guarantees that the allocated capacity does not exceed the remote computing capacity. Constraint (21) guarantees that the number of CPU cycles allocated does not exceed the number of remote CPU cycles. Constraint (22) guarantees that a winner's assignment does not time out. Constraint (23) guarantees that a winner gets resources from at most one MEC server. Constraint (24) guarantees that each VD can only get resources from the connected MEC. Constraint (25) indicates the integrity requirements of the variables.

To better illustrate our system model, we use the scenario depicted in Fig. 1 as a running example. We consider two types of resources ($R = 2$), three vehicle devices (VDs), and five vehicle device servers. The task request for $VD_1$ is $\theta_1 = (b_1 = 10, w_1 = 100, d_{11} = 4, d_{12} = 2, t_1 = 6, size_1 = 150)$. $VD_1$ can connect to MEC 1 and MEC 5 ($S_{11} = 1, S_{15} = 1$, others 0). The task request for $VD_2$ is $\theta_2 = (b_2 = 5, w_2 = 10, d_{21} = 4, d_{22} = 3, t_2 = 3, size_2 = 100)$. $VD_2$ can connect to MEC 1 and MEC 2 ($S_{21} = 1, S_{22} = 1$, others 0). The resource package for $VD_3$ is $\theta_3 = (b_3 = 6, w_3 = 100, d_{31} = 2, d_{32} = 1, t_3 = 1.6, size_3 = 150)$. $VD_3$ can connect to MEC 2, MEC 3, and MEC 4 ($S_{32} = 1, S_{33} = 1, S_{34} = 1$, others 0).

Without loss of generality, we assume that Mobile Edge Computing (MEC) servers has sufficient resources and low energy consumption to satisfy the demands of VDs. The resources are allocated as $x_{11} = 1, x_{21} = 1$, and $x_{32} = 1$. The MEC server can satisfy the VD's demand and hence constraints (20), (21), and (22) are satisfied. Based on constraint (23), each winner can obtain resources from up to one MEC server. For example, the $VD_2$ obtains resources from the MEC server 1, so she cannot obtain resources from the MEC server 2. Based on constraint (24), MEC server 1 can serve $VD_1$ and $VD_2$ because they are within its network coverage area. However, MEC server 1 cannot serve $VD_3$ since they are not in the same network coverage area. The social welfare is $b_1 + b_2 + b_3 = 21$.

## 2.4 Mechanism Properties

**Definition 1** (Individual Rationality): a mechanism is individually rational if any winner does not pay more than its bid.

**Definition 2** (Monotonicity): An allocation algorithm is said to be monotonic if it satisfies the following condition with respect to a bundle of VDs: if the allocation algorithm selects a $VD_i$ with $\theta_i$, then it also selects a VD with $\tilde{\theta}_i$ when $\tilde{\theta}_i \geq \theta_i$ and all other bundles of VDs are fixed.

**Definition 3** (Key Payment): if the allocation algorithm is monotonic, for each $\theta_i$, there will exist a unique value $pay_i^c$, called a key payment, such that $\theta_i$ is a winning statement when $b_i > pays_i^c$ and $\theta_i$ is a losing statement when $b_i < pay_i^c$.

**Definition 4** (Truthfulness): a mechanism is truthful (or incentive-compatible) if for each VD $\forall i \in \mathcal{N}$, for each statement of the other VDs $\theta_{-i}$, a truthful statement $\tilde{\theta}_i$ and any other statement of the VD $\theta_i$, we have $u_i(\tilde{\theta}_i, \theta_{-i}) \geq u_i(\theta_i, \theta_{-i})$.

**Definition 5** (Truthful Mechanism): a mechanism is Truthful if and only if its allocation algorithm is monotonic and its payment algorithm is based on key payments [13].

**Definition 6** (Computational Efficiency): a mechanism is computationally efficient if it runs in polynomial time.

# 3 Optimal Benchmark Mechanism: OPT-VCG

We first introduce an optimal mechanism based on the well-known Vickery-Clark-Groves (VCG) principles [7], termed OPT-VCG This mechanism serves as a theoretical benchmark, guaranteeing truthfulness while maximizing social welfare, although solving it optimally can be computationally expensive (NP-hard) for large problem instances. The OPT-VCG mechanism comprises two main components: an optimal allocation rule and a VCG payment rule.

**Optimal Allocation (Winner Determination):** This component finds the allocation x ∗ that yields the maximum possible social welfare by solving the Integer Program formulation of the ROTA problem (IP-RATO) defined in Sect. 2.3 (Eqs. 19–25). Let OPT* be the optimal social welfare value achieved by this allocation x*.

**VCG Payment Rule:** For each winning VD i (i.e., $\sum_{m \in \mathcal{M}} x_{im}^* = 1$), the payment $pay_i^*$ is calculated based on the externality it imposes on other VDs. Specifically, it is the difference between the optimal social welfare achievable *without* VD i's participation and the social welfare achieved by *other* VDs *with* VD i's participation:

$$\text{pay}_i^* = OPT' - \left(OPT^* - \sum_{m \in \mathcal{M}} x_{im}^* b_i\right) \qquad (26)$$

where OPT' is the optimal social welfare obtained by solving IP-RATO for the set of VDs N\{i}. This payment ensures truthfulness, as a VD's bid only affects whether they win, not how much they pay if they do win.

**Algorithm 1 OPT-VCG**

1: # Step 1: Declaration
2: /* Collecting bundle $\theta$ from VDs */
3: #Step 2: Allocation
4: $(OPT^*, \mathbf{x}^*)$ = solution of IP – RATO$(\theta)$;
5: #Step 3: Payment
6: for each $i \in \mathcal{N}$
7:    if $\sum_{m \in \mathcal{M}} x_{im}^* = 1$
8:      $OPT'$ = solution of IP – RATO $(\theta_{-i})$;
9:      $pay_i^* = OPT' - \left(OPT^* - \sum_{m \in \mathcal{M}} x_{im}^* b_i\right)$;
10: /*Allocating resources and payment*/

The OPT-VCG mechanism is summarized in Algorithm 1. The mechanism first collects request bundles from VDs (line 2). Then, it solves the integer programming ROTA (IP - RATO) in Eqs. (19)–(25) to obtain the optimal solution (line 4). Next, the mechanism calculates the payment for each winner (lines 6–9). Finally, the winner pays the fee and receives the requested resource (line 10).

While OPT-VCG provides theoretical optimality and truthfulness, solving the IP-RATO problem (which is NP-hard, as discussed later) multiple times makes this mechanism computationally expensive, especially for many VDs or servers. This computational challenge motivates the design of efficient approximation mechanisms, which we present in the following section.

## 4 Approximate Algorithm Design

The optimal OPT-VCG mechanism presented in Section III guarantees maximum social welfare and truthfulness but suffers from high computational complexity due to solving the NP-hard IP-RATO problem multiple times. To achieve practical applicability, we propose an efficient Approximate Mechanism designed. This mechanism unfolds in six sequential phases: declaration, initialization, winner determination, offloading decision I, offloading decision II and payment pricing.

In the declaration phase, VDs declare their request bundles $\theta_i$ (line 3). In the initialization phase, it computes the remote requirements (lines 4 - 7). Given $w_i$, $\forall i \in \mathcal{N}$, for the delay constraints to be satisfied, there exists a minimum frequency that satisfies the following equation:

$$\frac{w_i}{f_{im}} + t_{im}^{tra} + t_{im}^{down} = t_i^{req}, S_{im} = 1 \tag{27}$$

Thus, $f_{im}(\forall i \in \mathcal{N}, m \in \mathcal{M})$ is given by:

$$f_{im} = \begin{cases} \dfrac{w_i}{t_i^{req} - t_{im}^{tra} - t_{im}^{down}}, & \text{if } S_{im} = 1 \\ \infty, & \text{otherwise} \end{cases} \tag{28}$$

During the Winner Determination phase, the mechanism invokes the Winner Determination algorithm to obtain a winner (lines 8 - 9). Note that only the winner can offload its task to the MEC server for remote execution. The primary goal here is to identify VDs offering high overall value, using a metric (detailed in Algorithm 3) that considers both their bid (social welfare contribution) and potential energy savings. In the Offloading decision phase, the mechanism invokes the offloading decision I algorithm and Offloading decision II to determine the assignments (lines 10 - 13). Based on the winner's attributes, the offload decision algorithm assigns the winner's task to the appropriate MEC server to maximize energy savings. Thus, the second phase solves the social welfare problem and the third phase solves the energy consumption problem. In the pricing phase, the mechanism invokes the key payment algorithm to get paid (lines 14 - 15). Finally, the winner pays the price and offloads its tasks for remote execution (line 16).

| | **Algorithm 2 Approximation Algorithm** |
|---|---|
| 1: | # Step 1: Declaration |
| 2: | /*Collecting bundle $\theta_i$ from VD $i \in \mathcal{N}^*$ / |
| 3: | $\theta = (\theta_1, \ldots, \theta_N)$; |
| 4: | #Step 2: Initialization |
| 5: | for each $m \in \mathcal{M}$ |
| 6: | $f_{im} = \dfrac{w_i}{t_i^{req} - t_{im}^{tra} - t_{im}^{down}}, \forall S_{im} = 1;$ |
| 7: | $f_{im} = \infty, \forall S_{im} = 0$; |
| 8: | #Step 3: Winner determination |
| 9: | $(V, \mathbf{x}) = $ Winner-Determination $(\theta)$ ; |
| 10: | #Step 4: Offloading decision I |
| 11: | $(V, \mathbf{x}) = $ Offloading-Decision I $(\mathbf{x}, \theta)$ ; |
| 12: | #Step 5: Offloading decision II |
| 13 | $(V, \mathbf{x}) = $ Offloading-Decision II $(\mathbf{x}, \theta)$ |
| 14: | #Step 6: Pricing |
| 15: | pay $=$ Critical-Payment $(\mathbf{x}, \theta)$ ; |
| 16: | /*Allocating resources and payment*/ |

### 4.1 Winner Determination for Approximate Algorithm

The Winner-Determination algorithm (Algorithm 3) implements the crucial third phase of the approximation mechanism. Its objective is to greedily select a set of winning VDs that represent a favorable balance between socio-economic value (bid) and system efficiency (energy savings), normalized by resource cost. It comprises two main steps: Initialization and Greedy Allocation.

Step 1: Initialization (Lines 1–11):

The algorithm first initializes the necessary variables, including available server resources (Lines 1–2). It then iterates through all VDs and their connectable MEC servers to pre-calculate essential metrics for each potential assignment (i,m): the potential energy saving $E_{im}$, the task's relative resource footprint

$$D_{im} = \sum_{r \in \mathcal{R}} \frac{d_{ir}}{c_{mr}} + \frac{f_{im}}{F_m} \tag{29}$$

and a score $L_{im} = (b_i + E_{im})/2$. This score combines the bid $b_i$ and the potential energy saving $E_{im}$ (Lines 3–9). Based on these, a final sorting index

$$\prod_i = \frac{L_{im}}{D_{im}} \quad (30)$$

representing the value density, is computed for each VD (Lines 10–11).

Step 2: Greedy Allocation (Lines 12–27): This step performs the actual selection process (Line 12 marks the beginning). VDs are first sorted in descending order based on their value density index $\Pi_i$ (Line 13). In case of a tie, VDs with a lower original index are prioritized to ensure a deterministic ordering. The algorithm then processes the VDs one by one according to this sorted list (main loop starts at Line 14). For each $VD_i$, it evaluates all feasible MEC servers (inner loop starts at Line 16) by:

1. Initializing tracking variables for the best server choice (Line 15).
2. Checking if a connectable server m has sufficient currently available resources for the task's requirement (Line 17).
3. If feasible, calculating a server score to determine its suitability (Lines 18–19). This score calculation is crucial for balancing task value with resource utilization: First, an occupation_factor is calculated (Line 18): $1 - (\sum_{r \in R} \frac{d_{ir}}{\hat{c}_{mr}} + \frac{f_{im}}{\hat{F}_m})/2$. This factor estimates the server's relative remaining capacity after potentially allocating task i. The term $\frac{d_{ir}}{\hat{c}_{mr}}$ (or $\frac{f_{im}}{\hat{F}_m}$) represents the fraction of the server's currently available resource r (or CPU capacity) that task i would consume. Averaging these fractions and subtracting from 1 gives a measure where values closer to 1 indicate the server remains relatively lightly loaded by task i, while values closer to 0 indicate task i consumes a large portion of the available resources. Then, the final score is computed as $L_{im} \times$ occupation_factor (Line 19). The rationale here is to prioritize servers that not only suit a high-value task (high Lim) but also maintain a good level of remaining capacity. Multiplying by the occupation_factor effectively penalizes assigning the task to a server that would become heavily loaded as a result, promoting better load distribution across server.
4. Tracking the server m that yields the highest calculated score for the current VD$_i$ (Lines 20–21). After evaluating all potential servers for VD$_i$, if a suitable one was found (best_server $\neq -1$) (Line 22), the VD is allocated to that server (Line 23), and the server's available resources are updated (Lines 24–25). Finally, the algorithm returns the resulting allocation x (Line 27).

**Algorithm 3** Winner-Determination $(\theta)$

1: #Step 1: Initialization
2: $\mathbf{x} = \mathbf{0}, \hat{\mathbf{c}} = \mathbf{c}, \hat{\mathbf{F}} = \mathbf{F}$;
3: $E_{im}$ = calculate_saved_energy(i, m), $\forall i, m$ where $S_{im} = 1$
4: **for each** $i \in \mathcal{N}$
5:   **for each** $m \in \mathcal{M}$
6:     **if** $S_{im} = 1$
7:       $D_{im} = \sum_{r \in \mathcal{R}} \frac{d_{ir}}{c_{mr}} + \frac{f_{im}}{F_m}$;
8:       $L_{im} = (b_i + E_{im})/2$;
9:       Store $L_{im}$ and $D_{im}$ for $\mathcal{N}_i$;
10:   $m_i^* = \underset{m \in \{k|\, S_{ik}=1\}}{\mathrm{argmax}}\, L_{im}$;
11:   $\Pi_i = \frac{L_{im_i^*}}{D_{im_i^*}}$;
12: #Step 2: Greedy allocation
13: **sort** $\mathcal{N}$ in non-increasing order of $\Pi_i$;
14: **for each** $i \in \mathcal{N}$
15:   best_server = $-1$, best_score = $-1$;
16:   **for each** $m \in \mathcal{M}$
17:     **if** $d_{ir} \le \hat{c}_{mr}, \forall r \in \mathcal{R}$, $f_{im} \le \hat{F}_m$ **and** $S_{im} = 1 = 1s[i][m] = 1$
18:       occupation_factor = $1 - (\sum_{r \in \mathcal{R}} \frac{d_{ir}}{\hat{c}_{mr}} + \frac{f_{im}}{\hat{F}_m})/2$;
19:       score = $L_{im}$ *occupation_factor;
20:       **if** score > best_score
21:         best_server=m;
22:   **if** best_server $\ne -1$
23:     $x_{im} = 1$;
24:     $\hat{c}_{mr} = \hat{c}_{mr} - d_{ir}, \forall r \in \mathcal{R}$;
25:     $\hat{F}_m = \hat{F}_m - f_{im}$;
26: $V = \sum_{i \in \mathcal{N}} \sum_{m \in \mathcal{M}} x_{im} b_i$
27: **return**(V, x);

## 4.2 Offloading-Decision for Approximate Algorithm

Once the Winner-Determination phase (Algorithm 3) identifies an initial set of winning VDs ($\hat{\mathcal{N}}$), the Offloading-Decision phase aims to assign each winning VD's task to a specific connected MEC server to maximize the total energy savings achieved by offloading, compared to local execution. This phase specifically addresses the Maximum Energy Savings Problem (MESP), formulated as the integer program in Eqs. (33)–(38), considering only the winners $\hat{\mathcal{N}}$ and the available MEC server resources.

Let $\hat{\mathcal{N}}$ be the set of winners. We define the energy savings as

$$E_{im}^s = E_i^l - E_{im}^a \, \forall i \in \hat{\mathcal{N}}, m \in \mathcal{M} \tag{31}$$

Among them, the remote energy consumption

$$E_{im}^a = E_{im}^r + E_{im}^e + E_{im}^{down} = \rho_i t_{im}^{tra} + \kappa 2(\hat{f}_{im})^2 w_i + \rho_2 size_i / r_{2im} \tag{32}$$

The integer planning formulation of the Maximum Energy Savings Problem (IP - MESP) can be expressed as:

$$\max \sum_{i \in \hat{\mathcal{N}}} \sum_{m \in \mathcal{M}} x_{im} E_{im}^s \tag{33}$$

$$s.t. : \sum_{i \in \hat{\mathcal{N}}} x_{im} d_{ir} \leq c_{mr}, \, \forall m \in \mathcal{M}, \, r \in \mathcal{R} \tag{34}$$

$$\sum_{i \in \hat{\mathcal{N}}} \sum_{m \in \mathcal{M}} x_{im} f_{im} \leq F_m, \, \forall m \in \mathcal{M} \tag{35}$$

$$\sum_{m \in \mathcal{M}} x_{im} = 1, \, \forall i \in \hat{\mathcal{N}} \tag{36}$$

$$x_{im} = 0, \, \forall i \in \hat{\mathcal{N}}, \, m \in \mathcal{M} \text{ where } S_{im} = 0 \tag{37}$$

$$x_{im} \in \{0, 1\}, \, \forall i \in \hat{\mathcal{N}}, \, m \in \mathcal{M} \tag{38}$$

Maximum Energy Savings Problem (IP - MESP).

The goal (33) is to maximize energy savings. Constraints (34) and (35) guarantee that the allocated capacity of each MEC server does not exceed the available capacity. Constraint (36) guarantees that each winner gets the requested resources. Constraint (37) indicates that each winner can only get resources from the coverage of the MEC server Constraint (38) guarantees the integrity requirements of the variables.

The offloading decision algorithm is summarized in Algorithm 4. We modified the algorithm proposed in [14] to improve its energy saving efficiency and its proof more complete. Inspired in part by Caprara et al. [15], we modified the PTAS m-DKP algorithm from their work to fit our model and improve the efficiency of the algorithm. For the sake of realism, we only consider the problem of distributing the winners.

For the MEC server $m \in \mathcal{M}$, we relax constraints (38) and ignore constraints (36). The linear programming relaxation (LP - MESP - m) of the MEC server $m \in \mathcal{M}$ is modeled as:

$$\max \sum_{i \in \hat{\mathcal{N}}} \sum_{m \in \mathcal{M}} x_{im} E_{im}^s \tag{39}$$

$$\text{s.t.} : \sum_{i \in \hat{\mathcal{N}}} x_{im} d_{ir} \leq c_{mr}, \; r \in \mathcal{R} \tag{40}$$

$$\sum_{i \in \hat{\mathcal{N}}} x_{im} f_{im} \leq F_m \tag{41}$$

$$0 \leq x_{im} \leq 1, \; \forall i \in \hat{\mathcal{N}} \tag{42}$$

LP-MESP relaxation problem.

Specifically, the offloading decision algorithm is divided into the following steps:

1. Initial Check (Lines 1–4): It first calculates the energy savings V achieved by the initial allocation from Algorithm 3. It then solves the Linear Programming relaxation of the overall MESP (LP-MESP) to get an upper bound $O\tilde{P}T$ on the optimal energy savings. If the initial allocation V is already close enough to the upper bound (i.e., $V \geq (1-\epsilon) \cdot O\tilde{P}T$), this allocation is deemed sufficient, and the algorithm terminates early.
2. Initialization (Lines 5–6): If the initial check fails, the algorithm initializes variables to track the best global allocation found so far: $\hat{V} = 0$ (total energy savings) and $\hat{x} = \mathbf{0}$ (allocation matrix). It also confirms the set of winning VDs $\hat{\mathcal{N}}$ determined by Algorithm 3.
3. Iterating Through MEC Servers (Line 7): The algorithm then iterates through each MEC server $m \in \mathcal{M}$ to determine the allocation of VDs to that specific server. For each server, it performs the following steps:
    a. Per-Server Initialization (Lines 8–12):Initialize $Q = \emptyset$ (to store the best subset of VDs allocated to server m in this iteration) and $V = 0$ (to track the energy savings for this subset Q). Identify the set $\mathcal{N}_m$ of currently unallocated winning VDs ($\in \hat{\mathcal{N}}$) that can connect to server m ($S_{nm} = 1$).Sort $N_m$ in non-increasing order based on the potential energy saving $E_{im}$ if assigned to server m. Any ties are broken by selecting the VD with the smaller original index first to ensure deterministic behavior. Determine the parameter $q = \min\{\lceil (R+1)(1-\epsilon)/\epsilon \rceil, \mathcal{N}_m\}$. This parameter q controls the size of subsets considered in the enumeration steps, balancing approximation quality and computational complexity. R is the number of resource types. Calculate $\overline{OPT} = LP - MESP - m(\mathcal{N}_m, \mathbf{c}, F_m)$, which is the optimal value of the LP relaxation of the MESP restricted to only VDs in $\mathcal{N}_m$ and only server m. This serves as an upper bound for the energy savings achievable by allocating VDs from $\mathcal{N}_m$ to server m.

b. **Partial Allocation (Lines 13–17):** This step aims to find the optimal solution if the number of VDs assigned to server m in the true optimal solution is small (less than q). It enumerates all subsets $S \subset \mathcal{N}_m$ where $|S| \leq q - 1$. For each subset S that satisfies the resource constraints of server m (i.e., $\sum_{i \in S} d_{ir} \leq c_{mr}, \forall r \in \mathcal{R}$ and $\sum_{i \in S} f_{im} \leq F_m$), it calculates the total energy saving $\sum_{i \in S} E^s_{im}$. It keeps track of the feasible subset S that yields the highest energy saving found so far for server m, storing this best subset in Q and its corresponding energy saving in V.

c. **Approximate Allocation Phase (Lines 18–38):** This step handles cases where assigning q or more VDs to server m might be optimal. It iterates through each subset $S \subset \mathcal{N}_m$ with exactly $|S| = q$ that satisfies the resource constraints of server m (Line 20). For each such feasible 'core' set S: Determine the set of remaining VDs $\overline{\mathcal{N}} = \mathcal{N}_m \setminus S$ and calculate the server's remaining resources $\overline{c}, \overline{F}_m$, after allocating S (Lines 21–22). Solve the LP relaxation for the remaining VDs: obtain the (potentially fractional) solution $\overline{x'} = solution\ of\ LP-MESP-m(\overline{\mathcal{N}}, \overline{c}, \overline{F}_m)$ (Line 23). Process the fractional solution x': Identify the set $\mathcal{N}1 = \{i : \overline{x}_{im} = 1\}$ (integer part) and the set $\mathcal{NF} = \{i : \overline{x}_{im}! = 1 and \overline{x}_{im}! = 0\}$ (fractional part) (Line 24). Find the best feasible integer allocation derived from the fractional part: Initialize a potential best addition $P_2 = \mathcal{N}1$ and its energy saving best_S_energy (Line 25). Then, examine subsets $P \subset \mathcal{NF}$. For each combination $P_1 = P \cup \mathcal{N}1$ that is feasible under remaining resources, calculate its saving S_energy. Update $P_2$ to the feasible $P_1$ that yields the maximum S_energy (Lines 26–33). Now, $P_2$ represents the best integer allocation found for the VDs in $\overline{\mathcal{N}}$. Compare and update the best solution for server m: Calculate the total energy saving for the current branch as $E_{total} = \sum_{i \in S} E^s_{im} + \sum_{i \in P_2} E^s_{im}$. If $E_{total} > V$ (where V is the best saving found so far for server m, initialized in step 3.a and updated in step 3.b), update $V = E_{total}$ and set $Q = S \cup P_2$ (Lines 34–36). After checking a subset S, or after completing the inner loop (Lines 26–33), check for early termination: If the current best saving V for server m satisfies $V \geq (1- \epsilon)\overline{OPT}$ (where $\overline{OPT}$ is the per-server LP bound from step 3.a), break the loop for server m (Lines 37–38).

d. **Global Update (Lines 39–41):** Update $\hat{V} = \hat{V} + V$ and set the VD corresponding to the set in the allocation scheme to win at the current MEC server, i.e., $\hat{x}_{im} = 1, \forall i \in Q$. Remove the already processed VDs from the set of winners, i.e. $\hat{\mathcal{N}} = \hat{\mathcal{N}} \setminus Q$.

4. **Final Output (Lines 42–46):** Calculate the energy saving value of the total remaining $V' = \sum_{i \in \mathcal{N}} \sum_{m \in \mathcal{M}} x_{im} E^s_{im}$. Update $V' = \hat{V}, \mathbf{x} = \hat{\mathbf{x}}$, if $\hat{\mathcal{N}} = \emptyset$ and $\hat{V} > V'$, indicating that a better global solution has been found. Finally, return the final energy saving value and allocation scheme.

## Algorithm 4 Offloading-Decision I $(\mathbf{x}, \theta)$

1:   $V = \sum_{i \in \mathcal{N}} \sum_{m \in \mathcal{M}} x_{im} E_{im}^s$;
2:   $\tilde{OPT}$ = solution of $LP - MESP$
3:   **if** $V \geq (1-\epsilon) \cdot \tilde{OPT}$
4:     **return** $(V, \mathbf{x})$;
5:   $\hat{V} = 0, V' = \sum_{i \in \mathcal{N}} \sum_{m \in \mathcal{M}} x_{im} E_{im}^s$
6:   $\hat{\mathbf{x}} = \mathbf{0}, \hat{\mathcal{N}} = \{i : \sum_{m \in \mathcal{M}} x_{im} \geq 1\}$
7:   **for each** $m \in \mathcal{M}$
8:     #Step 1: Initialization
9:     $Q = \emptyset, V = 0, \mathcal{N}_m = \{n : \sum_{n \in \hat{\mathcal{N}}} S_{nm} = 1\}$
10:     sort $\mathcal{N}_m$ in non-increasing order of $E_{im}$;
11:     $q = \min\{\lceil (R+1)(1-\epsilon)/\epsilon \rceil, \mathcal{N}_m\}$
12:     $\overline{OPT} = LP - MESP - m(\mathcal{N}_m, \mathbf{c}, F_m)$
13:     #Step 2: Partial allocation
14:     **for each** $S \subset \mathcal{N}_m$ and $|S| \leq q-1$
15:       **if** $\sum_{i \in S} d_{ir} \leq c_{mr}, \forall r \in \mathcal{R}$ **and** $\sum_{i \in S} f_{im} \leq F_m$
16:         $Q = S$;
17:         $V = \sum_{i \in Q} E_{im}^s$;
18:     #Step 3: Approximation allocation
19:     **for each** $S \subseteq \mathcal{N}_m$ and $|S| = q$
20:       **if** $\sum_{i \in S} d_{ir} \leq c_{mr}, \forall r \in \mathcal{R}$ **and** $\sum_{i \in S} f_{im} \leq F_m$
21:         $\bar{\mathcal{N}} = \mathcal{N}_m \setminus S$
22:         $\bar{c}_{mr} = c_{mr} - \sum_{i \in S} d_{ir}, \forall r \in \mathcal{R}$;
23:         $\bar{F}_m = F_m - \sum_{i \in S} f_{im}$;
24:         $\overline{OPT}, \bar{x}$ = solution of $LP - MESP - m(\bar{\mathcal{N}}, \bar{\mathbf{c}}, \bar{F}_m)$
25:         $\mathcal{N}_1 = \{i : \bar{x}_{im} = 1\} \mathcal{NF} = \{i : \bar{x}_{im} \neq 1 \text{ and } \bar{x}_{im} \neq 0\}$
26:         $P_2 = \mathcal{N}_1 \text{ best}\_S\_energy = \sum_{i \in \mathcal{N}_1} E_{im}^s$
27:         **for each** $P \subset \mathcal{NF}$
28:           $P_1 = P \cup \mathcal{N}_1$
29:           **if** $\sum_{i \in P_1} d_{ir} \leq c_{mr}, \forall r \in \mathcal{R}$ **and** $\sum_{i \in P_1} f_{im} \leq F_m$
30:             $S\_energy = \sum_{i \in P_1} E_{im}^s$
31:             **if** $S\_energy \geq best\_S\_energy$
32:               $best\_S\_energy = S\_energy$
33:               $P_2 = P_1$
34:         **if** $\sum_{i \in S} E_{im}^s + \sum_{i \in P_2} E_{im}^s > V$
35:           $Q = S \cup P_2$;
36:           $V = \sum_{i \in Q} E_{im}^s$;
37:         **if** $V \geq (1-\epsilon) \overline{OPT}$
38:           **break**;
39:     $\hat{V} = \hat{V} + V$;
40:     $\hat{x}_{im} = 1, \forall i \in Q$;
41:     $\hat{\mathcal{N}} = \hat{\mathcal{N}} \setminus Q$;
42:   $V' = \sum_{i \in \mathcal{N}} \sum_{m \in \mathcal{M}} x_{im} E_{im}^s$;
43:   **if** $\hat{\mathcal{N}} = \emptyset$ **and** $\hat{V} > V'$
44:     $V' = \hat{V}$;
45:     $\mathbf{x} = \hat{\mathbf{x}}$;
46:   **return** $(V', \mathbf{x})$;

### 4.3 Offloading-Decision II for Approximate Algorithm

Offloading-Decision II is a supplementary heuristic to Offloading-Decision I, aimed at further reducing energy consumption. It iterates through winning VDs, seeking reassignments to alternative connected MEC servers that offer lower energy usage, feasible only if the target server has sufficient resources. This phase yields incremental energy benefits mainly in resource-abundant scenarios. Due to its straightforward implementation, its detailed pseudo-code is omitted for brevity.

### 4.4 Critical-Payment for Approximate Algorithm

To ensure the overall approximate mechanism is truthful (incentive-compatible), meaning VDs are best off bidding their true values, the Critical-Payment algorithm (Algorithm 5) is employed to determine the final payments. The purpose of the Critical-Payment is to find the lowest payment price at which the VD can still win. We have designed a payment price algorithm based on binary search, Critical-Payment. The fundamental idea is that for each winning VD, reduce the VD's bid $b_i$, and run the allocation algorithm again. If VDi can still win in the new allocation, then his bid will be reduced again; otherwise, the bid for VDi will be increased. If the difference between the upper and lower bounds is less than a very small value (for example, $10^{-6}$), the algorithm ends, and the upper bound is taken as the critical value and the final payment price. In the Critical-Payment algorithm, lines 1–15 calculate the final payment price for the winning VDs. For each winning VD, it changes his bid to half of what it was originally in line 2. The binary search-based lines 2–14 repeatedly call the Winner-Determination algorithm to find the final payment price for VDi. The payment price for all VDs who have not been allocated is set to 0 and they no longer participate in the payment algorithm.

**Algorithm 5** Critical-Payment $(x, \theta)$

1:     $\hat{\mathcal{N}} = \{i : \sum_{m \in \mathcal{M}} x_{im} \geq 1\}$
2:     **for all** $i \in \hat{\mathcal{N}}$ **do**
3:        $UB_i = b_i; LB_i = 0; pay_i = (UB_i + LB_i)/2;$
4:        **while** $\left(|UB_i - LB_i| \geq 10^{-6}\right)$ **do**
5:           $b_i = pay_i$
6:           $\hat{x}$ = Winner-Determination $\left(\hat{\theta}\right)$
7:           **if** $\sum_{m \in \mathcal{M}} \hat{x}_{im} \geq 1$ **then**
8:             $UB_i = pay_i$
9:             $pay_i = (UB_i + LB_i)/2$
10:          **else**
11:              $LB_i = pay_i$
12:             $pay_i = (UB_i + LB_i)/2$
13:          **end if**
14:        **end while**
15:        $pay_i = UB_i$
16:     **end for**
17:     **return** $pay$

### 4.5 Attribute

**Theorem 1**: The approximate ROTA mechanism is individually rational.

- Proof: A VD will never have negative utility. Losers pay zero. Winners pay their critical bid value determined by Algorithm 5, which, by construction of the binary search, cannot exceed their actual winning bid bi. Thus, $pay_i \leq b_i$ ensuring non-negative utility $u_i = b_i - pay_i \geq 0$.

**Theorem 2**: The Winner Determines that the algorithm is monotonic.

Assumption Scope: We assume that it is impossible for VDs to declare untruthful resource requirements and deployment constraints (the reasons have been analyzed in Sect. 2.2), but VDs can change their bids. Therefore, we need to prove monotonicity only with respect to the bid $b_j$.

-Proof: We must show that if a $VD_j$ wins when submitting request $\theta_j = \left(b_j, w_j, d_j, t_j^{req}, size_j\right)$, it must also win when submitting request $\tilde{\theta}_j = \left(\tilde{b}_j, w_j, d_j, t_j^{req}, size_j\right)$, where $\tilde{b}_j \geq b_j$, (assuming all other inputs $\tilde{\theta}_j$ remain fixed). Assume $VD_j$ wins with bid $b_j$ and is allocated resources on MEC server m by Algorithm 3. Now consider VD j submitting $\tilde{\theta}_j$ with $\tilde{b}_j \geq b_j$, The weighted value score

$\tilde{L}_{jm} = (\tilde{b}_j + E_{jm})/2 \geq (b_j + E_{jm})/2 = L_{jm}$ for all connectable servers m. Consequently, the sorting index $\tilde{\prod}_j$ must be greater than or equal to the original index $\prod_j$. Let $k_j$ and $\tilde{k}_j$ be the ranks (positions) of $VD_j$ in the list sorted by non-increasing $\prod$ value (Algorithm 3, Line 13) when bidding $b_j$ and $\tilde{b}_j$, respectively. Due to $\tilde{\prod}_j \geq \prod_j$, $VD_j$'s position in the sorted list will either stay the same or improve, meaning $\tilde{k}_j \leq k_j$. Now, consider the allocation process for server m where VD j initially won:

If $\tilde{k}_j = k_j$, $VD_j$ is considered at the same position in the sorted list. The set of VDs processed before it is identical in both scenarios. Therefore, the available resources $(\hat{c}, \hat{F})$ on server m when $VD_j$ is considered are exactly the same. Since $VD_j$ won with bid $b_j$, resources were sufficient then. As its resource requirements have not changed, resources are still sufficient, and it will be allocated. $VD_j$ wins.

If $\tilde{k}_j < k_j$, $VD_j$ is considered *earlier* in the sorted list when bidding $\tilde{b}_j$. Let R(k) denote the available resources on server m when the k-th VD in the list is considered. Because fewer (or the same) VDs have been processed before rank $\tilde{k}_j$ compared to rank $k_j$, the available resources $R(\tilde{k}_j)$ must be greater than or equal to $R(k_j)$. Since $VD_j$ won when considered at rank $k_j$, we know $R(k_j)$ was sufficient to meet its unchanged resource requirement. Therefore, $R(k_j)$ must also be sufficient. When $VD_j$ is processed at rank $\tilde{k}_j$, it will find server m (or potentially another suitable server) feasible and will be allocated. $VD_j$ wins. In both cases, if $VD_j$ wins with bid $b_j$, it also wins with any higher bid $\tilde{b}_j \geq b_j$. Therefore, the Winner-Determination algorithm (Algorithm 3) is monotonic with respect to bids.

Note that the offloading decision algorithm guarantees that each winner gets the required resources. Therefore, VD j will obtain resources from MEC server m and remain a winner.

Theorem 3: The Critical-Payment algorithm realizes the key payment.

PROOF: The Critical-Payment algorithm employs binary search to find the lowest price at which a VD can successfully deploy and allocate resources. The Critical-Payment algorithm ensures that if VD i's bid is above the critical value, the VD will win, and vice versa. Similarly, binary search guarantees that the VD's critical value is independent of their own bid but determined by the bids of other VDs, satisfying the definition of the critical value theory.

Theorem 4: The approximate ROTA mechanism is true.

PROOF: The winner determination algorithm is a monotone winner determination algorithm (Definition 2) and the key-payment algorithm realizes the key-payment (Definition 3). Therefore, the approximate ROTA mechanism satisfies the strategy proof property (Definition 5).

Theorem 5: The ROTA problem and the MESP problem are NP-hard.

Proof: without loss of generality, we assume $|\mathcal{M} = \{m\}| = 1$ and all VDs are fully connected. We ignore the constraints in the MESP problem (34–38). Then, the ROTA problem and the MESP problem can be modeled as multidimensional knapsack problems and are NP-hard.

Theorem 6 The approximation of Offloading-Decision I is $1 - \epsilon$ for a single MEC server.

Since we consider a single MEC server, we assume $\mathcal{M} = \{m\}$ and $|\mathcal{M}| = 1$. Let V be the solution obtained by Offloading-Decision. Let $x^*$ be the optimal allocation and $OPT = \sum_{i \in \mathcal{N}} x^*_{im} E^s_{im}$. If $\sum_{i \in \mathcal{N}} x^*_{im} \leq q$, it means that the algorithm finds the optimal solution because it considers all subsets $\mathcal{S}(|\mathcal{S}| \leq q)$ in the Offloading-Decision algorithm. If the algorithm terminates on line 4, we have $V \geq (1-\epsilon) OPT$. Let $\overline{OPT}$ be the optimal fraction solution. If the algorithm terminates on line 37, we have $V \geq (1-\epsilon)\overline{OPT} \geq OPT$. Otherwise, let $\{j_1^*, j_2^*, \ldots, j_q^*, \ldots\}$ be the set of VDs in an optimal solution ordered so that $E^s_{j_1^* m} \geq E^s_{j_2^* m} \geq \cdots \geq E^s_{j_q^* m} \geq \cdots$. In an iteration of step 3 in Offloading-Decision, the algorithm considers set $\mathcal{S}^* = \{j_1^*, j_2^*, \ldots, j_q^*\}$ and $\overline{\mathcal{N}^*} = \{i : i \in \mathcal{N} \setminus \mathcal{S}^*\}$. Let $\bar{x}$ be the allocation obtained by Offloading-Decision for $\overline{\mathcal{N}^*}$. Then, we have

$$V \geq \sum_{i \in S^*} E^s_{im} + \sum_{i \in \overline{\mathcal{N}^*}} \hat{x}_{im} E^s_{im} \qquad (43)$$

Let $\bar{x}^*$ be the optimal fraction allocation for $\overline{\mathcal{N}^*}$. We have

$$OPT = \sum_{i \in S^*} E^s_{im} + \sum_{i \in \overline{\mathcal{N}^*}} x^*_{im} E^s_{im} \leq \sum_{i \in S^*} E^s_{im} + \sum_{i \in \overline{\mathcal{N}^*}} \hat{x}^*_{im} E^s_{im} \qquad (44)$$

Let $\mathcal{D} = \{i : \hat{x}^*_{im} > \hat{x}_{im}, i \in \overline{\mathcal{N}^*}\}$. Since the basic solution has at most $R+1$ fraction variables, we have

$$|\mathcal{D}| \leq R + 1 \qquad (45)$$

Thus, we have

$$\sum_{i \in \mathcal{D}} E^s_{im} \leq (R+1) \max_{i \in \mathcal{D}} E^s_{im} \leq (R+1) \min_{i \in S} E^s_{im} \leq (R+1) \frac{\sum_{i \in S^*} E^s_{im}}{q} \qquad (46)$$

where the first inequality follows from (45); and the third inequality follows from the fact that $|S^*| = q$. Then

$$\sum_{i \in \overline{\mathcal{N}^*}} \hat{x}^*_{im} E^s_{im} \leq \sum_{i \in \overline{\mathcal{N}^*}} \hat{x}_{im} E^s_{im} + \sum_{i \in \mathcal{D}} E^s_{im} \leq \sum_{i \in \overline{\mathcal{N}^*}} \hat{x}_{im} E^s_{im} + (R+1) \frac{\sum_{i \in S^*} E^s_{im}}{q} \qquad (47)$$

where the second inequality follows from (46). Clearly,

$$OPT \leq \sum_{i \in S^*} E^s_{im} + \sum_{i \in \overline{\mathcal{N}^*}} \hat{x}^*_{im} E^s_{im} \leq \sum_{i \in S^*} E^s_{im} + \sum_{i \in \overline{\mathcal{N}^*}} \hat{x}_{im} E^s_{im} + (R+1) \frac{\sum_{i \in S^*} E^s_{im}}{q}$$

$$\leq V + (R+1) \frac{\sum_{i \in S^*} E^s_{im}}{q} \leq V \left(1 + \frac{R+1}{q}\right) \leq V \left(\frac{1}{1-\epsilon}\right) \qquad (48)$$

where the first inequality follows from (44); the second inequality follows from (47); the third inequality follows from (43); the fourth inequality follows from the fact that $V \geq \sum_{i \in S^*} E^s_{im}$; and the fifth inequality follows from the fact that.

Theorem 7: The time complexity of the winner determination algorithm is computationally efficient.

Proof. For each VD, the winner determination algorithm is first ordered with a time complexity of O (NlogN) then calculates each connectable MEC with a time complexity of O (NM). Therefore, the overall time complexity is O (NlogN + MN), which is a polynomial time complexity.

Theorem 8. The time complexity of the offloading decision algorithm is computationally efficient.

Proof: The offloading decision phase consists of two main parts: Offloading-Decision I (Algorithm 4) and the supplementary heuristic Offloading-Decision II. We analyze their complexities separately.

1. Offloading-Decision I (Algorithm 4): This algorithm is a polynomial-time approximation scheme (PTAS). Its complexity is determined by the step that enumerates subsets of winning VDs. The algorithm iterates through subsets S of size up to q, where q = min{$\lceil (R + 1)(1 - \epsilon)/\epsilon \rceil$, |Nm|}. In the worst case, the number of subsets to check is on the order of O(Nq). For each main iteration, a linear programming relaxation (LP-MESP-m) is solved. As stated in the paper, solving this LP relaxation can be done in polynomial time. Therefore, the overall time complexity of Offloading-Decision I is polynomial in N, and is specifically $O\big((R + 1)N^{(R+1)(1-\epsilon)/\epsilon}\big)$.
2. Offloading-Decision II: This phase is a supplementary heuristic designed to further reduce energy consumption. It works by iterating through the winning VDs (at most N VDs) and, for each one, attempting to reassign it to another connected MEC server (at most M servers) if the move is feasible and saves more energy. This process involves a nested loop structure, resulting in a time complexity of O(NM).

Since both Offloading-Decision I and Offloading-Decision II have polynomial-time complexities, the entire offloading decision algorithm is computationally efficient.

Theorem 9: The time complexity of the Critical-Payment algorithm is computationally efficient.

The Critical-Payment algorithm must invoke the Winner Determines algorithm for all winning VDs, so the time complexity of Critical-Payment is O ($N^2$ logN + $MN^2$).

## 5 Experiment

We evaluate the performance of the proposed mechanism in different scenarios. We consider a simulated environment that is able to capture the features of the MEC application scenario. The specific rules are provided as follows:

1. For each MEC server, we assume that the computational power, memory and storage are uniformly distributed between [15, 20] GHz, [512 MB, 1 GB] and [5 MB, 10 MB], respectively. For each VD, we assume that the local computational power, required computational power, memory, data size, cutoff time, and bid are uniformly distributed between [0.5, 1] GHz, [1200, 1500] megacycles, [20 MB, 50 MB], [100 kB, 500 kB], [1, 1.5] seconds, and [0.018, 0.34]. The selected value of $\epsilon$ is 0.4, corresponding to a

q-value of 5. If a higher energy saving approximation ratio is required, the value can be raised, but the corresponding calculation time will increase.
2. In our experiments, the parameters regarding the energy consumption and time delay

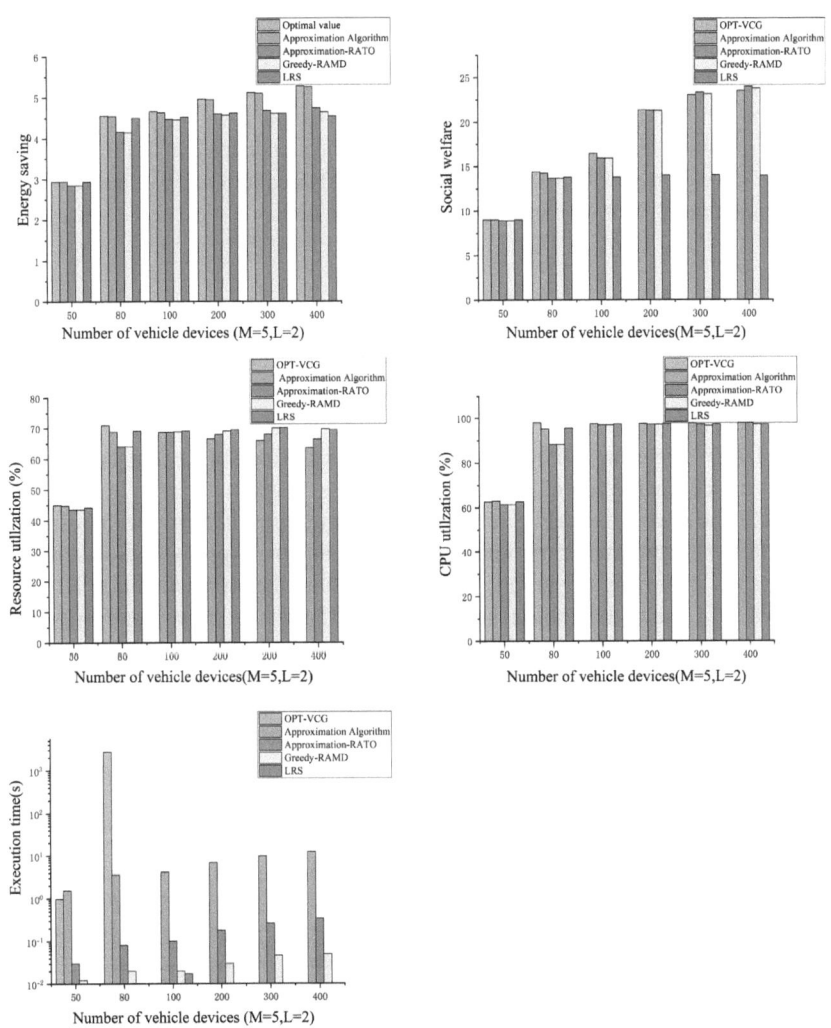

**Fig. 2.** The impact of the different numbers of VDs

of the MEC server and the VDs refer to [12]. The simulation parameters d denote the distance from the VD to the edge, taken as a random integer from 1 to 120, and $\vartheta$ denotes the path loss exponent, here taken as 4. h denotes the channel fading coefficient, which obeys a complex Gaussian distribution with zero-mean unit variance. The transmission bandwidth B is 20 MHz, the variance of the Gaussian white noise $\sigma^2$ is $3 \times 10^{-13}$, the transmission power of the VD $\rho_1$ is 0.5W, and the transmission power of the MEC server $\rho_2$ is 10W.

3. In order to eliminate the randomness of the data, we averaged the data points from 50 simulations for each metric of each algorithm in the experiment.
4. We compared Approximation Algorithm with OPT-VCG. The optimal solution of OPT-VCG and the optimal fractional solution of Approximation Algorithm are obtained by CPLEX. We compare the Approximation Algorithm with Approximation-RATO [14] and Greedy-RAMD-I [16]. Greedy-RAMD only considers the winner determination problem. In addition, we compare Approximation Algorithm with the baseline method LRS [17]. To make LRS suitable for this problem, we modified his algorithm so that its task always matches that of the MEC server with the lowest proportion of current resources. LRS cannot achieve authenticity, so we assume that all VDS are truthfully declared in LRS.

### 5.1 Impact of Different Amounts of VDs

This study explores a vehicle-connected scenario in which the number of vehicle devices (VDs) varies from 50 to 400, the number of MEC servers remains unchanged to 5, and the deployment constraint L is 2. When N is greater than 80, OPT-VCG cannot be solved in a limited time. Therefore, OPT-VCG will only be performed in the first 2 experiments. The results are compared in Fig. 2.

Figure 2(a) shows the energy savings achieved through different mechanisms. The optimal solution is the maximum energy saving under the Approximation Algorithm mechanism. By observing the graph, it can be seen that the Approximation Algorithm achieves a level close to the optimal energy saving. The results show that energy saving increases with the increase of VD quantity. The energy saving achieved by Approximation Algorithm is close to the optimal solution, and is better than Approximation-RATO, LRS and Greedy-RAMD. Therefore, it can be concluded that the Approximation Algorithm performs well in saving energy consumption.

Figure 2(b) shows a comparison of social welfare. By observing the graph, it can be seen that the Approximation Algorithm realizes a level close to the optimal social welfare. Compared with Approximation-RATO, Approximation Algorithm can obtain greater social welfare when $VD \leq 200$. Although there is a gap of about 1% between the social welfare at $VD > 200$ and the Approximation-RATO, the corresponding energy saving increases by about 8%, which is acceptable. When $VD \geq 300$, the social welfare obtained by Approximation Algorithm is slightly worse than that obtained by Approximation-RATO and Greedy-RAMD. This is due to the Approximation Algorithm that takes social welfare and energy savings into account. Compared with LRS, the approximate Algorithm has higher social welfare than LRS throughout the period.

Figures 2(c) and 2(d) show average resource utilization and average CPU utilization. The results show that as the number of VD increases, so does the percentage of resource utilization. As can be seen from the figure, the Approximation Algorithm is not always the optimal resource utilization, because our task is to find the VD with the greatest energy saving and social welfare, and does not care about the resource utilization.

Figure 2(e) shows the execution times of the winner determination problem on a logarithmic scale. It can be seen from the observation that the Approximation Algorithm mechanism has a high execution efficiency, while the OPT-VCG mechanism has a slow execution speed in large-scale problems. This is because the Approximation Algorithm does not need to search all possibilities. By synthesizing the data in Fig. 2(b) and 2(e), we can conclude that Approximation Algorithm mechanism can not only get close to the optimal solution, but also determine the winner within a reasonable time. It is worth noting that the time of Approximation Algorithm is higher than other approximation algorithms, because the time complexity of payment algorithm is relatively large.

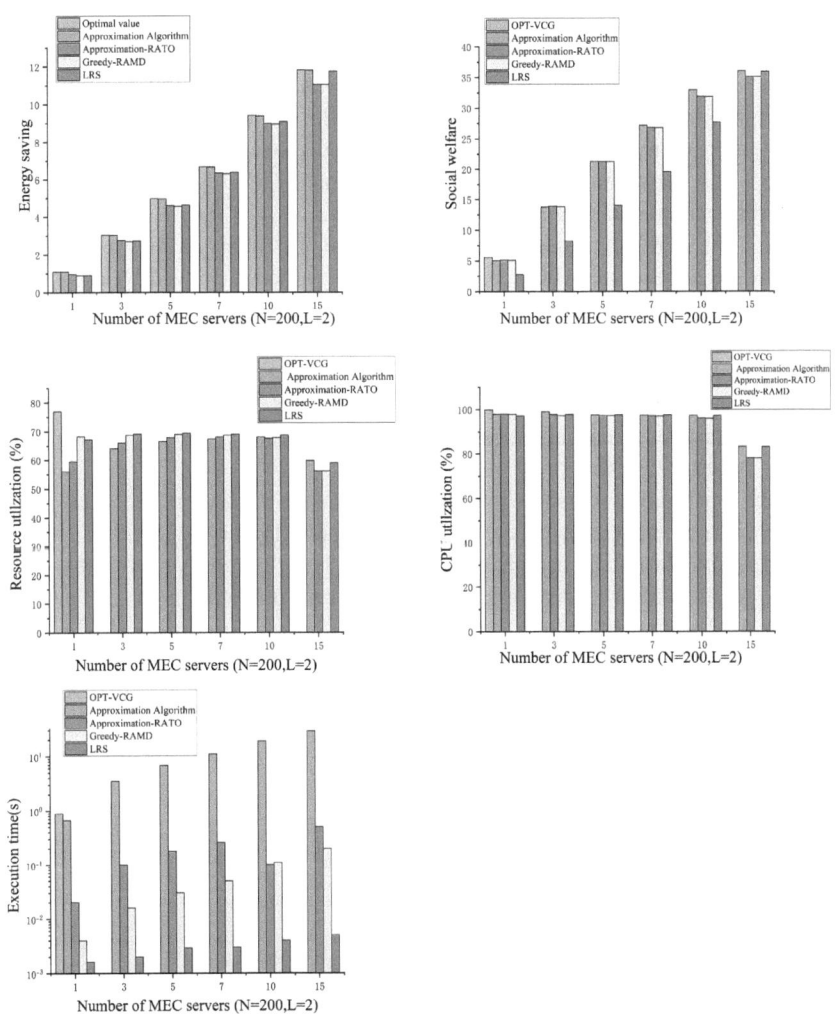

**Fig. 3.** The impact of the different numbers of MECs

## 5.2 Impact of Different Amounts of MECs

In this study, we explore a connected vehicle scenario where the number of MEC servers varies between 1 and 15, the number of vehicle devices (VDs) is 200, and the deployment constraint L is 2 (default is fully connected when M = 1). When M > 1, OPT-VCG cannot be solved in a limited time. Therefore, OPT-VCG will only be performed in the first experiment. The results of the comparative analysis are shown in Fig. 3.

Figure 3 (a) shows a comparison of energy savings. The results show that the energy saving effect of Approximation Algorithm is better than that of Approximation-RATO,LRS and Greedy-RAMD. It can be concluded that the Approximation Algorithm mechanism can effectively reduce energy consumption while ensuring the authenticity. It is noted that when M = 15, the energy saving effect achieved by LRS algorithm is close to the Approximate algorithm. As we mentioned above, LRS can achieve excellent energy savings without intense competition for resources. It is important to note that the LRS algorithm cannot achieve authenticity.

Figure 3 (b) shows the changes in social welfare. The analysis shows that with the increase in the number of MEC servers, the social welfare achieved by the proposed algorithm increases correspondingly. It can be observed that the social welfare achieved by the approximation algorithm is close to the optimal solution. Although in the case of intense resource competition (M < 5), it is about 1% lower than Approximation-RATO, the corresponding energy saving is improved by about 10%, which is acceptable. In the case of not intense resource competition (M > =5), the social welfare of Approximation Algorithm is better than that of all other algorithms.

Figures 3 (c) and 3 (d) show the average resource utilization and average CPU utilization. As can be seen from the figure, the Approximation Algorithm's resource utilization is not always the best, because our task is to find the VD with the greatest energy saving and social welfare, regardless of resource utilization.

Figure 3 (e) shows the change in execution time on a logarithmic scale. In the case of changes in the number of MEC servers, the Approximation Algorithm achieves near optimal social welfare in a reasonable time. Note that the Approximation Algorithm takes more time than other approximation algorithms because the payment algorithm calls the winner decision algorithm multiple times.

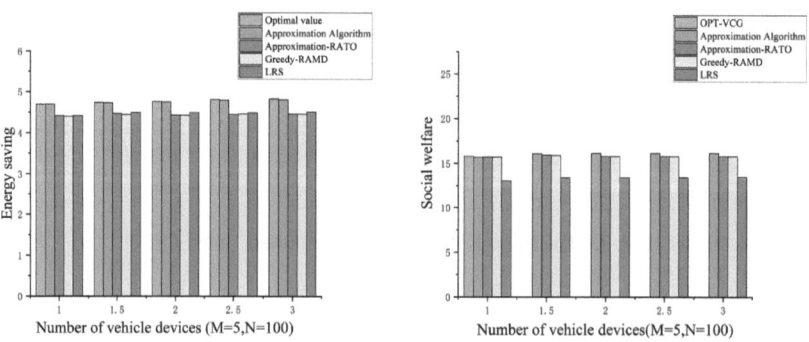

**Fig. 4.** The impact of the different deployment constraint L

## 5.3 Impact of Different Deployment Constraint L

In this research, we explored a connected vehicle scenario where the deployment constraint L varies between 1 and 3, with 100 Vehicle Devices (VDs) and the number of MEC servers (M) remains unchanged at 5. The parameter L defines the average number of distinct MEC servers (out of the M available) that each VD can connect to; thus, a higher L represents a scenario where VDs have more connection options to the fixed set of MEC servers. When L > 1, OPT-VCG cannot be solved within a finite timeframe. Therefore, OPT-VCG was only included in the first experiment where L was effectively 1 for it. The comparative analysis results are shown in Fig. 4.

Figure 4(a) displays the comparison of energy savings. Compared to Approximation-RATO, the Approximation Algorithm achieves over 6% improvement in energy savings across different deployment constraints, with the energy-saving effect slightly increasing as L increases. Similarly, the Approximation Algorithm's energy efficiency also outperforms both LRS and Greedy-RAMD. When comparing the Approximation Algorithm under different constraints, we observe that as deployment constraints increase, energy savings show a slight growth but no significant changes. We can conclude that different deployment constraints have minimal impact on the algorithm's energy-saving performance, and the Approximation Algorithm consistently demonstrates superior energy efficiency compared to other approximation algorithms.

Figure 4(b) illustrates the changes in social welfare. Analysis indicates that as the deployment constraint L increases, the social welfare achieved by the employed algorithms does not change significantly. We can observe that the social welfare achieved through the approximation algorithm approaches the optimal solution. Compared to Approximation-RATO, the Approximation Algorithm shows approximately 2% improvement in social welfare, with this improvement slightly increasing as the deployment constraint L grows, outperforming all other approximation algorithms. It is noted that when L = 1, the social welfare of the Approximation Algorithm will be slightly lower than that of the Approximation-RATO. This is because at this time each VD is only connected to one MEC, and the social welfare at this time is only related to the ranking index. Compared with the Approximation Algorithm that focuses on the comprehensive ranking index of social welfare and energy saving, the Approximation-RATO will obtain slightly better social welfare We can conclude that different deployment constraints have minimal impact on the algorithms' social welfare performance, and the Approximation Algorithm demonstrates superior social welfare compared to other algorithms.

The experimental results show that compared with Approximation-RATO, our algorithm can improve the energy saving effect by 8% to 11% in the environment of fierce resource competition, but only lose 1% to 2.5% of social welfare. In a low-competition environment, our algorithm can improve energy savings by 6% while improving social welfare by about 2%. Compared with other Approximation algorithms, the Approximation Algorithm can achieve better performance in social welfare and energy saving.

## 6 Conclusion and Future Work

This paper discusses the problem of joint resource allocation and task offloading in mobile edge computing. We considered the heterogeneous MEC server and multiple resource settings. The RATO problem includes the winner determination problem and the offloading decision problem. In the first problem, we propose a greedy approximation algorithm and show that it is individually rational and honest. We then analyzed the approximate ratios of the individual MEC servers. In the second problem, we propose an approximation algorithm based on the local search. We then analyzed the approximate ratios of the individual MEC servers. The experimental results show that our proposed approximation mechanism performs well under different conditions. For future work, we plan to extend the proposed mechanism to a time-varying environment or in real edge computing environments.

## References

1. Lin, F., Zhou, Y., Pau, G., Collotta, M.: Optimization-oriented resource allocation management for vehicular fog computing. IEEE Access **6**, 69294–69303 (2018)
2. Sun, J., Gu, Q., Zheng, T., Dong, P., Qin, Y.: Joint communication and computing resource allocation in vehicular edge computing. Int. J. Distrib. Sens. Networks **15**, 812336553 (2019)
3. Alrawais, A., Alhothaily, A., Yu, J., Hu, C., Cheng, X.: SecureGuard: a certificate validation system in public key infrastructure. IEEE Trans. Veh. Technol. 1 (2018)
4. Xu, X., et al.: An edge computing-enabled computation offloading method with privacy preservation for internet of connected vehicles. Futur. Gener. Comput. Syst. **96**, 89–100 (2019)
5. Reza Dibaj, S.M., Miri, A., Mostafavi, SeyedAkbar: A cloud priority-based dynamic online double auction mechanism (PB-DODAM). J. Cloud Comput. **9**(1), 1–26 (2020). https://doi.org/10.1186/s13677-020-00213-7
6. Zheng, X., Shah, S.B.H., Usman, S., Mahfoudh, S., Shemimks, F., Kumarshukla, P.: Resource allocation and network pricing based on double auction in mobile edge computing. J. Cloud Comput. (2192–113X). 12 (2023)
7. Eva, T.: Algorithmic game theory. Commun. ACM **53**, 78–86 (2007)
8. Mashayekhy, L., Nejad, M.M., Grosu, D.: Physical machine resource management in clouds: a mechanism design approach. IEEE Trans. Cloud Comput. **3**, 247–260 (2015)
9. Wang, X., Han, Y., Shi, H., Qian, Z.: JOAGT: latency-oriented joint optimization of computation offloading and resource allocation in D2D-assisted MEC system. IEEE Wireless Commun. Lett. **11**, 1780–1784 (2022)
10. Wang, M., Shi, S., Zhang, D., Wu, C., Wang, Y.: Joint computation offloading and resource allocation for MIMO-NOMA assisted multi-user MEC systems. IEEE Trans. Commun. 71 (2023)
11. Luo, Q., Hu, S., Li, C., Li, G., Shi, W.: Resource scheduling in edge computing: a survey. IEEE Commun. Surv. Tutorials **23**, 2131–2165 (2021)
12. Chen, M., Hao, Y., Hu, L., Huang, K., Lau, V.K.N.: Green and mobility-aware caching in 5G networks. IEEE Trans. Wireless Commun. **16**, 8347–8361 (2017)
13. Nisan, A.M.: Truthful approximation mechanisms for restricted combinatorial auctions. GAME Econ. Behav. (2008)
14. Liu, X., Liu, J., Li, W.: Truthful mechanism for joint resource allocation and task offloading in mobile edge computing. Comput. Netw. **254**, 110796 (2024)

15. Caprara, A., Kellerer, H., Pferschy, U., Pisinger, D.: Approximation algorithms for knapsack problems with cardinality constraints. Eur. J. Oper. Res. **123**, 333–345 (2000)
16. Liu, X., Liu, J., Wu, H., Dong, J.: A family of truthful mechanisms for resource allocation with multi-attribute demand in mobile edge computing. Clust. Comput. **27**, 11595–11610 (2024)
17. Liwang, M., Dai, S., Gao, Z., Tang, Y., Dai, H.: A truthful reverse-auction mechanism for computation offloading in cloud-enabled vehicular network. IEEE Internet Things **6**, 4214–4227 (2019)

# The State Transition Self-learning Framework Based on Generalized Intuitionistic Fuzzy Kripke Structure

Yuxuan He and Chao Yang[✉]

College of Information Engineering, Yangzhou University, Yangzhou 225127, China
mx120230565@stu.yzu.edu.cn, yangch12@yzu.edu.cn

**Abstract.** Based on generalized intuitionistic fuzzy Kripke structures (GIFKSs), we propose a novel state transition self-learning framework to address the problems of state modeling and parameter adaptability in dynamic systems. In this work, we assume that the states of GIFKS are unknown, and the only available knowledge is the sensor variables that exhibit ambiguous relationships with these states. To bridge the gap between these sensor variables and the states, we connect the sensor data to the atomic propositions representing the states using a set of intuitionistic fuzzy functions. The first learning model for GIFKS, called the GIFKS with Intuitionistic Fuzzifier Sets (GIFKS - IFSs), combines a standard GIFKS model with a collection of intuitionistic fuzzy functions that link the system's states to various sensor variables. These intuitionistic fuzzy functions allow for more flexible handling of uncertainty by considering both membership and non-membership degrees in the fuzzy relations between the sensor data and system states. To optimize the parameters of the intuitionistic fuzzy function that describes the state transition mechanism and the elements of the atomic propositional transition matrix, we derive learning algorithms based on stochastic gradient descent. The proposed self-learning model demonstrates superior performance in both theoretical and experimental settings, offering strong parameter adaptability and algorithmic convergence.

**Keywords:** Generalized intuitionistic fuzzy Kripke structure · Intuitionistic fuzzy logic · State transition learning · Intuitionistic fuzzy systems

## 1 Introduction

The Kripke structure [2] has long served as a foundational tool for formally modeling the dynamic behavior of discrete - event systems. It represents systems as a graph of state nodes and transitions, offering a formal framework for system analysis. However, binary logic in classical Kripke structures proves inadequate for modeling systems with uncertain or imprecise information.

While extensions such as the possibility Kripke structure [4-6] address some of these challenges by incorporating possibility theory or probability distributions, they remain constrained by the normalization condition of transition probabilities. This limitation restricts their ability to capture and represent complex uncertainties effectively.

Recent advances in fuzzy modeling have provided solutions to these issues. Zadeh's possibility theory [23] laid the foundation for the generalized possibility Kripke structure (GPKS) [9–11,15], which replaces binary transitions with possibility matrices. Building on this framework, Liu [14] proposed the generalized possibility Kripke structure with Fuzzy Sets (GPKS - FS), linking sensor variables to atomic propositions via Gaussian membership functions. However, its single - membership framework lacks the interpretability needed to model "rejection" or "uncertainty" states, limiting its application in more complex environments.

This study presents a new approach [22] to tackle these problems by integrating Intuitionistic Fuzzy Sets (IFS) [1] into the GPKS framework. The resulting model, Generalized Intuitionistic Fuzzy Kripke Structure with Intuitionistic Fuzzy Sets (GIFKS - IFS), not only overcomes the limitations of the traditional Kripke structure in system modeling but also offers greater flexibility and interpretability in system modeling [16,18]. Utilizing intuitionistic fuzzy functions, this model can effectively handle uncertainty in sensor data. Furthermore, an online learning method based on stochastic gradient descent is proposed to optimize the model parameters, thereby enhancing both the stability and accuracy of the system. This approach provides a promising new framework for modeling uncertainty in dynamic systems, with both theoretical depth and practical application potential.

The remainder of this paper is organized as follows: Section 2 introduces $t$-norms, $t$-conorms, intuitionistic fuzzy theory and GIFKS. Section 3 presents GIFKS with intuitionistic fuzzy sets (GIFKS - IFS). In Section 4, the learning algorithm for optimizing all model parameters is derived based on the stochastic gradient descent principle. Section 5 presents experimental results and analyzes the learning performance. Finally, Sect. 6 concludes the paper.

## 2 Preliminaries

In the following study, $\vee$ and $\wedge$ are used to denote the maximum and minimum operations on $[0,1]$, respectively. Additionally, $\bigvee X$ and $\bigwedge X$ represent the supremum and infimum of subset $X$ contained in $[0,1]$, respectively.

Now, we recall some basic notions of $t$-norms and $t$-conorms.

*Definition 1:* ([13]) A $t$-norm $\otimes$ is a binary operation on $[0,1]$ fulfilling commutativity, associativity, nondecreasing in each argument and with neutral element 1.

*Definition 2:* ([13]) A $t$-conorm $\oplus$ is a binary operation on $[0,1]$ fulfilling commutativity, associativity, nondecreasing in each argument and with neutral element 0.

Some common notations for $t$-norms and $t$-conorms are as follows:

1. Standard: $a \otimes_S b = a \wedge b$, $a \oplus_S b = a \vee b$,
2. Product: $a \otimes_P b = ab$, $a \oplus_P b = a + b - ab$,

where $a, b \in [0, 1]$.

For the reader's convenience, we proceed by reviewing the definition of intuitionistic fuzzy sets and by introducing the concept of generalized intuitionistic fuzzy Kripke structures.

*Definition 3:* ([1]) Let $X$ be a set. Then an intuitionistic fuzzy set $A$ on $X$ is defined as:

$$A = \{(x, \mu_A(x), \gamma_A(x)) \mid x \in X\},$$

where $\mu_A$ and $\gamma_A$ are fuzzy subsets of $X$, that is, they are functions from $X$ to $[0, 1]$, and $\mu_A(x)$ and $\gamma_A(x)$ refer to as the degree of membership and the degree of nonmembership of $x \in X$ to $A$, respectively. Additionally, for all $x \in X$, it holds that $0 \leq \mu_A(x) + \gamma_A(x) \leq 1$. The hesitancy degree $\pi_A(x) = 1 - \mu_A(x) - \gamma_A(x)$ quantifies the uncertainty of $x$ belonging to $A$. For simplicity, we always write the expression of $A$ as $A = (\mu_A, \gamma_A)$ and for any $x \in X$, $A(x) = (\mu_A(x), \gamma_A(x))$.

*Definition 4:* A Generalized Intuitionistic Fuzzy Kripke Structure (GIFKS) is a quintuple $\mathcal{M} = (S, P, I, AP, L)$, where:

1. $S$ is a countable, nonempty set of states;
2. $P$ is an intuitionistic fuzzy set on $S \times S$ and called the intuitionistic fuzzy transition function;
3. $I$ is an intuitionistic fuzzy set on S and called the intuitionistic fuzzy initial distribution function;
4. $AP$ is a set of atomic propositions;
5. $L$ is an intuitionistic fuzzy set on $S \times AP$ and called the inituitionistic fuzzy labeling function.

Specially, if the intuitionistic fuzzy transition and initial distributions are regular (i.e., $\bigvee_{s' \in S} P(s, s') = (1, 0)$, $\bigvee_{s \in S} I(s) = (1, 0)$) and the labeling function $L$ is crisp (i.e., $L : S \times AP \to \{(1, 0), (0, 1)\}$), then GIFKS $\mathcal{M}$ is called regular.

## 3 Dual-Channel Fuzzy State Space Modeling

A Generalized Intuitionistic Fuzzy Kripke Structure with Intuitionistic Fuzzy Sets(GIFKS-IFSs) model comprises a standard GIFKS and a group of intuitionistic fuzzy sets that link the states of the model to external sensor variables.

*Definition 5 (GIFKS-IFSs):* Let the following components be formally specified:

- **Sensor measurement space**: $V \subseteq \mathbb{R}^m$ where $m \in \mathbb{N}$, with concrete measurement vectors denoted as $\mathbf{v} = [x_1, x_2, \ldots, x_m] \in V$.
- **Atomic propositions**: Finite set $AP = \{AP_1, AP_2, \ldots, AP_n\}$ with $|AP| = n$.

A GIFKS-IFS is a tuple $\mathcal{G} = (\lambda, \mathcal{M}_\lambda, \text{Fuzzifier})$, defined as:

1. **Parameter** $\lambda \in \mathbb{N}$ specifies the modeling precision index:

$$\mathbb{D}_\lambda = \{k \times 10^{-\lambda} \mid k \in \mathbb{Z},\ 0 \leq k \leq 10^\lambda\}.$$

2. **Model** $\mathcal{M}_\lambda$ is a GIFKS with state space:

$$S_\lambda = \left\{ s : AP \to \mathbb{D}_\lambda \times \mathbb{D}_\lambda \mid \forall AP_i \in AP,\ s(AP_i) = (\mu_i, \gamma_i),\ \mu_i + \gamma_i \leq 1 \right\},$$

where each state $s \in S_\lambda$ maps atomic propositions to intuitionistic fuzzy values.

3. **Fuzzifier**: $V \to S_\lambda$ is a function induced by a family of intuitionistic fuzzy membership functions

$$\Theta = \{(\theta_i^\mu, \theta_i^\gamma)\}_{i \in \{1,2,\cdots,n\}},$$

where $\theta_i^\mu : V \to [0,1]$ and $\theta_i^\gamma : V \to [0,1]$ satisfy $\theta_i^\mu(\mathbf{v}) + \theta_i^\gamma(\mathbf{v}) \leq 1$ for all $\mathbf{v} \in V$.

For each sensor measurement $\mathbf{v} \in V$, the Fuzzifier constructs a state $s_\mathbf{v} \in S_\lambda$ such that:

$$s_\mathbf{v}(AP_i) = (\theta_i^\mu(\mathbf{v}), \theta_i^\gamma(\mathbf{v})) \quad \forall AP_i \in AP.$$

Here, $\theta_i^\mu(\mathbf{v})$ and $\theta_i^\gamma(\mathbf{v})$ represent the membership and non-membership degrees of the sensor measurement $\mathbf{v}$ satisfying the proposition $AP_i$, respectively. Together, they form an intuitionistic fuzzy set over the atomic propositions $AP$, parameterized by the sensor input $\mathbf{v}$.

In this framework, Gaussian-type functions are selected for IFS membership functions $\theta^\mu$ and IFS non-membership functions $\theta^\gamma$ due to their close alignment with real-world sensor behaviors. By adjusting the mean and standard deviation, the Gaussian function can flexibly adapt to the distribution of sensor data and variations in system state. Compared to the GPKS with Fuzzy Sets (GPKS-FS) [14], GIFKS-IFSs provides enhanced expressiveness by distinguishing between non-membership and hesitation, making it better suited for applications requiring fine-grained uncertainty quantification.

*Example 1.* Consider a rotating machinery health monitoring system implementing GIFKS-IFS with two atomic propositions:

- $AP_1$: "Bearing vibration within safety range"
- $AP_2$: "Lubricant temperature normal"

Let $\lambda = 3$ define the discretization precision:

$$\mathbb{D}_3 = \{0.000, 0.001, \ldots, 1.000\}.$$

The Gaussian parameters are configured as:

$$AP_1 : \begin{cases} \mu\text{-function} & (g_1 = 2.0 \text{ mm/s}, \ h_1 = 0.5) \\ \gamma\text{-function} & (r_1 = 5.0 \text{ mm/s}, \ \sigma_1 = 1.0) \end{cases}$$

$$AP_2 : \begin{cases} \mu\text{-function} & (g_2 = 75 \ ^\circ\text{C}, \ h_2 = 5) \\ \gamma\text{-function} & (r_2 = 90 \ ^\circ\text{C}, \ \sigma_2 = 10) \end{cases}$$

where $g_j/r_j$ represent the means, and $h_j/\sigma_j$ represent the standard deviations. For sensor measurements $\mathbf{v} = [3.2 \text{ mm/s}, \ 82 \ ^\circ\text{C}]$:

$$\theta_1^\mu(3.2) = \exp\left(-\frac{(3.2-2.0)^2}{2(0.5)^2}\right) = 0.278$$

$$\theta_1^\gamma(3.2) = \exp\left(-\frac{(3.2-5.0)^2}{2(1.0)^2}\right) = 0.486$$

$$\text{Hesitation}_1 = 1 - 0.278 - 0.486 = 0.236$$

$$\theta_2^\mu(82) = \exp\left(-\frac{(82-75)^2}{2(5)^2}\right) = 0.263$$

$$\theta_2^\gamma(82) = \exp\left(-\frac{(82-90)^2}{2(10)^2}\right) = 0.527$$

$$\text{Hesitation}_2 = 1 - 0.263 - 0.527 = 0.21$$

The constructed system state is:

$$\mathbf{s} = [(0.278, 0.486)_{\mathbb{D}_3}, \ (0.263, 0.527)_{\mathbb{D}_3}]$$

Table 1. Comparison between GPKS-FS and GIFKS-IFS

| Method | $\mu$-Degree | $\gamma$-Degree | Hesitation |
|---|---|---|---|
| GPKS-FS | 0.278 | N/A | N/A |
| GIFKS-IFS | 0.278 | 0.486 | 0.236 |

## 3.1 State Description

In dynamic systems, state transitions are critical for understanding behavior. We define a pair of states: the current state $s$ and the next state $t$. The degrees of the state $s$ are determined by a family of sensor variables $X_s$, while the degrees of state $t$ are described by a family of sensor variables $Y_t$ [21]. This relationship is formalized as:

$$X_s \Rightarrow s \xrightarrow{P(s,t)} t \Leftarrow Y_t. \tag{1}$$

Let $s = [(m_1, n_1), (m_2, n_2), \ldots, (m_n, n_n)]$ represent the current state, where $m_i$ and $m_i$ are the membership and non-membership degrees, respectively, inferred from sensor data $X_i$ using Gaussian membership and non-membership functions. To balance their influence, both weights are set to 0.5, ensuring impartiality in fuzzy reasoning, i.e.,

$$m_j = 0.5\theta_j^\mu(x_j \mid g_j, h_j) = 0.5e^{-\frac{(x_j - g_j)^2}{2h_j^2}}, \tag{2}$$

$$n_j = 0.5\theta_j^\gamma(x_j \mid r_j, \sigma_j) = 0.5e^{-\frac{(x_j - r_j)^2}{2\sigma_j^2}}, \tag{3}$$

Parameters $g_j$ and $r_j$ represent the means for the membership and non-membership degrees, respectively, while $h_j$ and $\sigma_j$ represent the standard deviations for the non-membership and membership degrees, respectively. The parameters $g_j$ and $h_j$ for the membership and non-membership degrees are learned through algorithms described in the subsequent sections. On the other hand, the parameters $r_j$ and $\sigma_j$ for the non-membership degrees are set based on real-world knowledge and expert input, and are therefore considered known in the experiments presented later. For the next state $t = [(p_1, q_1), (p_2, q_2), \ldots, (p_n, q_n)]$, estimated values $\hat{t} := [(\hat{p}_1, \hat{q}_1), (\hat{p}_2, \hat{q}_2), \ldots, (\hat{p}_n, \hat{q}_n)]$ are linked to sensor variables $Y_t = [y_1, y_2, \ldots, y_n]$ via inverse Gaussian functions.

$$\hat{y}_j^\mu = \theta_j^{\mu(-1)}(\hat{y}_j^\mu \mid g_j, h_j) = g_j \pm h_j\sqrt{-2\ln 2\hat{p}_j}, \tag{4}$$

$$\hat{y}_j^\gamma = \theta_j^{\gamma(-1)}(\hat{y}_j^\gamma \mid r_j, \sigma_j) = r_j \pm \sigma_j\sqrt{-2\ln 2\hat{q}_j}. \tag{5}$$

In Eq. (4), the + sign is used if $\hat{p}_j \geq g_j$, otherwise the − sign is applied. In Eq. (5), the + sign is used if $\hat{q}_j \geq r_j$, otherwise the − sign is applied. These rules will be consistently applied throughout the article to any formula involving the ± sign.

### 3.2 Atomic Propositional Transition Matrix

For the current state $s$, it will transition to a certain and unique next state $t$, provided that the state transition mechanism is known. However, many systems in the real world involve ambiguous and nondeterministic state transitions. We do not have full knowledge of the specific transition mechanism from one state to another, which often behaves as a black - box system. For example, in clinical trials, a drug treatment may change a patient from a bad state to a good state, although the mechanism of the drug is usually not known or needs to be known (the mechanism may be a chemical reaction between the molecular structure of the drug and the body). To describe such uncertain transitions, we use atomic propositions to represent each fuzzy state and model the transitions between states via an atomic propositional transition matrix(APTM). APTM $T$ is a matrix that describes the probability or law of the system transferring from atomic propositions to another, thus succinct capturing the complex state transition mechanism. Specifically, $T$ is defined as a $n \times n$ intuitionistic fuzzy matrix, and its matrix representation is

$$T = \begin{pmatrix} (\tau_{11}^{\mu}, \tau_{11}^{\gamma}) & \cdots & (\tau_{1n}^{\mu}, \tau_{nn}^{\gamma}) \\ \vdots & \ddots & \vdots \\ (\tau_{n1}^{\mu}, \tau_{n1}^{\gamma}) & \cdots & (\tau_{1n}^{\mu}, \tau_{nn}^{\gamma}) \end{pmatrix}$$

where $n = |AP|$, $\tau_{ij}^{\mu}$ represents the membership degree transition parameter, and $\tau_{ij}^{\gamma}$ represents the non - membership degree transition parameter. Then the process of the mechanism of transition between intuitionistic fuzzy state $s = [(m_1, n_1), (m_2, n_2), \ldots, (m_n, n_n)]$ and $\hat{t} = [(\hat{p}_1, \hat{q}_1), (\hat{p}_2, \hat{q}_2), \ldots, (\hat{p}_n, \hat{q}_n)]$ can be expressed as $s \circ T = \hat{T}$. The symbol $\circ$ represents the intuitionistic fuzzy composition operation. After comparing several simulation experiments, it appears that using the product t-norm ($\otimes$) to calculate membership and using the probabilistic sum t-conorm ($\oplus$) to calculate non-membership are more effective methods for simulating the transition mechanism of intelligent systems.

Hence

$$\hat{p}_j = \bigvee_{i=1}^{n} m_i \otimes_S \tau_{ij}^{\mu}, \tag{6}$$

$$\hat{q}_j = \bigwedge_{i=1}^{n} n_i \oplus_P \tau_{ij}^{\gamma}. \tag{7}$$

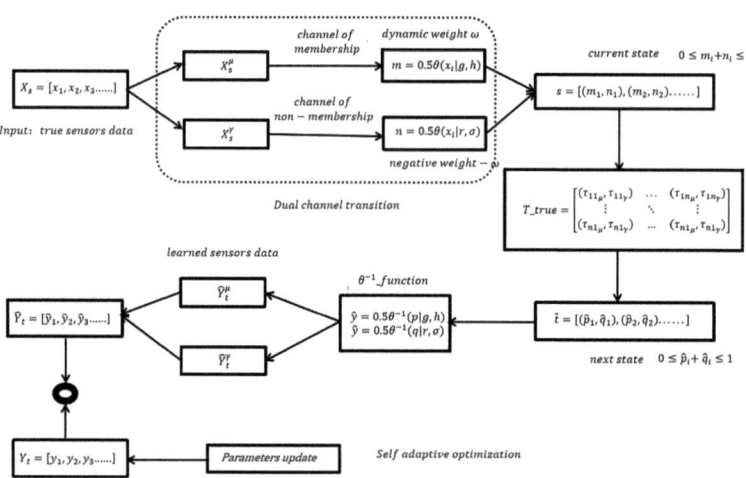

**Fig. 1.** Framework diagram of the GIFKS-IFS model.

For numerical stability, log-sum-exp (LSE) [3,17] approximations are applied:

$$\hat{p}_j \approx \frac{1}{\beta} \ln \left( \sum_{i=1}^{n} e^{\beta m_i \tau_{ij}^{\mu}} \right), \tag{8}$$

$$\hat{q}_j \approx -\frac{1}{\beta} \ln \left( \sum_{i=1}^{n} e^{-\beta(n_i + \tau_{ij}^{\gamma} - n_i \tau_{ij}^{\gamma})} \right). \tag{9}$$

where the constant $\beta > 0$ is a hyper-parameter that determines the accuracy of the approximation, and $m_j = 0.5\theta_j^{\mu}(x_j \mid g_j, h_j)$, $n_j = 0.5\theta_j^{\gamma}(x_j \mid r_j, \sigma_j)$.

The GIFKS-IFS model is the first GIFKS learning model in the literature that links the variables external to the system, and Fig. 1 provides the learning framework of the GIFKS-IFS model.

## 4 Dual-Channel Gradient Learning Algorithm

Given $R$ state sample pairs $\{(x_i, \hat{y}_j)\}_{i=1}^{R}$, this work aims to learn the atomic propositional transition matrix $T$ and fuzzification parameters $g_j$, $h_j$ in the GIFKS-IFS model to approximate their true values, while optimizing $\hat{y}_j$ to match the target output $y_j$.

To achieve supervised online learning, we minimize the following loss function [24]:

$$L = \frac{1}{2} \sum_{j=1}^{n_{AP}} (y_j - \hat{y}_j)^2. \tag{10}$$

Due to the independence of membership($\mu$) and non-membership($\gamma$) degrees, gradients are computed separately to avoid optimization bias from parameter coupling.

### 4.1 Membership-Related Learning

1. *Update Rule for $g_j$*:

$$g_j^{\text{new}} = g_j - \lambda_g \frac{\partial L}{\partial g_j} \tag{11}$$

In the rest of the paper, the superscript "new" is used to denote the new value of the same parameter after it has been updated in a learning iteration. The hyperparameter $\lambda_g$ is the learning rate of $g_j$. The following $\lambda_h, \lambda_\tau$ is used to denote the learning rates of $h_j$ and $\tau_{ij}$, respectively.
By (11):

$$\frac{\partial L^{\mu}}{\partial g_j} = \frac{\partial L^{\mu}}{\partial \hat{y}_j} \frac{\partial \hat{y}_j}{\partial g_j} = (y_j^{\mu} - \hat{y}_j^{\mu}) \frac{\partial \hat{y}_j}{\partial g_j} \tag{12}$$

Let $\Delta^\mu = y_j^\mu - \widehat{y}_j^\mu$.
Utilizing (4):

$$\frac{\partial \widehat{y}_j}{\partial g_j} = 1 \pm \frac{\partial \widehat{y}_j}{\partial \widehat{p}_j}\frac{\partial \widehat{p}_j}{\partial g_j} = 1 \mp \frac{h_j}{\widehat{p}_j\sqrt{-2\ln 2\widehat{p}_j}}\frac{\partial \widehat{p}_j}{\partial g_j} \qquad (13)$$

By (8):

$$\frac{\partial \widehat{p}_j}{\partial g_j} = \frac{\partial \widehat{p}_j}{\partial m_j}\frac{\partial m_j}{\partial g_j} = \tau_{jj}^\mu \frac{e^{\beta m_j \tau_{jj}^\mu}}{\sum_{i=1}^n e^{\beta m_i \tau_{ij}^\mu}}\frac{\partial m_j}{\partial g_j} \qquad (14)$$

Let:

$$\omega_{jj} = \frac{e^{\beta m_j \tau_{jj}^\mu}}{\sum_{i=1}^n e^{\beta m_i \tau_{ij}^\mu}}, \qquad (15)$$

and also (2):

$$\frac{\partial m_j}{\partial g_j} = 0.5\theta_j(x_j)\frac{(x_j - g_j)}{h_j^2}. \qquad (16)$$

According to the above equation:

$$\frac{\partial L^\mu}{\partial g_j} = \Delta^\mu \left(1 \mp \frac{\tau_{jj}^\mu \omega_{jj} \theta_j(x_j)(x_j - g_j)}{h_j \widehat{p}_j \sqrt{-2\ln 2\widehat{p}_j}}\right). \qquad (17)$$

2. *Update Rule for $h_j$*:

$$h_j^{\text{new}} = h_j - \lambda_g \frac{\partial L^\mu}{\partial h_j}. \qquad (18)$$

Based on (11),

$$\frac{\partial L^\mu}{\partial h_j} = \frac{\partial L^\mu}{\partial \widehat{y}_j}\frac{\partial \widehat{y}_j}{\partial h_j} = \Delta^\mu \frac{\partial \widehat{y}_j}{\partial h_j}. \qquad (19)$$

Note that,

$$\frac{\partial \widehat{y}_j}{\partial h_j} = \pm\sqrt{-2\ln 2\widehat{p}_j} \mp \frac{h_j}{\widehat{p}_j\sqrt{-2\ln 2\widehat{p}_j}}\frac{\partial \widehat{p}_j}{\partial h_j}. \qquad (20)$$

By (15) and (4),

$$\frac{\partial \widehat{p}_j}{\partial h_j} = \frac{\partial \widehat{p}_j}{\partial n_j}\frac{\partial n_j}{\partial m_j}\frac{\partial m_j}{\partial h_j} = \frac{\tau_{jj}^\mu \omega_{jj}\theta_j(x_j)(x_j - g_j)^2}{2h_j^3}. \qquad (21)$$

According to the above equation:

$$\frac{\partial L^\mu}{\partial h_j} = \Delta^\mu \left(\pm\sqrt{-2\ln 2\widehat{p}_j} \mp \frac{\tau_{jj}^\mu \omega_{jj}\theta_j(x_j)(x_j - g_j)^2}{h_j^2 \widehat{p}_j \sqrt{-2\ln 2\widehat{p}_j}}\right). \qquad (22)$$

3. **Update Rule for** $\tau_{ij}^{\mu}$:

$$(\tau_{ij}^{\mu})^{\text{new}} = \tau_{ij}^{\mu} - \lambda_{\tau^{\mu}} \frac{\partial L^{\mu}}{\partial \tau_{ij}^{\mu}}. \tag{23}$$

$$\frac{\partial L^{\mu}}{\partial \tau_{ij}^{\mu}} = \frac{\partial L^{\mu}}{\partial \widehat{y}_j} \frac{\partial \widehat{y}_j}{\partial \tau_{ij}^{\mu}} = \Delta^{\mu} \frac{\partial \widehat{y}_j}{\partial \tau_{ij}^{\mu}}. \tag{24}$$

$$\frac{\partial \widehat{y}_j}{\partial \tau_{ij}^{\mu}} = \frac{\partial \widehat{y}_j}{\partial \widehat{p}_j} \frac{\partial \widehat{p}_j}{\partial \tau_{ij}^{\mu}} = \mp \frac{h_j}{\widehat{p}_j \sqrt{-2 \ln 2 \widehat{p}_j}} \frac{\partial \widehat{p}_j}{\partial \tau_{ij}^{\mu}}. \tag{25}$$

$$\frac{\partial \widehat{p}_j}{\partial \tau_{ij}^{\mu}} = m_i \omega_{jj}. \tag{26}$$

Hence,

$$\frac{\partial L^{\mu}}{\partial \tau_{ij}^{\mu}} = \mp \frac{\Delta^{\mu} h_j m_i \omega_{jj}}{\widehat{p}_j \sqrt{-2 \ln 2 \widehat{p}_j}}. \tag{27}$$

### 4.2 Non-membership-Related Learning

Since the non-membership function is known, we only need to learn $\tau_{ij}^{\gamma}$ of the atomic proposition matrix, the idea of gradient descent is similar to the derivation of membership, the main difference is in (7), namely,

$$(\tau_{ij}^{\gamma})^{\text{new}} = \tau_{ij}^{\gamma} - \lambda_{\tau^{\gamma}} \frac{\partial L^{\gamma}}{\partial \tau_{ij}^{\gamma}}. \tag{28}$$

$$\frac{\partial L^{\gamma}}{\partial \tau_{ij}^{\gamma}} = \frac{\partial L^{\gamma}}{\partial \widehat{q}_j} \frac{\partial \widehat{q}_j}{\partial \tau_{ij}^{\gamma}} = (q_j^{\gamma} - \widehat{q}_j^{\gamma}) \frac{\partial \widehat{q}_j}{\partial \tau_{ij}^{\gamma}}. \tag{29}$$

Let $\Delta^{\gamma} = q_j^{\gamma} - \widehat{q}_j^{\gamma}$.

$$\frac{\partial \widehat{q}_j}{\partial \tau_{ij}^{\gamma}} = \frac{(1 - n_i) e^{-\beta(n_i + \tau_{ij}^{\gamma} - n_i \tau_{ij}^{\gamma})}}{\sum_{i=1}^{n} e^{-\beta(n_i + \tau_{ij}^{\gamma} - n_i \tau_{ij}^{\gamma})}} \tag{30}$$

Let

$$\omega_{jj}^{*} = \frac{e^{-\beta(n_i + \tau_{ij}^{\gamma} - n_i \tau_{ij}^{\gamma})}}{\sum_{i=1}^{n} e^{-\beta(n_i + \tau_{ij}^{\gamma} - n_i \tau_{ij}^{\gamma})}} \tag{31}$$

Hence,

$$\frac{\partial L^{\gamma}}{\partial \tau_{ij}^{\gamma}} = \Delta^{\gamma} \omega_{jj}^{*} (1 - n_i) \tag{32}$$

## 4.3 Improved Learning for $j_j, h_j, \tau_{ij}^\mu$ and $\tau_{ij}^\gamma$

In this study, the learned parameters are divided into three layers based on their relative position in the error signal $y_j - \hat{y}_j$. The first layer contains $g_j$ and $h_j$ parameters, which are closest to the error signal, and the second layer consists of $\tau_{ij}^\mu$ and $\tau_{ij}^\gamma$ parameters, which are slightly distant from the error signal, while the third layer farthest from the error signal is also composed of $g_j$ and $h_j$ parameters. According to the derived learning algorithm, the update of the parameters of the second layer depends on the parameters of the first layer, while the learning of the parameters of the third layer is influenced by both the parameters of the first and the second layer.

Although we use smooth functions instead of max and min functions in the derivation process, and the analysis shows that the algorithm is correct in theory, the performance of the algorithm is not always ideal in the actual learning process, especially in the learning of atomic proposition transition matrix. The reason is that the gradient calculation in the algorithm involves a smooth function, and the value of the function depends on the learning of the parameters of the first layer. This may cause the calculated gradient to be close to zero, thus causing the parameter updates in equations to almost stall. Since the parameters of the third layer are a bridge connecting the first layer and the third layer, if these parameters are not updated, the effect of the whole learning process will be affected, resulting in poor learning performance.

This parameter dependence problem [7,8] is not limited to our model. In the learning algorithm of the FDES model [19,20], Ying et al. first discovered this problem, while Liu proposed a similar solution in the GPKS model [14] by enhancing the parameter update effect in the learning process through certain formulas.

Although this paper has the uniqueness of intuitionistic fuzzy sets and we need to enhance $\omega_{jj}$ in the membership parameters and $\omega_{jj}^*$ in the nonmembership parameters, respectively, we can take a similar approach, that is, enhance $\omega_{jj}$ and $\omega_{jj}^*$ by the following formula:

$$\omega_{jj} := \frac{e^{\beta m_j \tau_{jj}^\mu}}{\bigwedge_{i=1}^n e^{\beta m_i \tau_{ij}^\mu}}, \tag{33}$$

$$\omega_{jj}^* = \frac{e^{-\beta(n_i + \tau_{ij}^\gamma - n_i \tau_{ij}^\gamma)}}{\bigvee_{i=1}^n e^{-\beta(n_i + \tau_{ij}^\gamma - n_i \tau_{ij}^\gamma)}}, \tag{34}$$

and use above $\omega_{jj}$ and $\omega_{jj}^*$ to replace previous $\omega_{jj}$ and $\omega_{jj}^*$ in (16) and (32). Note that $\omega_{jj}$ is now in $[1, e^\beta]$ and $\omega_{jj}^*$ is now in $(0, 1]$, which mean they cannot be zero. This addresses effectively the parameter dependency problem in the later computer simulations.

## 5 Experiment Design and Result Analysis

The above theoretical analysis of GIFKS-IFS model mainly verifies its feasibility, but to fully evaluate the learning performance of the model [12], it still needs to rely on computer simulation experiments. Similar to many iterative optimization problems, the learning performance of GIFKS model is greatly affected by many parameters, including but not limited to the setting of the initial value, the adjustment of the learning rate and the size of the sample data. It is important to note that the simulation experiments carried out in this paper are abstract in nature and are not directly related to any specific fuzzy system. However, this abstractness does not affect its applicability for testing learning performance. Through these simulation experiments, we can effectively evaluate and verify the learning performance of GIFKS model.

### 5.1 Learning Accuracy Criteria

In the process of model parameter learning, it is crucial to evaluate the accuracy and goodness of fit of the parameters. For complex models such as generalized intuitionistic fuzzy Kripke structures (GIFKS), the learning process of the model can still be regarded as a traditional parameter optimization problem, where the goal is to adjust the parameters to minimize the prediction error and fit the real data as accurately as possible. In order to check the effectiveness of the learning process, we mainly measure the learning effect by several criteria, including mean absolute error (MAE) and transition matrix convergence error.

MAE measures the deviation between the predicted values of the model and the true observed values. The formula is defined as follows:

$$\text{MAE} = \frac{1}{n} \sum_{i=1}^{n} |y_i - \hat{y}_i|. \tag{35}$$

Similarly, the convergence error between APTM $T$ and possibility matrix $P$ is defined as follows:

$$\text{ERROR } T = \frac{1}{n^2} \sum_{i=1}^{n} \sum_{j=1}^{n} |\tau_{ij} - \hat{\tau}_{ij}|, \tag{36}$$

where $R$ is the number of samples, $n$ is the number of atomic propositions, and $N$ is the total number of states.

In practice, since we cannot directly obtain the true APTM $T$, the effect of model learning is usually measured by the error. Usually the error $T$ will be implicit in the goodness of fit of the evolution matrix of atomic propositions, reflecting the extent to which the transition between states deviates from the true value. Therefore, the smaller error $T$ is, the more credible $T$ is.

### 5.2 Simulation Settings

The purpose of this experiment is to verify the effectiveness of GIFKS in modeling state transitions of dynamic systems. To achieve this goal, we learn the parameters and generate the sample pairs $\{(x_i, \hat{y}_i)\}_{i=1}^{n}$ needed to evaluate the learning performance. The hardware environment of the experiment is Intel Core i7-9750H 2.60 GHz CPU, 64GB DDR4 memory, and the software environment is Python 3.8 and NumPy 1.21.

1. *Initialization:* We first generate the state space $S$ based on the number of $AP$ and precision, and initialize the APTM $T$ and the possibility matrix $P$. Then, by combining 70% of the samples drawn from a normal distribution with 30% of random numbers sampled from a uniform distribution, we generate $R$ input-output sample pairs $\{(X_i, Y_i)\}_{i=1}^{R}$, which represent the variables of the true current sensor. The incorporation of a small proportion of uniform random number data aims to more accurately reflect the characteristics of real-
2. *Training Process:* During model training, the forward propagation is performed first. In the state transition step, the current state $s$ obtains the membership degree and non-membership degree of the next state $\hat{t}$ through the estimated APTM $\hat{T}$. On this basis, the inverse of Gaussian fuzzy sets $\theta_j^{-1}$ with $g_j$ and $h_j$ to create true next variables $\hat{t}_i$ for $i = 1, 2, \ldots, R$ via (8)(9). Since (4)(5) is a one-to-two function, $\hat{t}_i$ is computed by alternating the $+$ and $-$ operations in (4)(5), to prevent skewing and unbalancing the distribution of $\hat{t}_i$. Next, the state prediction error and the matrix convergence error are calculated. In the back propagation, the two-channel gradient calculation is performed firstly, and the gradients of membership and non-membership are calculated respectively.

## 5.3 Simulation Results

Here, we only randomly selected the learning results of a representative GIFKS-IFS model to verify the feasibility of the framework. We set the number of atomic propositions of the model to 3 ($AP = \{a_1, a_2, a_3\}$) to construct a two-dimensional state space. The precision is set to 1, and the corresponding state space step is 0.1. The number of samples is 200. The training period was set to 300 times. The initial value of hyper-parameter $\beta$ was 3.5. We manually investigated the impact of different values of these hyper-parameters on learning performance and adopted plausible values in subsequent evaluation simulations, without systematically trying to explore the best values of these hyper-parameters, as a full search of the high-dimensional parameter space can take a long time.

To facilitate further analysis, we set the true standard deviation of membership as $g = [0.25, 0.5, 0.8]$ and $h = [0.35, 0.25, 0.15]$; the true standard deviation of non-membership is set as $r = [0.35, 0.5, 0.7]$ and $\sigma = [0.1, 0.2, 0.3]$; APTM $T$ is set as

$$\begin{bmatrix} [[0.3, 0.15] & [0.2, 0.25] & [0.35, 0.2]] \\ [[0.2, 0.15] & [0.4, 0.3] & [0.45, 0.3]] \\ [[0.35, 0.2] & [0.3, 0.2] & [0.3, 0.2]] \end{bmatrix},$$

the above data are randomly generated and do not have uniqueness, which can be modified according to specific application scenarios.

The MAE, calculated using equations (35)–(36), is $2.59 \times 10^{-5}$. Figure 2 shows that the trend of the error decreasing with the rounds indicates that the model converges stably and decreases with the learning rounds.

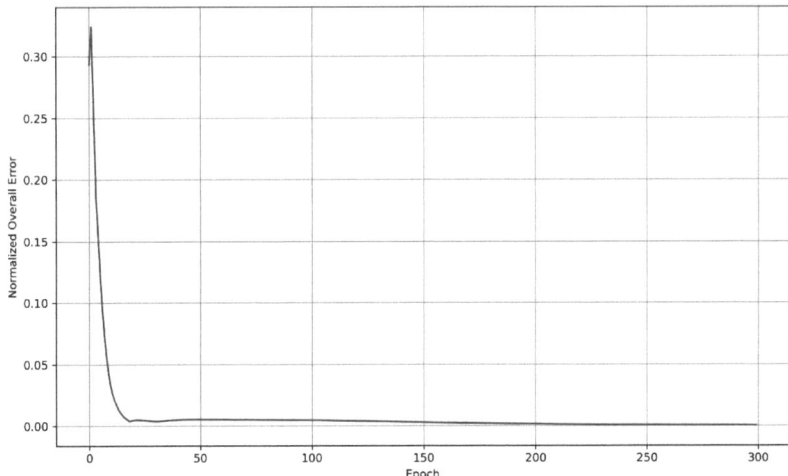

**Fig. 2.** Progressive decrease of the normalized overall error.

Finally, the learned APTM $\widehat{T}$ is obtained:

$$\begin{bmatrix} [[0.301, 0.150] & [0.232, 0.250] & [0.350, 0.199]] \\ [[0.186, 0.150] & [0.399, 0.299] & [0.450, 0.300]] \\ [[0.351, 0.200] & [0.302, 0.200] & [0.146, 0.199]] \end{bmatrix}$$

Figures 3–11 illustrate the learning progression of each element in the APTM $T$ matrix. The solid line represents the true value, while the dotted line indicates the learned value. It is evident that the nine elements of the $T$ matrix, which do not involve membership degrees, progressively approach their true values with each round of training. In contrast, the membership degree exhibits a slight deviation. This phenomenon primarily arises because the non-membership functions adhere to a known Gaussian distribution, whereas the membership function must first learn this distribution before determining the elements of the $T$ matrix. Despite this, the overall observation demonstrates satisfactory performance. For clarity, states nearing convergence are omitted from the figure.

Figure 12 show the error analysis obtained by decomposing the membership and non-membership degrees, which verifies the above content.

After the epochs of learning, the final estimated value of each parameter is $\hat{g} = [0.280\ 0.517\ 0.766]$ and $\hat{h} = [0.317\ 0.260\ 0.144]$, which shows the gap with the true value is small, and the effect is good.

Figure 13 and Fig. 14 exhibit the learning progress of means $g_j$ and standard deviations $h_j$. They can be found to have only a small deviation from their true values.

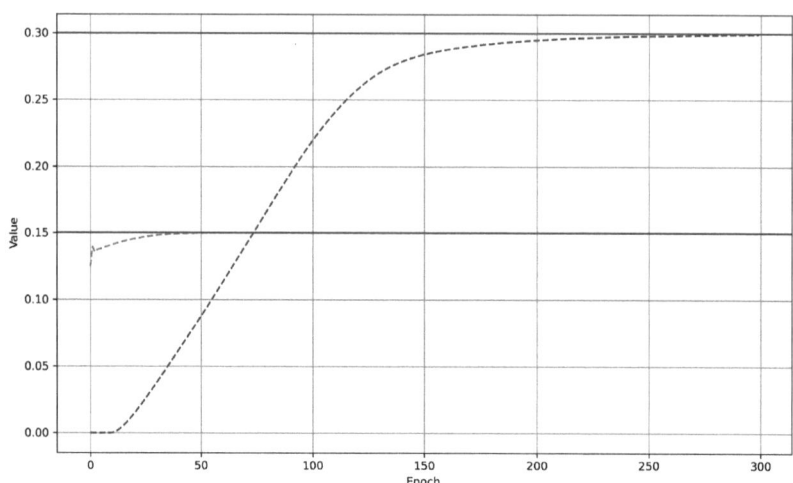

**Fig. 3.** Learning progress of $\tau_{11}$.

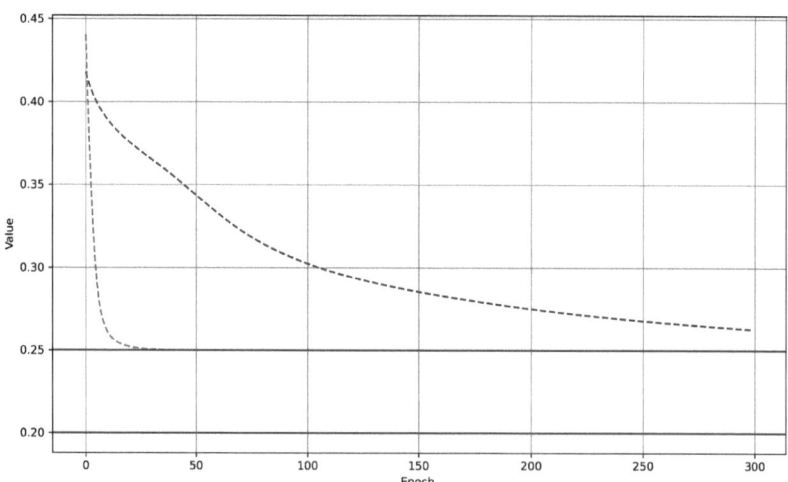

**Fig. 4.** Learning progress of $\tau_{12}$.

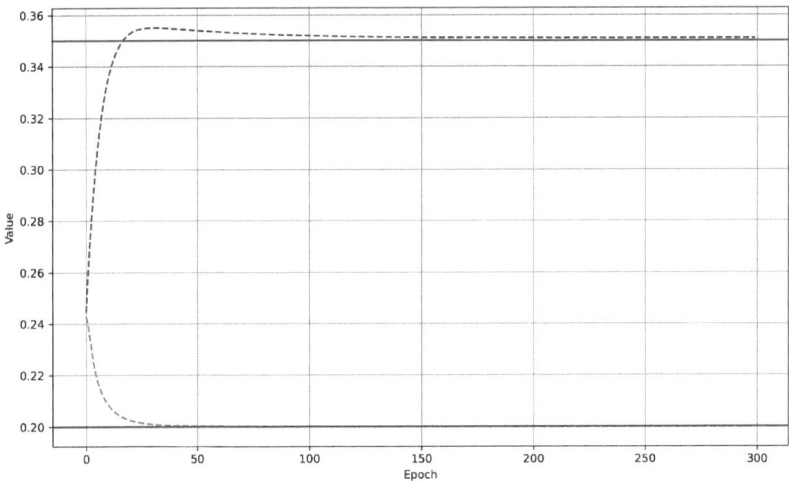

**Fig. 5.** Learning progress of $\tau_{13}$.

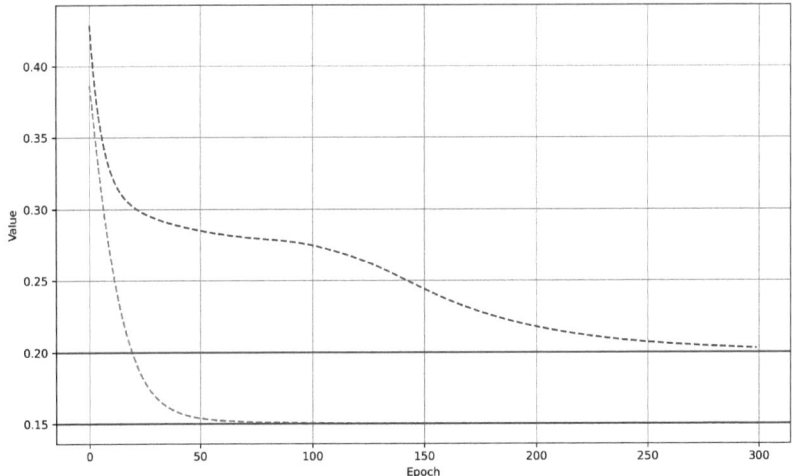

**Fig. 6.** Learning progress of $\tau_{21}$.

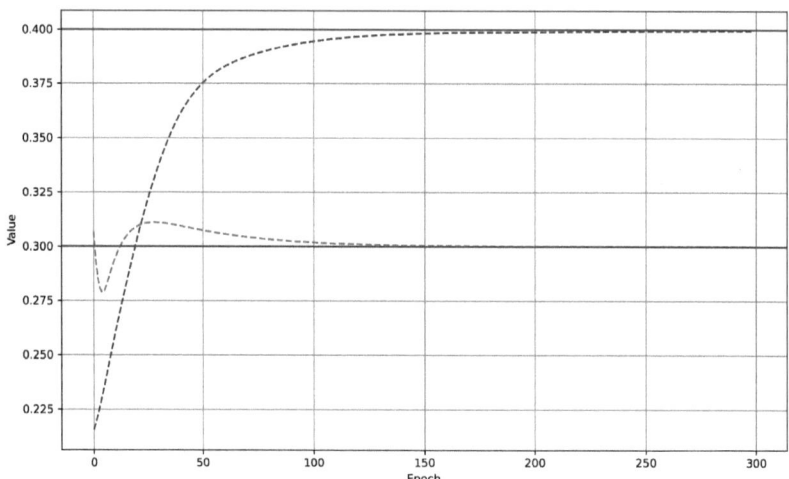

**Fig. 7.** Learning progress of $\tau_{22}$.

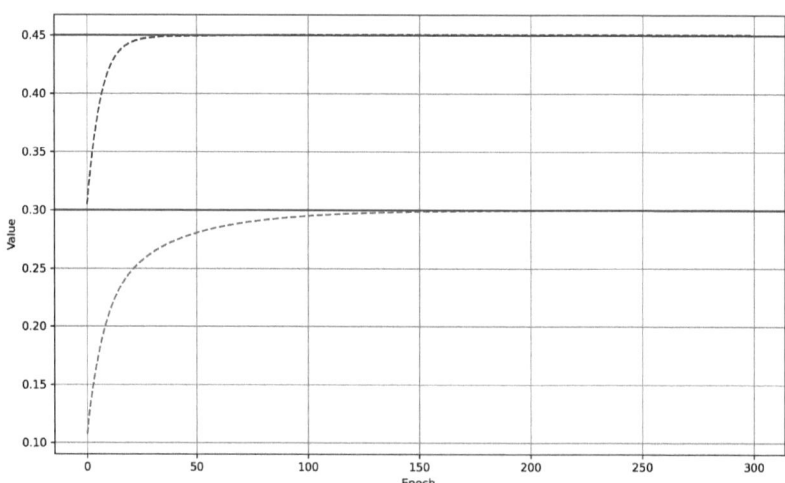

**Fig. 8.** Learning progress of $\tau_{23}$.

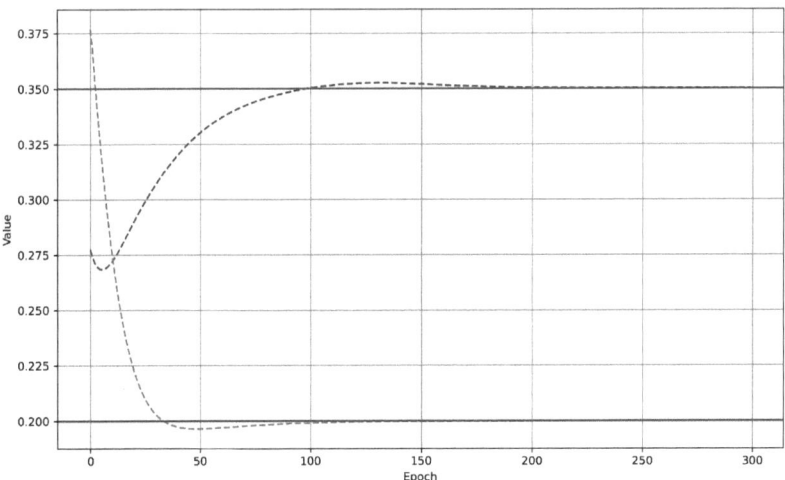

**Fig. 9.** Learning progress of $\tau_{31}$.

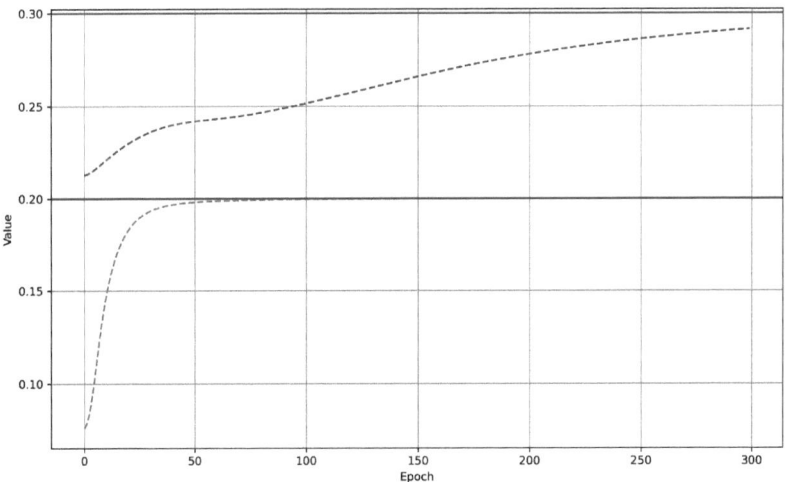

**Fig. 10.** Learning progress of $\tau_{32}$.

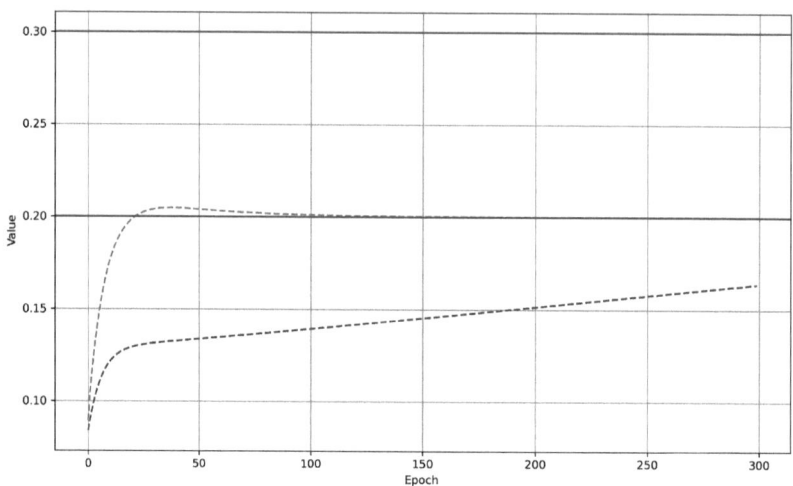

**Fig. 11.** Learning progress of $\tau_{33}$.

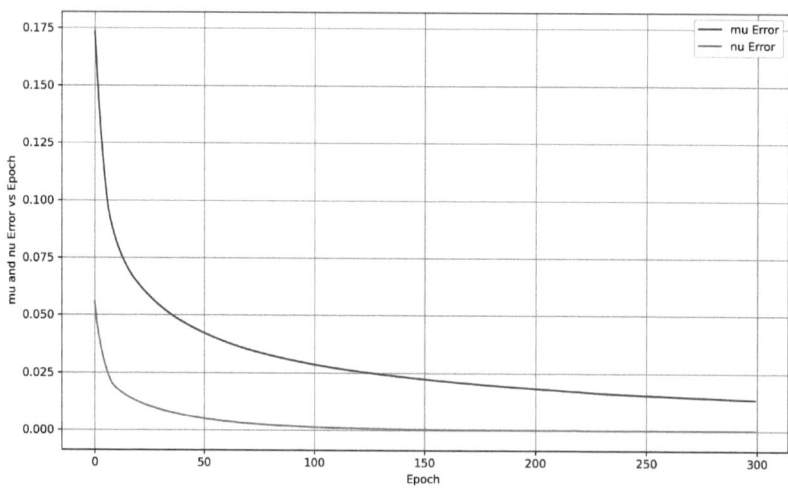

**Fig. 12.** Progressive decrease of the membership and non-membership errors.

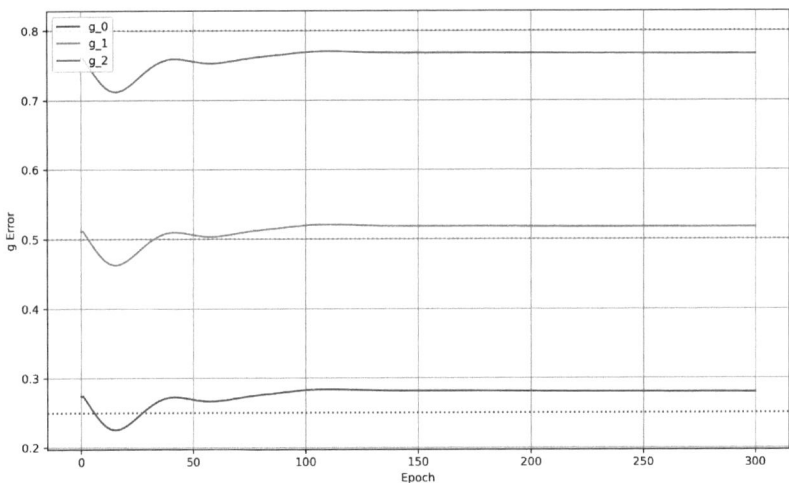

**Fig. 13.** Normalized means $g$ error.

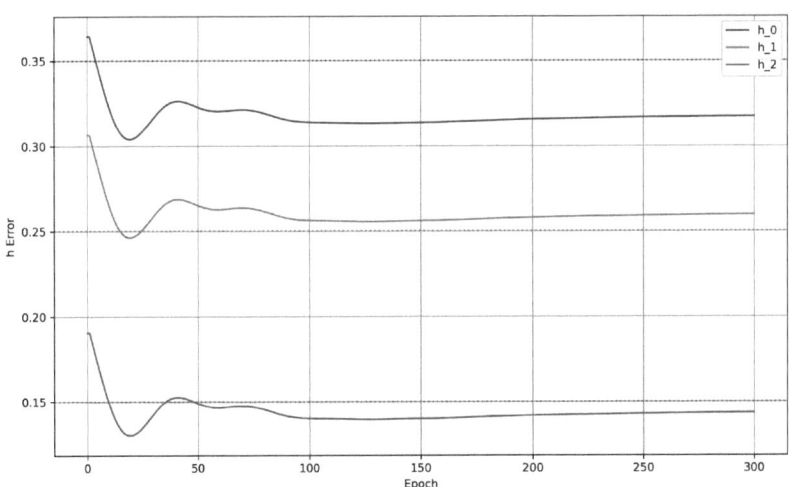

**Fig. 14.** Normalized standard deviations $h$ error.

## 6 Conclusion

This paper proposes a self-learning framework (GIFKS-IFS) first integrating intuitionistic fuzzy sets' dual-channel evidence expression into the formal Kripke framework. This enables modeling fuzzy states and autonomous evolution of transition rules in dynamic environments, with smooth functions ensuring parameter convergence and stability. Experimental results demonstrate its strong performance in parameter adaptability, convergence, and learning efficiency for state transition paths in dynamic environments. Though validated primarily on synthetic data, the framework offers theoretical novelty in integrating the two paradigms and practical value through its approach to modeling fuzzy states and rule evolution. However, it faces challenges with computational overhead in high-dimensional data and initialization dependence impacting stability in complex systems. Future work will validate with real datasets (e.g., intelligent transportation, medical management) to enhance real-world applicability, while exploring cross-domain applications and integration with deep learning to boost intelligence and self-learning.

**Acknowledgments.** This paper was supported by the National Natural Science Foundation of China under Grant 12301596 and the Research Proiect of the Fundamental Science (Natural Science) for Higher School in Jiangsu under Grant 21KJD520001.

## Appendix

**Table A1.** Glossary of Key Symbols

| Symbol | Definition | Location |
|---|---|---|
| $\mu_A(x)$ | Membership degree of $x$ in intuitionistic fuzzy set $A$ | §2.1 (Def. 3) |
| $\gamma_A(x)$ | Non-membership degree of $x$ in $A$ | §2.1 (Def. 3) |
| $M = (S, P, I, AP, L)$ | GIFKS quintuple | §2.2 (Def. 4) |
| $\Theta = (\theta_i^\mu, \theta_i^\gamma)$ | Family of intuitionistic fuzzy functions (membership and non-membership) | §3 (Def. 5) |
| $X_s$ | a family of input sensor variables | §3.1 (Eq. 1) |
| $Y_t$ | a family of output sensor variables | 3.1 (Eq. 1) |
| $m, n$ | Membership and non-membership degrees of the current state $s$ | §3.1 (Eq. 2–3) |
| $g_j, h_j$ | Mean and standard deviation of Gaussian membership function for $AP_j$ | §3.1 (Eq. 2) |
| $r_j, \sigma_j$ | Mean and standard deviation of Gaussian non-membership function for $AP_j$ | §3.B (Eq. 3) |
| $\hat{p}, \hat{q}$ | Estimated membership and non-membership degrees of the next state $\hat{t}$ | §3.2 (Eq. 6–7) |
| $\tau^\mu, \tau^\gamma$ | Membership and non-membership transition parameters in APTM $T$ | §3.2 |
| $\beta$ | Hyperparameter for log-sum-exp approximation | §3.2 (Eq. 8–9) |
| $\omega_{jj}, \omega_{jj}^*$ | Weight term for membership and non-membership gradient | §4.3 (Eq. 15, Eq. 31) |
| $\Delta^\mu, \Delta^\gamma$ | Membership and non-membership prediction error | §4.3 (Eq. 17, Eq. 32) |

# References

1. Atanassov, K.T.: Intuitionistic fuzzy sets. Fuzzy Sets Syst. **20**, 87–96 (1986)
2. Baier, C., Katoen, J.P.: Principles of Model Checking. MIT Press, Cambridge, MA (2008)
3. Bertsekas, D.P.: Minimax methods based on approximation. In: Proceedings of the Johns Hopkins Conference on Information Sciences and Systems, pp. 1–6 (1976)
4. Chechik, M., Easterbrook, S., Petrovykh, V.: Model-checking over multi-valued logics. In: Proceedings of the International Symposium on Formal Methods Europe, pp. 72–98 (2001)
5. Chechik, M., et al.: Multi-valued symbolic model-checking. ACM Trans. Softw. Eng. Methodol. **12**, 371–408 (2003)
6. Chechik, M., et al.: Data structures for symbolic multi-valued model-checking. Formal Methods Syst. Design **29**, 295–344 (2006)
7. Kingma, D.P., Ba, J.: Adam: a method for stochastic optimization. In: Proceedings of the International Conference on Learning Representations, pp. 1–15 (2015)
8. Li, X., Yue, Y.: Review of gradient descent algorithm. J. Softw. Eng. **23**, 1–4 (2020)
9. Li, Y.: Quantitative model checking of linear-time properties based on generalized possibility measures. Fuzzy Sets Syst. **320**, 17–39 (2017)
10. Li, Y., et al.: Quantitative model checking of linear-time properties based on generalized possibility measures. IEEE Trans. Fuzzy Syst. **23**, 2034–2047 (2015)
11. Li, Y., et al.: Quantitative computation tree logic model checking based on generalized possibility measures. Inf. Sci. **485**, 87–113 (2019)
12. Li, Y., et al.: Warehouse robot path planning based on artificial bee colony-adaptive genetic algorithm. J. Instrum. Measur. Technol. **43**, 282–290 (2022)
13. Li, Y.M.: Analysis of Fuzzy Systems. Academic Press, Beijing (2005)
14. Liu, W., et al.: Self-learning modeling in possibilistic model checking. IEEE Trans. Emerg. Topics Comput. Intell. **8**, 264–278 (2024)
15. Pan, H., et al.: Model checking fuzzy computation tree logic. Fuzzy Sets Syst. **262**, 60–77 (2015)
16. Wang, J.: Interval-valued intuitionistic fuzzy multi-criteria decision-making method under incomplete information. Control Decision **21**, 1253–1256 (2006)
17. Xu, S.: Smoothing methods for min-max problems. Comput. Optim. Appl. **20**, 267–279 (2001)
18. Xu, Z.: Intuitionistic fuzzy preference information-based multi-attribute decision-making approaches. Syst. Eng. Theory Pract. **27**, 62–71 (2007)
19. Ying, H., Lin, F.: Online self-learning fuzzy discrete event systems. IEEE Trans. Fuzzy Syst. **28**, 2185–2194 (2020)
20. Ying, H., Lin, F.: Learning fuzzy automaton's event transition matrix when post-event state is unknown. IEEE Trans. Cybern. **52**, 4993–5000 (2022)
21. Ying, H., Lin, F.: Self-learning fuzzy automaton with input and output fuzzy sets for system modeling. IEEE Trans. Emerg. Topics Comput. Intell. **7**, 500–512 (2023)
22. Yu, X., et al.: Intuitionistic fuzzy measure computation tree logic. J. Exploratory Comput. Sci. **9**, 1523–1530 (2017)
23. Zadeh, L.A.: Fuzzy sets as a basis for a theory of possibility. Fuzzy Sets Syst. **1**, 3–28 (1978)
24. Zhao, W., et al.: A new gradient descent approach for local learning of fuzzy neural models. IEEE Trans. Fuzzy Syst. **21**, 30–44 (2013)

# Spiking Neural Network Based on Bidirectional Variational Anomaly Detection for Knowledge Tracing

Jinru Hu, Mingkun Chen, Yige Zhu, and Jianrui Chen(✉)

School of Artificial Intelligence Computer Science, Shaanxi Normal University, Xi'an 710199, China
jianrui_chen@snnu.edu.cn

**Abstract.** Knowledge Tracing is a core technology in educational data mining and intelligent education systems. It aims to predict future personal ability by analyzing the interaction history between learners and learning systems, and dynamically modeling the evolution process of their knowledge states. Despite significant progress in knowledge tracing research, there are still abnormal interactions at the data level, such as guessing, slipping and cheating, etc. These anomalies interfere with the model's estimation of the real knowledge state, and reduce the accuracy of the prediction. To address these issues, we propose a spiking neural network based on bidirectional variational anomaly detection to enhance the accuracy of the model by interactive denoising (i.e., denosing abnormal data). Specifically, we design a bidirectional variational detector to the answer sequence of learners. The underlying distribution of normal interactions is learned by an encoder-decoder mechanism, and the reconstruction error is calculated to identify abnormal behaviors that deviate from the sequence distribution. Finally, the spiking neural network is introduced for temporal decision-making, and its event-driven characteristics are utilized to perform pulse coding on interactions after denoising. Extensive experiments on three real datasets show that the proposed method can dynamically denoise and improve the robustness of the knowledge tracing model, which is suitable for sparse and noisy data in real education scenarios.

**Keywords:** Knowledge Tracing · Abnormal Interactions · Spiking Neural Network · Bidirectional Variational Detector · Denoising

## 1 Introduction

With the advancement of AI and big data technologies, online learning has become an integral part of modern education. Knowledge Tracing (KT) is the core technology of online learning systems [1]. It dynamically captures the changes in learners' knowledge mastery status by analyzing their historical interaction data (such as answer records and response times), and predicts future performance (such as the probability of getting the answer right for the following question) [2]. Based on these insights, online learning platforms adjust teaching strategies in real time, and significantly enhances learning efficiency and personalization levels [3].

The early stage of probabilistic models lay the theoretical foundation. Bayesian knowledge tracing models knowledge states as latent variables through Hidden Markov models [4], but its strict assumption of independence limits the expressive power of the model. To break through this limitation, researchers introduce the logistic regression framework and context features, the prediction accuracy has been significantly improved [5]. However, such methods are still limited by manual features [6]. The rise of deep learning has brought about a paradigm breakthrough. Deep knowledge tracing is the first to use recurrent neural networks to process time series data, which achieves end-to-end feature learning [7]. Subsequently, the dynamic key-value memory network better simulates the dynamic change process of human knowledge through a separated memory storage mechanism [8]. In recent years, the introduction of the Transformer architecture has enabled models to capture longer-term dependencies [9], while graph knowledge tracing has demonstrated unique advantages in cognitive diagnosis by explicitly modeling the correlation networks between knowledge points [10].

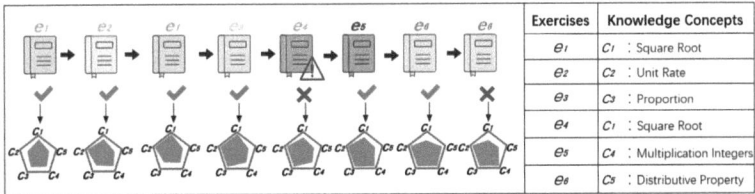

**Fig. 1.** The interaction record of a student's and the corresponding knowledge status.

Although most current methods give priority to optimizing the network structure to improve the prediction accuracy of future students' performance, they still face significant challenges when dealing with abnormal interactions [11]. Abnormal interaction problems refer to the behavioral data that deviates from the normal learning mode during the interaction process between learners and the education system [12]. These abnormalities interfere with the model's estimation of the real knowledge state, and reduces the accuracy of prediction and recommendation. The root cause of this abnormal learning interaction may manifest as unexpected mistakes or random guesses regarding the mastered content [12]. As illustrated in Fig. 1, as a student provides two inconsistent responses to the same exercise in quick succession, it suggests his grasp of the underlying concept is either tenuous or conflicted. This inconsistency may stem from gaps in foundational knowledge, misinterpretation of instructions, or an inability to apply theoretical understanding in practice. In addition, it is seen from the radar chart that the student has a solid grasp of the knowledge point of "*Square Root*". However, in the actual problem-solving process, he still makes mistakes in $e_4$ related questions, which shows obvious abnormal interaction. This phenomenon may include the reasons such as the lack of detail processing, the deviation of the meaning understanding or the operation error.

In fact, resolving inconsistent learning behaviors (e.g., rapid shifts in responses) is a key driver of personalized education efficacy. Addressing such anomalies requires integrating real-time diagnostics with adaptive instruction to stabilize understanding and bridge cognitive gaps [13]. Anomaly detection of time series data aims to identify the anomaly points that deviate from the normal pattern in the time dimension, so as to discover potential problems or abnormal events in a timely manner [14]. The existing methods are mainly be classified into three categories: statistical methods, machine learning methods and deep learning methods. Statistical methods usually assume that the data follows a specific distribution by detecting outliers that deviate from the threshold, but they may perform inadequately in complex or nonlinear time series [15]. Machine learning methods introduce ways of model training, such as cluster-based detection (such as k-means) or supervised learning to learn the features of time series [16]. These methods have stronger adaptability than statistical methods, but they rely on a large amount of labeled data or feature engineering. In recent years, commonly used models based on deep learning include recurrent neural networks, long short-term memory networks, and autoencoders [17]. These models can capture multi-scale and multi-varying abnormal patterns by automatically learning the complex temporal relationships and latent features in time series. To sum up, deep learning methods have gradually become the mainstream direction of time series anomaly detection, but in practical applications, model optimization still needs to be carried out in combination with domain knowledge [18]. Traditional coding and reconstruction methods can effectively capture the potential characteristics of students during the learning process, but they often lack the simulation of temporal information and the learning mechanism of the nervous system. In recent years, as a computing model imitating biological nervous system, Spiking Neural Network (SNN) process temporal information more naturally, has the ability of time encoding, and shows excellent time dynamic processing ability [19].

Based on the above discussion, we detect and filter the abnormal interactions among students in the KT field. The main contributions are as follows.

- A bidirectional variational encoder architecture combining bidirectional long short-term memory network is introduced to filter the abnormal interactions among students behaviors.
- Spiking neural network is used to simulate complex dynamic temporal behaviors and neuronal discharge mechanisms, and capture the potential characteristics of students' behaviors.
- Diverse experiments have proved that this model has superior performance in the complex and changeable student interaction data environment and outperforms the existing methods in several indices.

The remainder of this article is organized as follows. Section 2 provides the detailed descriptions to our proposed algorithm. Subsequently, the experimental results are presented in Sect. 3. Finally, Sect. 4 provides the conclusions and sketches future work.

## 2 Method

In this section, we first provide an overall overview of the framework. Subsequently, we gave a detailed explanation of the model.

Figure 2 shows the overall framework of the model, which consists of four main components, including the embedding layer, the bidirectional variational anomaly detector, the SNN and the prediction layer.

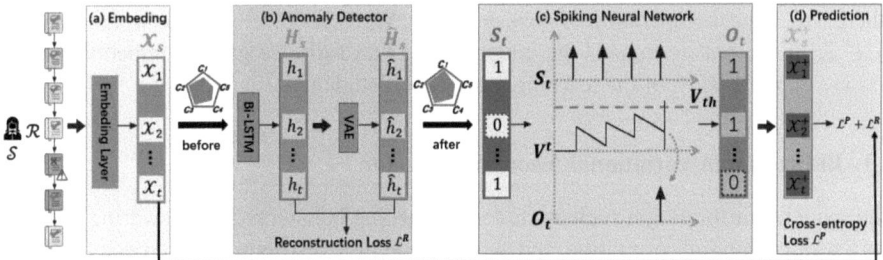

**Fig. 2.** The overall framework of the model.

### 2.1 Problem Formalization

The set of exercises is denoted as $\mathcal{E} = \{e_1, e_2, \ldots, e_m\}$, where $e_t (t = 1, \ldots, m)$ is the exercise that the student answers at step $t$. The set of knowledge concepts is $\mathcal{C} = \{c_1, c_2, \ldots, c_k\}$. Each exercise is associated with specific knowledge concepts and the $Q$-matrix $\mathcal{Q} = \{q_{ij}\}_{m \times k}, (q_{ij} \in \{0, 1\})$ is utilized to indicate the relationship between exercises $e_i$ and knowledge concepts $c_j$. $q_{ij} = 1$ if exercise $e_i$ involves concept $c_j$ and $q_{ij} = 0$ otherwise. In the learning process, there exist learning sequences in which different students answer the allocated exercises. For each student, the sequence is formalized as $\mathcal{R} = \{(e_1, c_1, a_1), (e_2, c_2, a_2), \ldots, (e_t, c_t, a_t)\}$, where $a_t = 1(t = 1, \ldots, m)$ indicates that the exercise $e_t$ is answered correctly at step $t$, otherwise $a_t = 0$, and the triplet $(e_t, c_t, a_t)$ is the $t$-th learning interaction behavior.

Given the historical answer sequences $\mathcal{R} = \{(e_1, c_1, a_1), (e_2, c_2, a_2), \ldots, (e_t, c_t, a_t)\}$ of a student, KT aims to determine the level of knowledge mastery of student at this stage and predict the probability of the student correctly answers the question at the next stage $t + 1$, i.e., $p(a_{t+1} = 1 | e_{t+1}, \mathcal{R})$.

### 2.2 Embedding Layer

When dealing with students' interaction behavior data, the embedding layer aims to transform each element of discrete triples $(e_t, c_t, a_t)$ into continuous dense vectors. Specifically, the exercises $e_t$ and answers $a_t$ are represented as one-hot vectors and then multiplied by the trained embedding matrix and mapped to a continuous embedding space.

$$x_{e_t} = e_t W^E, x_{a_t} = a_t W^A, \tag{1}$$

where $e_t \in \mathbb{R}^m$ and $a_t \in \mathbb{R}^{2k}$ are the one-hot encoding of the exercises and responses, respectively. $W^E \in \mathbb{R}^{m \times d_e}$ and $W^A \in \mathbb{R}^{2c \times d_a}$ are the embedding matrices of the exercises and responses, respectively. $d_e$ and $d_a$ are corresponding dimensions. $x_{e_t} \in \mathbb{R}^{d_e}$ and $x_{a_t} \in \mathbb{R}^{d_a}$ stand for their embedding representations. Finally, to express the interactive information between students and knowledge points more comprehensively, the exercise representation and the answer state representation are combined.

$$x_t = [x_{e_t} || x_{a_t}] W_1 + b_1, \tag{2}$$

where $\parallel$ denotes the operation of concatenating, $W_1 \in \mathbb{R}^{(d_e+d_a) \times d}$ is the weight matrix, $b_1 \in \mathbb{R}^d$ is the bias term, $d$ is the dimension. As a result, we get the embedding $x_s = [x_1, x_2, ..., x_t] \in \mathbb{R}^{t \times d}$ of the learning sequence of student $s$.

### 2.3 Bidirectional Variational Anomaly Detector

The sequence information such as students' learning behaviors and answering patterns has a strong temporal correlation, and there are potential distribution differences between normal behaviors and abnormal behaviors. We introduce a bidirectional variational coding architecture combining Bi-LSTM and VAE. In this study, the bidirectional variational anomaly detector aims to identify the abnormal behavior of students and improve the robustness of behavior reconstruction combined with a denoising mechanism. Anomaly detection is defined based on the distribution of latent characteristics of student behavior, related to the degree of deviation from normal behavior.

Firstly, Bi-LSTM [20] is utilized to extract deep features containing temporal contexts and enhance the understanding ability of behavioral sequences. The representation of the learning sequence $x_s$ is shown as:

$$h_s^F, h_s^B = Bi - LSTM(x_s, \Theta_1), \tag{3}$$

$$h_s = h_s^F \oplus h_s^B, \tag{4}$$

where $h_s^F$ and $h_s^B$ represent the forward and backward hidden state representations of the student sequence obtained after *Bi-LSTM* processing, respectively. $\Theta_1$ is a trainable parameter of *Bi-LSTM* and is optimized through gradient descent during training. $\oplus$ is the vector concatenation operation that concatenates forward and backward hidden states into a more comprehensive representation. $h_s = [h_1, h_2, ..., h_t] \in \mathbb{R}^{t \times d_s}$ denotes the knowledge state matrix.

Secondly, as a generative model, VAE [21] is capable of learning the latent distribution of data and capturing the implicit features behind normal behaviors. As the interaction sequence of students conforms to the learned latent distribution, the reconstruction error of the model is low, which indicates its behavior is consistent with the normal pattern. As abnormal behaviors deviate from the normal distribution, the reconstruction error will increase significantly. Thus, we obtain the reconstructed student hidden embedding $\hat{h}_s$.

$$\hat{h}_s \sim N\left(\mu_s, diag\left(\sigma_s^2\right)\right), \tag{5}$$

where $\mu_s = MLP_\mu(h_s)$ and $\sigma_s = MLP_\sigma(h_s)$ are the mean and standard deviation obtained from the learning process, respectively. $diag(\cdot)$ represents a diagonal matrix. $MLP_\mu(\cdot)$ and $MLP_\sigma(\cdot)$ are two multilayer perceptrons, which are used to output the mean and standard deviation of the latent space respectively. That means $\hat{H}_s$ is the relative true state after denoising.

## 2.4 Spiking Neural Network

The reconstructed hidden state $\hat{h}_s$ is then feed to SNN to capture the detailed information of the behavioral time pulses. In this study, the SNN is composed of multiple layers of voltage-based neurons. Each neuron responds to external input pulses and generates emission pulses through dynamically evolving membrane potentials, then transmits the information to the next layer in a time-coded manner.

Firstly, for each element of the hidden state vector, we set a threshold $\gamma$. As the element value is greater than this threshold, output pulse 1; otherwise, output 0:

$$S_t = \begin{cases} 1, & \hat{h}_s^i < \gamma \\ 0, & \hat{h}_s^i \geq \gamma \end{cases} \tag{6}$$

Then, $S_t$ is taken as the input and passed into the LIF neuron model [22]. With the dynamic evolution of membrane potential, the process of neurons emitting pulses is simulated.

$$V^t = V^{t-1} + \frac{1}{\tau}\left(V_{reset} - V^{t-1} + W \cdot S_t\right), \tag{7}$$

$$O^t = \Theta(V^t - V_{th}), \tag{8}$$

$$V^t = O^t V_{reset} + (1 - O^t) V^t. \tag{9}$$

Here, $V^t$ represents the membrane potential at time $t$, and $\tau$ is a membrane-related hyperparameter to control how fast the membrane potential decays, which leads to the membrane potential charges and discharges exponentially in response to the inputs. Typically, the initial membrane potential $V^0$ be set to the resting potential of a biological neuron, between -65mV and -70mV. Once $V^t$ exceeds the firing threshold $V_{th}$, the neuron will file a spike expressed by $O^t$. Then, the membrane potential $V^t$ will be reset to reset potential $V_{reset}$, typically set to zero. The decision to fire and generate a spike in the neuron output is carried out according to the Heaviside step function, which is defined by $\Theta(x) = 1$ if $x \geq 0$ and 0 otherwise. Finally, we obtain the output $O^t$, which is a binary (0 or 1) pulse signal, indicating whether the neuron has emitted a pulse at time $t$.

About learning mechanism, without using the model of error back propagation, but using the pulse sequence dependent plasticity rules (such as STDP) or reinforcement learning algorithm, dynamic adjustment of synaptic weights $W$, to enhance the performance capability of the network. The update of synaptic weights depends on the temporal relationship of the pulses emitted by neurons, thereby achieving effective learning and adaptation.

## 2.5 Response Prediction

We now obtain the denoised signal $O^t$ and apply it to the embedded representation $x_s$ of the learned sequence, thereby enhancing the model's focus on the real signal and suppressing noise interference. In this way, a screened or corrected representation is formed for subsequent tasks.

$$x_s^+ = O^t \odot x_s, \tag{10}$$

where $\odot$ represents the element-level product (Hadamard product). To predict the outcome of the current interaction, $x_s^+$ is mapped to the probability that the student will give the correct response to $e_i$ at the next step $t + 1$, as follows:

$$y = \sigma(z) = \frac{1}{1 + e^{-z}}, \tag{11}$$

where $\ddagger = \omega x_s^+ + b$ is the *Logit* probability. $\omega$ and $b$ are the readout weight and bias parameters, respectively. To jointly learn all model parameters, a cross-entropy loss between the predicted response $y$ and the true response $a$ is:

$$\mathcal{L}^P = -\sum\nolimits_{i=1}^{t}(a_i \log y_i + (1 - a_i)\log(1 - y_i)). \tag{12}$$

Meanwhile, in LSTM, the training objective not only includes minimizing the reconstruction error, but also must make the distribution of the latent variables conform to a certain prior distribution. Here, we calculate the reconstruction loss:

$$\mathcal{L}^R = \frac{1}{t}\sum\nolimits_{i=1}^{t}\left(\hat{h}_i - h_i\right)^2 + \mathcal{L}^{kl}, \tag{13}$$

$$\text{here, } \mathcal{L}^{kl} = \sum\nolimits_{1 \leq i \leq t}(\mu_i^2 + \sigma_i^2 - \log(\sigma_i)). \tag{14}$$

Then, we obtain the overall loss for training process:

$$\mathcal{L} = \mathcal{L}^P + \mathcal{L}^R \tag{15}$$

The network is trained with the Adam optimizer. The choice of the Adam optimizer [22] for training is particularly beneficial due to its adaptive learning rate feature, which adjusts the learning speed for each parameter dynamically. This adaptability accelerates convergence and is especially effective in environments with noisy gradients, such as those encountered in educational data.

## 3 Experiments

To verify the effectiveness of the proposed method, we conduct systematic experiments on three different datasets, aiming to comprehensively evaluate the adaptability and generalization performance of the model. Through tests in multiple practical application scenarios, the robustness and universality of the method is better demonstrated, which provides a solid foundation for subsequent analysis and discussion.

### 3.1 Datasets

In this study, to fully evaluate the generalization ability and practical application effect of the proposed method, we select three representative datasets: Junyi, ASSISTment17 and ASSISTment09. The properties of the datasets are shown in Table 1.

**Table 1.** Properties of different datasets.

| Datasets | Junyi | ASSISTment17 | ASSISTment09 |
| --- | --- | --- | --- |
| #Students | 10,000 | 1,709 | 4,151 |
| #Concepts | 734 | 3,162 | 16,891 |
| #Exercises | 734 | 102 | 101 |
| #Interactions | 408,057 | 942,816 | 247,596 |

### 3.2 Experimental Settings

In the proposed model, The membrane-related hyperparameter $\tau$ is 1.0 for all datasets, the membrane reset potential $V_{reset}$ is 0, and the firing potential $V_{th}$ is 1.0 for all datasets. In terms of evaluation indicators, this paper adopts two commonly used and representative indicators: AUC and ACC.

### 3.3 Experimental Baselines

In order to comprehensively evaluate the performance of the proposed method and ensure its superiority, we select six deep learning-based baselines for comparison, specifically including: AKT [9], SAKT [24], DKT [7], DKVMN [8], DGEKT [25] and HawkesKT [26].

### 3.4 Overall Performance

According to the experiment settings, we conduct performance comparison, and the experimental results are shown in Table 2.

Overall, the performance of our model has been significantly improved. On all datasets, the performance of traditional sequence models (DKT, DKVMN) is significantly inferior to that of our model. For example, on the Junyi dataset, the AUC of DKT is 0.7384 and the ACC is 0.7269; The AUC of our method is 0.7721 and the ACC is 0.7693, with significant improvement. It indicates that the traditional sequence model has limitations in capturing variable interactions and complex behaviors, while our model makes full use of deep and multi-angle feature information. On the more complex dataset, ASSISTment17, our model also outperforms the models based on attention mechanisms (AKT, SAKT), which demonstrates a more accurate ability to capture students' answering behaviors. Meanwhile, on ASSISTment17, the results of our model outperforms those of DGEKT, with the AUC of 0.7563 and the ACC of 0.7059. This verifies that in diverse scenarios and complex temporal dynamic environments, our model has stronger adaptability and predictive capabilities. In ASSISTment09, our model demonstrates a stronger discrimination ability, especially the improvement of ACC, from 0.7496 to 0.7537, which indicates the denoising mechanism of this model plays a significant role in identifying abnormal behaviors of students.

**Table 2.** Prediction performance of different models.

| Models | Junyi | | ASSISTment17 | | ASSISTment09 | |
|---|---|---|---|---|---|---|
|  | AUC | ACC | AUC | ACC | AUC | ACC |
| AKT | 0.7698 | 0.7405 | 0.7240 | 0.6779 | 0.7458 | 0.7087 |
| SAKT | 0.7687 | 0.7377 | 0.7180 | 0.6705 | 0.7399 | 0.7240 |
| DKT | 0.7384 | 0.7269 | 0.6879 | 0.6685 | 0.7334 | 0.6681 |
| DKVMN | 0.7264 | 0.7175 | 0.6691 | 0.6570 | 0.7394 | 0.7156 |
| DGEKT | 0.7640 | 0.7503 | 0.7551 | 0.6870 | 0.7724 | **0.7579** |
| HawkesKT | 0.7612 | 0.7582 | 0.7213 | 0.6897 | 0.7603 | 0.7454 |
| SVAKT | **0.7721** | **0.7693** | **0.7563** | **0.7059** | **0.7789** | 0.7537 |

### 3.5 Parameter Sensitivity Analysis

To test the influence of different hyperparameters, we conduct the parameter sensitivity test, presented in Fig. 3. In the hyperparameter tuning experiments conducted on the Junyi dataset, the final selection is obtained based on the AUC performance metric system evaluation. As shown in Fig. 3 (a), as the dimension gradually increases from 16 to 128, the model's ability to capture interaction features is significantly enhanced, especially as the dimension is 128. It can be observed from Fig. 3 (b) that the selection of batch size presents an inverted U-shaped curve, and the setting of 64 achieves the best balance between training efficiency and model stability. As shown in Fig. 3 (c), the comparison of dropout rates is particularly crucial. The setting of 0.1 alleviates overfitting compared to the absence of dropout, while retaining more effective features compared to the more aggressive 0.25. The collaborative optimization of these three parameters enables the model to perform outstandingly.

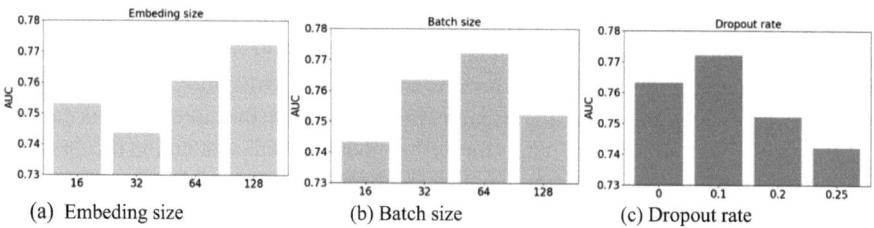

**Fig. 3.** Impact of different hyperparameters.

### 3.6 Ablation Study

Then, we conduct an in-depth analysis of the performance differences among different variants to verify the contribution of each component to the overall model. Table 3 shows the results. *SVAKT-d* removes the variational anomaly detector in the basic model,

*SVAKT-s* replaces SNN with the traditional convolutional neural network. *SVAKT-f* substitutes the denoising mechnism to forgetting function [27]. These ablation experiments validate the effectiveness of two key innovations in the model, the variational anomaly detector and the SNN. The variational detector significantly reduces the noise of abnormal behaviors on model predictions and enhances the true expression of behaviors. SNN focus on learning real and representative student behaviors, thereby enhancing the robustness and prediction accuracy of the model.

Table 3. The performance comparison of different modules.

| Variants | Junyi | | ASSISTment17 | | ASSISTment09 | |
|---|---|---|---|---|---|---|
| | AUC | ACC | AUC | ACC | AUC | ACC |
| SVAKT-d | 0.7647 | 0.7506 | 0.7441 | 0.6972 | 0.7668 | 0.7480 |
| SVAKT-s | 0.7632 | 0.7589 | 0.7465 | 0.6905 | 0.7699 | 0.7440 |
| SVAKT-f | 0.7641 | 0.7569 | 0.7473 | 0.6954 | 0.7674 | 0.7469 |
| SVAKT | 0.7721 | 0.7693 | 0.7563 | 0.7059 | 0.7789 | 0.7537 |

## 4 Conclusions

This paper focuses on the data anomaly problem in KT and proposes an SNN method based on bidirectional variational anomaly detection, aiming to enhance the robustness of the model when facing sparse and noisy data. To address the interference of abnormal behaviors such as guessing and cheating on the estimation of knowledge states, we design a bidirectional variational detector. By learning the latent distribution of the learner's answer sequence and using the encoder-decoder mechanism to calculate the reconstruction error, we identify abnormal interactions that deviate from the normal distribution. Overall, this study provides a promising processing solution for complex and real interaction data in the smart education system, and offers new ideas for future research in anomaly detection and model robustness of educational data. Although the model in this paper has achieved remarkable results in terms of robustness, it currently mainly focuses on anomaly detection and denoising. The root cause analysis behind abnormal behaviors and personalized intervention strategies have not been deeply explored yet. In the future, more diverse psychological and behavioral characteristics are combined to achieve a deep understanding and intelligent intervention of abnormal behaviors.

**Acknowledgements.** This research was supported through National Natural Science Foundation of China (No. 62273219); Program for Innovative Research Team in Universities of Inner Mongolia Autonomous Region (NMGIRT2317).

## References

1. Mohzana, M., Murcahyanto, H., Haritani, H.: The effectiveness of online learning on the level of understanding of international course material. Interdisc. J. Educ. **2**(1), 1–11 (2024)

2. Liu, Q., Shen, S., Huang, Z., Chen, E., Zheng, Y.: A survey of knowledge tracing. arXiv preprint arXiv:2105.15106
3. Cully, A., Demiris, Y.: Online knowledge level tracking with data-driven student models and collaborative filtering. IEEE Trans. Knowl. Data Eng. **32**(10), 2000–2013 (2020)
4. Bulut, O., Shin, J., Yildirim-Erbasli, S.N., et al.: An introduction to Bayesian knowledge tracing with pyBKT. Psych **5**(3), 770–786 (2023)
5. Abdelrahman, G., Wang, Q., Nunes, B.: Knowledge tracing: a survey. ACM Comput. Surv. **55**(11), 1–37 (2023)
6. Pavlik, P.I., Eglington, L.G., Harrell-Williams, L.M.: Logistic knowledge tracing: a constrained framework for learner modeling. IEEE Trans. Learn. Technol. **14**(5), 624–639 (2021)
7. Piech, C., Bassen, J., Huang, J., et al.: Deep knowledge tracing. Adv. Neural Inf. Process. Sys. **28** (2015)
8. Zhang, J., Shi, X., King, I., et al.: Dynamic key-value memory networks for knowledge tracing. In: Proceedings of the 26th International Conference on World Wide Web, pp. 765–774 (2017)
9. Ghosh, A., Heffernan, N., Lan, A.S.: Context-aware attentive knowledge tracing. In: Proceedings of the 26th ACM SIGKDD International Conference on Knowledge Discovery & Data Mining, pp. 2330–2339 (2020)
10. Yang, Y., Shen, J., Qu, Y., et al.: GIKT: a graph-based interaction model for knowledge tracing. In: Machine learning and knowledge discovery in databases: European conference, ECML PKDD 2020, Ghent, Belgium, September 14–18, 2020, proceedings, part I. Springer International Publishing, pp. 299–315 (2021)
11. Ma, H., Yang, Y., Qin, C., et al.: HD-KT: advancing robust knowledge tracing via anomalous learning interaction detection. Proc. ACM Web Conf. **2024**, 4479–4488 (2024)
12. Guo, T., Bai, X., Tian, X., et al.: Educational anomaly analytics: features, methods, and challenges. Front. Big Data **4**, 811840 (2022)
13. Abdulaal, A., Liu, Z., Lancewicki, T.: Practical approach to asynchronous multivariate time series anomaly detection and localization. In: Proceedings of the 27th ACM SIGKDD Conference on Knowledge Discovery & Data Mining, pp. 2485–2494 (2021)
14. Fu, H., Cao, X., Tu, Z.: Cluster-based co-saliency detection. IEEE Trans. Image Process. **22**(10), 3766–3778 (2013)
15. Samariya, D., Thakkar, A.: A comprehensive survey of anomaly detection algorithms. Ann. Data Sci. **10**(3), 829–850 (2023)
16. Su, Y., Zhao, Y., Niu, C., Liu, R., Sun, W., Pei, D.: Robust anomaly detection for multivariate time series through stochastic recurrent neural network. In: Proceedings of the 25th ACM SIGKDD International Conference on Knowledge Discovery & Data Mining, pp. 2828–2837 (2019)
17. Deng, A., Hooi, B.: Graph neural network-based anomaly detection in multivariate time series. In: Proceedings of the AAAI Conference on Artificial Intelligence, vol. 35, no. 5, pp. 4027–4035 (2021)
18. Zhao, H., et al.: Multivariate time-series anomaly detection via graph attention network. In: 2020 IEEE International Conference on Data Mining (ICDM), pp. 841–850. IEEE (2020)
19. Ding, J., Yu, Z., Tian, Y., et al.: Optimal ANN-SNN conversion for fast and accurate inference in deep spiking neural networks. arXiv:2105.11654 (2021)
20. Shahid, F., Zameer, A., Muneeb, M.: Predictions for COVID-19 with deep learning models of LSTM, GRU and Bi-LSTM. Chaos Solitons Fractals **140**, 110212 (2020)
21. Dai, B., Wipf, D.: Diagnosing and enhancing VAE models. arXiv:1903.05789 (2019)
22. Bu, T., Ding, J., Yu, Z., Huang, T.: Optimized potential initialization for low-latency spiking neural networks. Proc. AAAI Conf. Artif. Intell. **36**(1), 11–20 (2022)
23. Kingma, D.P., Ba, J.: Adam: a method for stochastic optimization arXiv:1412.6980 (2014)

24. Pandey, S., Karypis, G.: A self-attentive model for knowledge tracing. arXiv:1907.06837 (2019)
25. Cui, C., Yao, Y., Zhang, C., et al.: DGEKT: a dual graph ensemble learning method for knowledge tracing. ACM Trans. Inf. Syst. **42**(3), 1–24 (2024)
26. Wang, C., Ma, W., Zhang, M., et al.: Temporal cross-effects in knowledge tracing. In: Proceedings of the 14th ACM International Conference on Web Search and Data Mining, pp. 517–525 (2021)
27. Murre, J.M.J., Dros, J.: Replication and analysis of Ebbinghaus' forgetting curve. PLoS ONE **10**(7), e0120644 (2015)

# Author Index

**B**
Bao, Liyong 123

**C**
Chandrasekaran, Neelakandan 94
Chen, Jianrui 204
Chen, Mingkun 204
Chen, Zhigang 77
Cheng, Zi 35

**G**
Guo, Bin-bin 94

**H**
He, Qing 50
He, Xing 153
He, Yuxuan 182
Hu, Jinru 204

**K**
Kang, Le 94

**L**
Li, Wenhao 94
Li, Yongming 50
Liu, Wuniu 50
Liu, Xi 153
Luo, Qingyu 20

**M**
Mao, Yimin 94
Miao, Decheng 94

**P**
Pi, Hongyu 153

**Q**
Qi, Tangquan 77

**R**
Rong, Guozhen 3

**S**
Shi, Feng 3
Si, Yonghui 123
Sun, Yunyun 3

**W**
Wu, Guangwei 3

**Y**
Yang, Chao 182
Yang, Haiyan 123
Yang, Xutao 153
Yang, Yaru 20
Yaser, A 94
Yu, Yongang 77

**Z**
Zhang, LeFei 35
Zhang, Xintong 50
Zhao, Kang 3
Zhou, Dongming 123
Zhu, Yige 204

MIX
Papier aus verantwortungsvollen Quellen
Paper from responsible sources
FSC® C105338

If you have any concerns about our products,
you can contact us on
**ProductSafety@springernature.com**

In case Publisher is established outside the EU,
the EU authorized representative is:
**Springer Nature Customer Service Center GmbH
Europaplatz 3, 69115 Heidelberg, Germany**

Printed by Libri Plureos GmbH
in Hamburg, Germany